The College Panda
10 Practice Tests
for the
SAT Math

ISBN: 978-0-9894964-4-5

*SAT is a registered trademark of the College Board, which does not endorse this product.

For more information, visit thecollegepanda.com

Discounts available for teachers and companies. Please contact thecollegepanda@gmail.com for details.

Table of Contents

1

Practice Test 1

Math Test --- No Calculator

25 Minutes, 20 Questions

Reference

$A = \pi r^2$
$C = 2\pi r$

$A = lw$

$A = \dfrac{1}{2}bh$

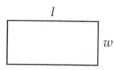

$c^2 = a^2 + b^2$

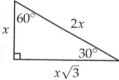

Special Right Triangles

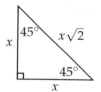

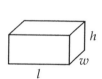

$V = lwh$

$V = \pi r^2 h$

$V = \dfrac{4}{3}\pi r^3$

$V = \dfrac{1}{3}\pi r^2 h$

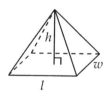

$V = \dfrac{1}{3}lwh$

There are 360 degrees of arc in a circle.
There are 2π radians of arc in a circle.
The sum of the measures of the angles of a triangle, in degrees, is 180.

3 **3**

1

The volume of a balloon is given by the equation $V = t^2 - 3t + 3$. What is the volume of the balloon after 3 seconds?

A) 3

B) 6

C) 9

D) 12

9 -

2

Which of the following is equivalent to $\dfrac{\frac{1}{x}}{x+3}$?

A) $\dfrac{1}{x(x+3)}$

B) $\dfrac{x}{x+3}$

C) $\dfrac{x+3}{x}$

D) $x(x+3)$

x(x+3)

3

If

$$(x-2)^2 + (y-3)^2 + (z+4)^2 = 0$$

what is the value of $x + y + z$?

A) -4

B) 0

C) 1

D) 2

4

If $3^{x-3} = 27$, what is the value of x ?

A) 0

B) 3

C) 6

D) 9

5

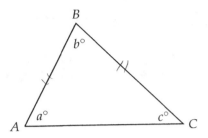

Note: Figure not drawn to scale.

The triangle above is isosceles and $b > a$. Which of the following must be FALSE?

A) $AB = BC$

B) $AB = AC$

C) $AC = BC$

D) $a = c$

6

A rectangular field has a perimeter of p meters. The length of the field is 9 meters shorter than its width. Which of the following expresses the width, in meters, of the field in terms of p ?

A) $\dfrac{p-9}{2}$

B) $\dfrac{p-18}{4}$

C) $\dfrac{p+9}{2}$

D) $\dfrac{p+18}{4}$

3 **3**

7

In the xy-plane, the line $y = mx - 7$ is parallel to the line $2x + 3y = 6$. What is the value of m ?

A) $-\dfrac{3}{2}$

B) $\dfrac{3}{2}$

C) $-\dfrac{2}{3}$

D) $\dfrac{2}{3}$

$3y = -2x + 6$

$-\dfrac{2}{3}$

8

For a lemonade stand, the total cost c, in dollars, of selling n cups of lemonade is given by $c = 100 + 1.5n$. What is the best interpretation of the number 100 in this equation?

A) The cost of each cup of lemonade

B) The number of cups of lemonade sold on the first day

C) The initial cost of setting up the lemonade stand

D) The maximum total cost of running the lemonade stand

9

Which of the following is equal to $(5 + 2i)(5 - 2i)$? (Note: $i = \sqrt{-1}$)

A) 21

B) 29

C) $21 - 20i$

D) $29 + 20i$

$25 - 4i^2$

$\downarrow 4$

10

The graph of a parabola in the xy-plane has x-intercepts at $\dfrac{3}{5}$ and $-\dfrac{1}{2}$. Which of the following could be the equation of the parabola?

A) $y = (5x - 1)(2x + 3)$

B) $y = (5x + 1)(2x - 3)$

C) $y = (5x - 3)(2x + 1)$

D) $y = (5x + 3)(2x - 1)$

11

During a trip, Jonathan had driven a total of 75 miles by 6:20 PM and a total of 85 miles by 6:40 PM. He drove at the same rate for the entire trip. At what time had he driven a total of 140 miles?

A) 7:30 PM

B) 8:00 PM

C) 8:30 PM

D) 9:00 PM

$10\,mi \quad 20min$

$5mi \quad 10min$

110

12

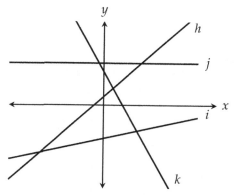

In the figure above, lines $h, i, j,$ and k are graphed in the xy-plane. Which of the following correctly orders them by their slope from least to greatest?

A) $k < j < i < h$

B) $k < i < j < h$

C) $k < j < h < i$

D) $j < k < i < h$

3 **3**

13

$$\left(\frac{1}{m}\right)^2 - 2\left(\frac{1}{m}\right)\left(\frac{1}{n}\right) + \left(\frac{1}{n}\right)^2$$

Which of the following is equivalent to the expression shown above?

A) $\left(\dfrac{1}{\sqrt{m}} - \dfrac{1}{\sqrt{n}}\right)^4$

B) $\left(\dfrac{1}{m} - \dfrac{1}{n}\right)^2$

C) $\dfrac{1}{(m-n)^2}$

D) $\dfrac{2}{m^2 - mn + n^2}$

14

The equation $\dfrac{kx^2 + 14x - 20}{3x - 2} = 5x + 8 - \dfrac{4}{3x - 2}$

is true for all values of $x \neq \dfrac{2}{3}$, where k is a constant. What is the value of k?

A) 8
B) 9
C) 11
D) 15

15

$$x^2 + 3x - 1 = y$$
$$x = y - 2$$

The system of equations above is graphed in the xy-plane. If the ordered pair (a, b) represents an intersection point of the graphs of the two equations, which of the following is a possible value of b?

A) -3
B) -1
C) 1
D) 5

16

If $g(x) = bx^2 + 2x + 1$, where b is a whole number greater than 3 and less than 7, what is one possible value of $g(2)$?

$4 \cdot 4 + 4 + 1$
$16 + 4 + 1$

21

17

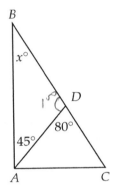

Note: Figure not drawn to scale.

In the figure above, what is the value of x?

85

8

18

Eric can put together a bookshelf in two steps. The first step requires 5 wooden boards and 9 nails. The second step requires 3 wooden boards and 6 nails. If Eric has 70 wooden boards and 110 nails available in his workshop, what is the maximum number of bookshelves he could put together?

[handwritten: x   y.]
[handwritten: 10 x + 6 y = 70.]
[handwritten: 9x + 6y = 110]
[handwritten: so x = 30]
[handwritten: y =]
[handwritten: 8]

[handwritten margin:]
1st   5w   9n
2nd   3w   6n

70   110
8 x = 70   15y = 110
x = 8   y =

19

x	$f(x)$
1	0
2	h
h	k

In the table above, if $f(x) = x^2 + x - 2$, what is the value of k?

[handwritten: 4 + 2 - 2]
[handwritten: h = 4.]
[handwritten: 16 + 4 - 2]
[handwritten: 18]

20

$$x^3 - 3x^2 + 3x - 9 = 0$$

For what real value of x is the equation above true?

[handwritten: $x^2(x-3) + 3(x-3)$]
[handwritten: $(x^2+3)(x-3) = 0$]
[handwritten: 3]

4 🖩 **4**

Math Test --- Calculator
55 Minutes, 38 Questions

Reference

$A = \pi r^2$
$C = 2\pi r$

$A = lw$

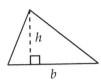

$A = \frac{1}{2}bh$

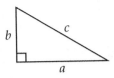

$c^2 = a^2 + b^2$

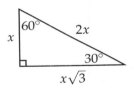

Special Right Triangles

$V = lwh$

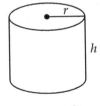

$V = \pi r^2 h$

$V = \frac{4}{3}\pi r^3$

$V = \frac{1}{3}\pi r^2 h$

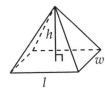

$V = \frac{1}{3}lwh$

There are 360 degrees of arc in a circle.
There are 2π radians of arc in a circle.
The sum of the measures of the angles of a triangle, in degrees, is 180.

1

Last Saturday, Maya drove from her house to the bookstore, where she stayed for several hours before driving back home. Which of the following graphs could represent Maya's trip?

A)

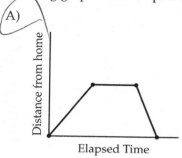

B)

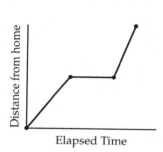

C)

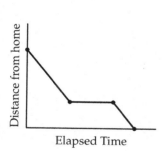

D)

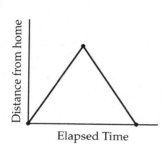

2

A giant sequoia tree weighs 3,700 tons. If a ton is equivalent to 2,000 pounds, what is the weight of the tree in pounds?

A) 3.7×10^3

B) 7.4×10^3

C) 7.4×10^6

D) 7.4×10^7

3700×2000
7400000

3

Before a big test, James memorized 10 percent more words than Zach. Zach memorized 30 percent more words than Amy. If Amy memorized a words, how many words did James memorize in terms of a ?

A) $(1.10)(1.30)a$

B) $\dfrac{a}{(1.10)(1.30)}$

C) $\dfrac{a}{(0.9)(0.7)}$

D) $1.40a$

$Z \cdot 1.1 = J$
$A \cdot 1.3 = Z$
$J = A \cdot 1.3 \cdot 1.1$

4

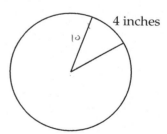

4 inches

A certain pizza restaurant cuts slices out at every 4 inches along the edge of a pizza, as shown in the figure above. What is the maximum number of full pizza slices that can be cut out from a circular pizza with a radius of 10 inches?

A) 7

B) 8

C) 14

D) 15

20π

| 4   🖩   **4 |**

5

The function f is defined by $f(x) = x^2 + bx + c$, where b and c are constants. If the graph of f has x-intercepts at -5 and 3, which of the following correctly gives the values of b and c?

A) $b = -5, c = 3$

B) $b = -3, c = 5$

C) $b = -2, c = -15$

D) $b = 2, c = -15$

$(x+5)(x-3)$
$x^2 + 2x - 15$

6

In the xy-plane, the line $y = mx + b$, where m and b are constants, is a reflection of line l across the y-axis. At which of the following points do the two lines intersect?

A) $(0, b)$

B) $(0, -b)$

C) $(0, m)$

D) $(m, 0)$

7

Rocket	Fuel burned (liters)
Rocket 1	7
Rocket 2	12
Rocket 3	17
Rocket 4	23
Rocket 5	29
Rocket 6	32
Rocket 7	35

The distance d, in meters, traveled by a rocket depends on the amount of fuel f, in liters, it burns according to the equation $d = \frac{2}{3}f$. Based on the table above, how many rockets traveled more than 20 meters?

A) One

B) Two

C) Three

D) Four

8

The table below summarizes student enrollment at three different universities.

University	Under-graduate	Graduate	Total
State	32,791	5,835	38,626
A&M	26,802	4,631	31,433
Southwest	19,443	2,918	22,361
Total	79,036	13,384	92,420

A researcher decides to interview a student who attends either State University or Southwest University. Which of the following is closest to the probability that the chosen student is an undergraduate at Southwest University?

A) 0.21

B) 0.25

C) 0.32

D) 0.54

$\dfrac{19443}{79.036}$

9

A grocery store has two recycling machines outside. The first recycling machine took in 240 plastic bottles and 180 metal cans. The second took in 30 percent more plastic bottles but 10 percent less metal cans. The second machine recycled what percent more items than the first (rounded to the nearest percent)?

A) 9%

B) 11%

C) 13%

D) 15%

(handwritten: 13 240 p. 12 m; 108; 312 p. 162; 420 54)

10

Ashley estimates that there are a marbles in a jar. Harry, who knows the actual number of marbles in the jar, b, notes that Ashley's estimate is within 15 marbles (inclusive) of the actual number of marbles. Which of the following inequalities represents the relationship between Ashley's estimate and the actual number of marbles in the jar?

A) $-15 \leq a - b \leq 15$

B) $a \leq b + 15$

C) $a \geq b - 15$

D) $a + b \geq 15$

11

A circle in the xy-plane is centered at $(1, 2)$ and contains the point $(4, 6)$. Which of the following could be the equation of the circle?

A) $(x - 1)^2 + (y - 2)^2 = 5$

B) $(x - 1)^2 + (y - 2)^2 = 25$

C) $(x + 1)^2 + (y + 2)^2 = 5$

D) $(x + 1)^2 + (y + 2)^2 = 25$

Questions 12-13 refer to the following information.

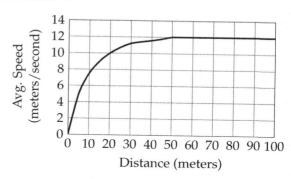

John is training for the 100-meter-dash, a sprint race in track and field competitions. The graph above shows his average speed at different points during his last race.

12

According to the graph, what percentage of the race had John completed before he reached his maximum average speed?

A) 10%

B) 20%

C) 40%

D) 50%

13

Which of the following best describes John's performance during his last race?

A) John maintained a constant speed throughout the entire race.

B) John accelerated to his maximum speed and maintained it for the rest of the race.

C) John accelerated to his maximum speed and then maintained a lower constant speed for the rest of the race.

D) John accelerated to his maximum speed and then slowed down in the middle of the race before reaching his maximum speed again.

4 🖩 **4**

14

If $\dfrac{x}{5} = \dfrac{k}{y}$, where k is a constant, and $y = 3$ when $x = 10$, what is the value of y when $x = 2$?

A) 10

B) 12

C) 15

D) 18

15

The value of a stock is going up by 200% every hour. Which of the following best describes the relationship between time (in hours) and the value of the stock?

A) Increasing linear

B) Decreasing linear

C) Exponential growth

D) Exponential decay

16

A sports equipment manufacturer produced 3,600 footballs and 2,200 basketballs during the fall. In the winter, it produced 3,060 footballs and a certain number of basketballs. If the manufacturer decreased the production of basketballs by the same percentage as it did for footballs, how many basketballs did it produce in the winter?

A) 1,810

B) 1,870

C) 1,920

D) 1,950

17

The number of books in a warehouse can be found using the expression $4,000 + 100bd$, where b is the number of boxes of books the warehouse receives each day over a period of d days. What is the best interpretation of the number 100 in the expression?

A) The number of books in each box

B) The number of books received each day

C) The number of boxes received that contain books

D) The number of days it takes to receive each box

18

If $\sqrt{x} + \sqrt{y} = 4\sqrt{y}$, where $x > 0$ and $y > 0$, what is x in terms of y?

A) $16y$

B) $9y$

C) $6y$

D) $4y$

19

Richard has seven times as many pineapples as Fred. Nathan has three times as many pineapples as Fred. Richard has 32 more pineapples than Nathan. How many pineapples does Fred have?

A) 7

B) 8

C) 11

D) 12

20

During a high school basketball game, Michael scores 30 times for a total of 68 points. If he ended the game with x two-pointers and y three-pointers, solving which of the following systems of equations gives x and y ?

A) $x + y = 30$
$2x + 3y = 68$

B) $x + y = 68$
$2x + 3y = 30$

C) $x + y = 30$
$3x + 2y = 68$

D) $x + y = 68$
$3x + 2y = 30$

21

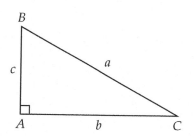

Given right triangle ABC above, which of the following is equal to $\dfrac{c}{b}$?

A) $\tan B$

B) $\dfrac{1}{\tan B}$

C) $\cos B$

D) $\dfrac{1}{\cos B}$

22

To determine whether low lighting affects reading speed, a researcher randomly selected 30 subjects to participate in a study. Half of the subjects were randomly assigned to read an article under low lighting (400 lumens) while the other half read the same article under normal lighting (900 lumens). The resulting data showed that the subjects who read the article under low lighting took significantly longer than those who read the article under normal lighting. Based on the design and results of the study, which of the following is an appropriate conclusion?

A) Low lighting is harmful to the eyes.

B) Everyone reads slower under low lighting.

C) Low lighting is likely to cause a decrease in reading speed.

D) High lighting (1,200 lumens) is likely to cause an increase in reading speed.

23

A train traveling at an average speed of 80 miles per hour takes 8 hours to complete a given trip. How much time would it take the train to complete the same trip if it traveled at an average speed of 120 miles per hour?

A) 4 hours

B) 4 hours and 30 minutes

C) 5 hours and 20 minutes

D) 5 hours and 30 minutes

4 **4**

Questions 24-25 refer to the following information.

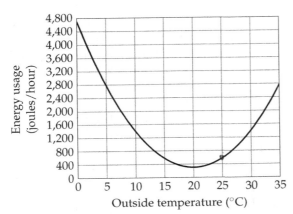

Outside temperature (°C)

An aquarium relies on an energy source to keep it at room temperature. The aquarium is cooled when the outside temperature is greater than room temperature and heated when the outside temperature is less than room temperature. The graph above gives the aquarium's energy usage, in joules per hour, at different outside temperatures, in degrees Celsius.

24

At an outside temperature of 25° Celsius, which of the following is closest to the total amount of energy, in joules, used by the aquarium over 3 hours?

A) 600

B) 1,800

C) 3,600

D) 5,400

25

$$E(x) = a(x - 20)^2 + 300$$

The function E, defined above, is used to model the aquarium's energy usage, in joules per hour, at an outside temperature of $x°$ Celsius. For which of the following values of a does E best approximate the values given by the graph?

A) 8

B) 11

C) 14

D) 25

26

A six-sided die with faces numbered one through six is rolled 40 times. The outcomes are summarized in the table below.

Outcome	Frequency
1	4
2	2
3	12
4	10
5	4
6	8

Which of the following correctly relates the mean, median, and mode of the outcomes?

A) mode < median < mean

B) mean < mode < median

C) mode < mean < median

D) median < mode < mean

27

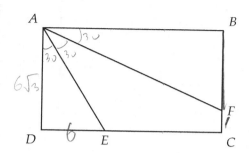

In rectangle $ABCD$ above, E is on $\overline{DC}$, F is on $\overline{BC}$, $DE = 6$, and $FC = 1$. If angle A is trisected (divided into three equal angles) by $\overline{AE}$ and $\overline{AF}$, what is the length of $\overline{BF}$?

A) 5

B) $5\sqrt{2} - 1$

C) $5\sqrt{3} - 1$

D) $6\sqrt{3} - 1$

28

$$x - 3y = 4$$
$$2(x - 1) - 6(y + 2) = -6$$

How many solutions (x, y) are there to the system of equations above?

A) Zero

B) One

C) Two

D) More than two

Questions 29-30 refer to the following information.

$$f_{obs} = f_s \left(\frac{v_w}{v_w - v_a} \right)$$

An ambulance is moving at a velocity v_a, in meters per second, towards an observer standing still on a sidewalk. Because of this movement, the actual frequency of the sound waves emitted by the ambulance's siren f_s, in hertz, is perceived by the observer to be a different frequency f_{obs}. The siren's sound waves travel at a velocity v_w, in meters per second. The formula above shows the relationship between these variables.

29

Which of the following expresses the velocity of the ambulance in terms of the other variables?

A) $v_a = \dfrac{f_s v_w}{f_{obs} v_w}$

B) $v_a = \dfrac{f_{obs} v_w}{f_{obs} + f_s v_w}$

C) $v_a = \dfrac{f_s v_w - f_{obs} v_w}{f_{obs}}$

D) $v_a = \dfrac{f_{obs} v_w - f_s v_w}{f_{obs}}$

30

If the velocity of the siren's sound waves is 340 meters per second, the velocity of the ambulance is 22 meters per second, and the observer perceives the frequency of the siren's sound waves to be 500 hertz, which of the following is closest to the actual frequency of the siren's sound waves?

A) 468

B) 496

C) 507

D) 535

4   4

31

A financial analyst started tracking the value of a stock on March 1 at 9:00 AM. The stock lost half its value each day until it was worth $2.75 on March 6 at 9:00 AM. What was the value, in dollars, of the stock on March 1 at 9:00 AM?

1 2 3 4 5 6
88 44 22 11 5.5 2.75

88

32

$$(3x + 2y)^2$$

If the expression above can be written as $ax^2 + bxy + cy^2$, where $a, b,$ and c are constants, what is the value of $a + b + c$?

9 12 4

25

33

$$g(x) = \sqrt{(x-1)(x-2)}$$

What is one possible value of x for which the function g above is undefined?

1.5

34

At a certain pizza restaurant, 8 ounces of cheese is enough for $\frac{2}{3}$ of a pizza. Given that there are 16 ounces in a pound, how many pizzas can be produced with 12 pounds of cheese?

192 oz s   12 oz / pizza

16 p

35

Beginner	
Intermediate	60
Advanced	
Total	180

An after-school program offers three different swimming classes: beginner, intermediate, and advanced. The incomplete table above shows the number of students in each class. If the number of students in the advanced class is $\frac{3}{5}$ the number of students in the beginner class, how many students are in the beginner class?

75   45

75

4   **4**

36

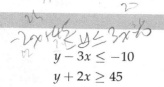

$$y - 3x \leq -10$$
$$y + 2x \geq 45$$

In the xy-plane, a point with coordinates (h, k) lies in the solution set of the system of inequalities above. What is the minimum possible value of h?

12

▼

Questions 37-38 refer to the following information.

Male crickets vary their chirp rate according to the temperature. The scatterplot below shows the relationship between chirp rate and temperature for 9 crickets. The line of best fit is also shown.

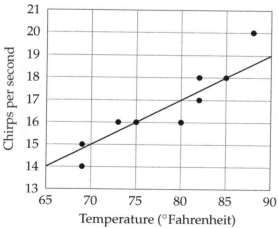

37

Based on the line of best fit, what is the predicted male cricket chirp rate, in chirps per second, at a temperature of 80 degrees Fahrenheit?

17

38

What is the chirp rate, in chirps per second, of the male cricket represented by the data point that is farthest from the line of best fit?

20

▲

2

Practice Test 2

Math Test --- No Calculator

25 Minutes, 20 Questions

Reference

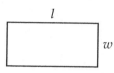

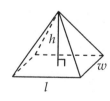

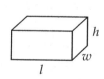

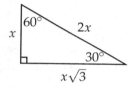

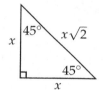

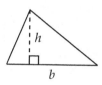

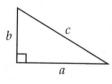

$A = \pi r^2$
$C = 2\pi r$

$A = lw$

$A = \frac{1}{2}bh$

$c^2 = a^2 + b^2$

Special Right Triangles

$V = lwh$

$V = \pi r^2 h$

$V = \frac{4}{3}\pi r^3$

$V = \frac{1}{3}\pi r^2 h$

$V = \frac{1}{3}lwh$

There are 360 degrees of arc in a circle.
There are 2π radians of arc in a circle.
The sum of the measures of the angles of a triangle, in degrees, is 180.

1

Which of the following expressions is NOT equivalent to $ab(c + d)$?

A) $abd + abc$

B) $ab(d + c)$

C) $ba(c + d)$

D) $abc + bd$

2

At a movie theater, an adult ticket costs $10 and a bag of popcorn costs $6. If a group of adults bought tickets to a movie and 4 bags of popcorn, what expression could be used to determine how much in total the group spent, in dollars?

A) $10x + 6$, where x is the number of adults

B) $10x + 24$, where x is the number of adults

C) $16x$, where x is the number of adults

D) $6x + 10$, where x is the number of bags of popcorn purchased

3

If $xy = 5$, which of the following CANNOT be a value for x ?

A) -6

B) -5

C) 0

D) 1

4

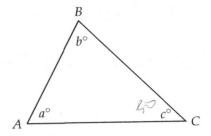

Note: Figure not drawn to scale.

In the figure above $AB = AC$ and $c = 50°$. What is the value of a ?

A) 65

B) 70

C) 75

D) 80

5

Barbara has x dolls in her doll collection. If Barbara has half as many dolls as Tanya does and Tanya has y dolls, which of the following equations must be true?

A) $y = x + 2$

B) $y = \dfrac{1}{2}x$

C) $y = 2x$

D) $xy = 2$

6

What is the sum of the solutions to $2x^2 - 6x + 2 = 0$?

A) -3

B) -1

C) 1

D) 3

3 **3**

7

Let the function f be defined by $f(x) = 2x^3 - 1$, and let the function g be defined by $g(x) = x^2 + 3$, what is the value of $f(g(1))$?

A) 4

B) 23

C) 56

D) 127

8

$$ax + 4y = 14$$
$$5x + 7y = 8$$

In the system of equations above, a is a constant and x and y are variables. If the system has no solution, what is the value of a ?

A) $\dfrac{20}{7}$

B) $\dfrac{35}{4}$

C) $-\dfrac{35}{4}$

D) $-\dfrac{20}{7}$

9

On Friday, Janice read x pages every 30 minutes for 4 hours, and Kim read y pages every 15 minutes for 5 hours. Which of the following represents the total number of pages read by Janice and Kim on Friday?

A) $4x + 5y$

B) $8x + 20y$

C) $20x + 8y$

D) $120x + 75y$

10

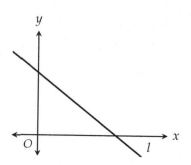

The graph of line l is shown in the xy-plane above. The equation of line n (not shown) is $y = mx + b$, where m and b are constants. If line l is perpendicular to line n, which of the following must be true?

A) $m < 0$

B) $m > 0$

C) $b > 0$

D) $b < 0$

11

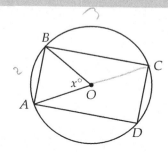

Note: Figure not drawn to scale.

In the figure above, rectangle $ABCD$ is inscribed in a circle with center O. If the ratio of the length of arc $\overgroup{AB}$ to the length of arc $\overgroup{BC}$ is 2:3, what is the value of x ?

A) 45

B) 60

C) 72

D) 108

3   **3**

12

$$x^2 + kx + 9 = (x + a)^2$$

In the equation above, k and a are positive constants. If the equation is true for all values of x, what is the value of k?

A) 0

B) 3

C) 6

D) 9

13

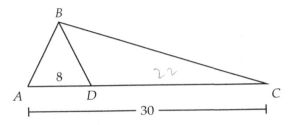

The area of triangle ABC above is 75. If $AD = 8$ and $AC = 30$, what is the area of triangle BDC?

A) 40

B) 45

C) 50

D) 55

14

If $27^{81} = 3^x$, what is the value of x?

A) 27

B) 84

C) 100

D) 243

15

To restock the supplies in the office, Fabiano needs to order at least 16 printer cartridges. He is given a $300 budget for black and white cartridges and a $400 budget for color cartridges. Each black and white cartridge costs $25 and each color cartridge costs $35. Which of the following systems of inequalities models this situation in terms of b and c, where b is the number of black and white cartridges and c is the number of color cartridges?

A) $b + c \leq 16$
$0 \leq 25b + 35c \leq 700$

B) $b + c \geq 16$
$0 \leq 25b + 35c \leq 700$

C) $b + c \leq 16$
$0 \leq 25b \leq 300$
$0 \leq 35c \leq 400$

D) $b + c \geq 16$
$0 \leq 25b \leq 300$
$0 \leq 35c \leq 400$

16

If $\dfrac{1}{2}x - \dfrac{1}{3}x = 1 + \dfrac{1}{2}$, what is the value of x?

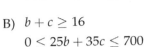

17

A pet turtle is fed several times a day. Each meal consists of either 8 food pellets or 5 pieces of shrimp. If there are 120 food pellets and 63 pieces of shrimp left in the turtle's food supply, how many more full meals will the turtle be able to have before the supply runs out?

8f · 120   15
5s   63   12

12

18

x	$f(x)$	$g(x)$
1	4	0
2	6	2
3	5	6
4	2	4

Four values for the functions f and g are shown in the table above. If $g(m) = 6$, what is the value of $f(m)$?

5

19

$$\frac{3x+10}{x(x-3)^2} - \frac{3}{x(x-3)}$$

For all $x \neq 3$, the expression above is equivalent to $\dfrac{k}{x(x-3)^2}$, where k is a positive constant. What is the value of k ?

3x+10 -(3(x-3))
       -3x+9

19

20

$$x^2 - 5x + c = 0$$

In the quadratic equation above, c is a constant. If the equation has two solutions for x, one of which is -3, what is the value of the other solution?

-2

4 📱 **4**

Math Test --- Calculator

55 Minutes, 38 Questions

Reference

$A = \pi r^2$
$C = 2\pi r$

$A = lw$

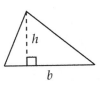

$A = \frac{1}{2}bh$

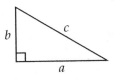

$c^2 = a^2 + b^2$

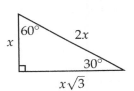

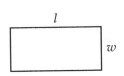

Special Right Triangles

$V = lwh$

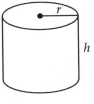

$V = \pi r^2 h$

$V = \frac{4}{3}\pi r^3$

$V = \frac{1}{3}\pi r^2 h$

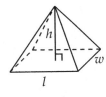

$V = \frac{1}{3}lwh$

There are 360 degrees of arc in a circle.
There are 2π radians of arc in a circle.
The sum of the measures of the angles of a triangle, in degrees, is 180.

4 **4**

1

A small shop can manufacture 4 windows every 5 hours. At that rate, how long will it take the shop to manufacture 7 windows?

A) 8 hr

B) 8 hr 15 min

C) 8 hr 30 min

D) 8 hr 45 min

2

If the area of a circle is $\frac{\pi}{4}$, what is the diameter of the circle?

A) $\frac{1}{4}$

B) $\frac{1}{2}$

C) 1

D) $\frac{3}{2}$

3

An analyst determines that the cost of an order depends on the quantity ordered in the following way: $C = 3600 - 400q + 20q^2$, where $q \geq 0$. According to this model, for which of the following values of q would the cost of an order be the lowest?

A) 5

B) 10

C) 15

D) 20

$20\left(q^2 - 20q + 100\right) + 3600 - 2000$

1600

4

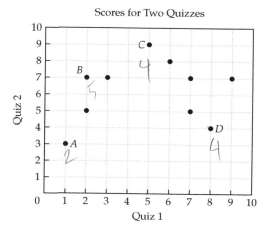

Scores for Two Quizzes

Ten students in a class have taken two quizzes so far. For each student, the score for the first quiz was plotted against the score for the second quiz in the grid shown above. Which labeled grid point represents the student for whom the difference between the scores of the two quizzes was greatest?

A) A

B) B

C) C

D) D

5

The perimeter of one face of a cube is $2k$, where k is a positive constant. Which of the following gives the surface area of the cube?

A) $\frac{k^2}{4}$

B) $\frac{3}{2}k^2$

C) $3k^2$

D) $24k^2$

$\frac{k}{2}$ $\frac{k^2}{4} \times 6 = \frac{3}{2}$

---

4 **4**

6

If X is 20% of Y and Y is 30% of Z, then what percent of Z is X ?

A) 5%

B) 6%

C) 8%

D) 12%

[handwritten: X = 0.2Y, Y = 0.3Z, .0.6]

7

A fiberoptic cable can transfer d megabytes of data in t seconds, where $d = 8t^2$. Which of the following gives the average data transfer speed of the cable, in megabytes per second, over k seconds?

A) $8k$

B) $8k^2$

C) $\dfrac{8}{k}$

D) $16k$

[handwritten: $\dfrac{8k^2}{k}$]

▼

Questions 8-9 refer to the following information.

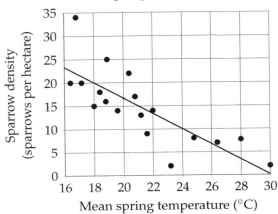

Sparrow Density and Spring Temperature

The scatterplot above shows the sparrow densities of 19 forests, in sparrows per hectare, with respect to their mean spring temperatures in degrees Celsius (°C). The line of best fit is also shown.

8

According to the scatterplot, which of the following statements is true about the relationship between the sparrow density of a forest and its mean spring temperature?

A) Forests that have higher mean spring temperatures tend to have lower sparrow populations.

B) Forests that have higher mean spring temperatures tend to have higher sparrow populations.

C) Forests that have lower mean spring temperatures tend to have lower sparrow densities.

D) Forests that have lower mean spring temperatures tend to have higher sparrow densities.

9

According to the line of best fit, which of the following best approximates the sparrow density, in sparrows per hectare, of a forest that has a mean spring temperature of 20 degrees Celsius?

A) 10

B) 17

C) 18

D) 20

▲

4 **4**

$\times 33.8 = 120$

10

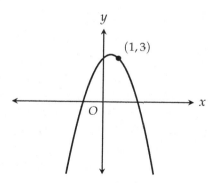

The graph of the function g in the xy-plane is shown above. If f is another function defined in the same xy-plane and $f(1) = 1$, then g could be which of the following?

A) $f - 1$

B) $f - 2$

C) $f + 1$

D) $f + 2$

11

This year, Roger beat Rafael in 25% of their tennis matches. If Rafael won 18 matches, how many matches did Roger win?

A) 2

B) 3

C) 4

D) 6

$18 \cdot 75\% $

$6.$

12

One calorie is equivalent to 4.184 joules of energy. One calorie also represents the amount of energy required to raise the temperature of 1 gram of water by 1° Celsius. Based on this information, raising the temperature of 1 gram of water by 120° Fahrenheit would require how many joules of energy, to the nearest hundredth? (1° Celsius = 33.8° Fahrenheit)

A) 12.76 $120°F = 3.55°C$

B) 13.88

C) 14.32

D) 14.85

13

At the start of a semester, 150 students enroll in a course for which the regular tuition fee is $5,400. The school finds that for every $200 discount on the tuition fee for the course, the student enrollment increases by 9. Which of the following equations gives the student enrollment E when the tuition fee for the course is discounted by d dollars?

A) $E = 150 + 0.045d$

B) $E = 150 + 9d$

C) $E = 150 + 0.045(5,400 - d)$

D) $E = 150 + 9(5,400 - 200d)$

4 ▯ **4**

14

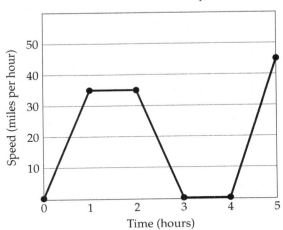

Alicia's Road Trip

The graph above shows Alicia's speed during a road trip. She stopped at a rest stop during her trip to take a nap. Based on the graph, Alicia stopped for her nap after how many hours of driving?

A) 1
B) 2
C) 3
D) 4

---▼---

Questions 15-16 refer to the following information.

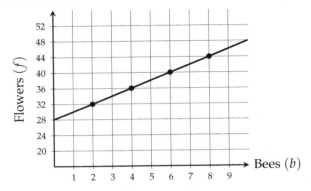

A botanist uses the graph above to show the number of flowers f that blossom in a garden with b bees.

15

What is the meaning of the f-intercept?

A) The average number of flowers that blossom
B) The maximum number of flowers that blossom
C) The number of flowers that blossom per bee
D) The number of flowers that blossom in a garden without any bees

16

Which of the following describes the relationship between f and b ?

A) $f = 28 + 0.5b$
B) $f = 28 + 2b$
C) $b = 28 + 0.5f$
D) $b = 28 + 2f$

---▲---

17

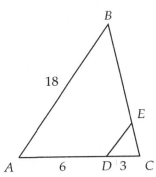

In the figure above, $\overline{DE}$ is parallel to $\overline{AB}$. If $AD = 6$, $DC = 3$, and $AB = 18$, what is the length of $\overline{DE}$?

A) 3
B) 6
C) 9
D) 12

4 **4**

18

A school district wants to make at least 600 but no more than 700 computers available to students. To meet this goal, the superintendent puts aside a budget to install 8 new computers every month. If there is a total of 200 computers available at the schools in the district currently, which of the following inequalities gives the possible number of months t for which the school district can continue to add new computers? Assume t is an integer.

A) $50 \le t \le 62$

B) $50 \le t \le 63$

C) $75 \le t \le 87$

D) $75 \le t \le 88$

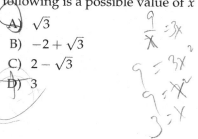

19

If $a = x^2 - 5x + 2$ and $b = 3x^3 + 4x^2 - 6$, what is $3a - b$ in terms of x ?

A) $4x^2 - 15x + 12$

B) $-3x^3 - x^2 - 15x + 12$

C) $-3x^3 - x^2 - 15x$

D) $-3x^3 + 7x^2 - 15x + 12$

20

$$\frac{9}{x - 2} = 3(x - 2)$$

Based on the equation above, which of the following is a possible value of $x - 2$?

A) $\sqrt{3}$

B) $-2 + \sqrt{3}$

C) $2 - \sqrt{3}$

D) 3

21

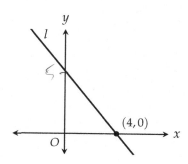

In the xy-plane above, line l has slope $-\dfrac{5}{4}$. What is the area of the triangle bounded by line l, the x-axis, and the y-axis?

A) 5

B) 8

C) 10

D) 16

22

The price of a textbook this year is 20% greater than the price last year. If this year's price is p, what was last year's price in terms of p ?

A) $\dfrac{1}{5}p$

B) $\dfrac{4}{5}p$

C) $\dfrac{5}{6}p$

D) $\dfrac{6}{5}p$

4 **4**

23

$$y = x^2 - 2x - 3$$

A parabola in the xy-plane is given by the equation above. Which of the following equivalent forms of the equation displays the coordinates of the vertex of the parabola as constants or coefficients?

A) $y = (x - 1)^2 - 4$
B) $y = (x - 1)^2 - 2$
C) $y = (x - 3)(x + 1)$
D) $y + 3 = x(x + 2)$

24

$$T = 2\pi\sqrt{\frac{L}{9.8}}$$

The time it takes a clock pendulum to repeat its motion is called its period. The formula above shows the relationship between T, the period of the pendulum, in seconds, and L, the length of the pendulum, in meters. Which of the following is closest to L when T is 8?

A) 14.4
B) 15.9
C) 16.3
D) 17.1

25

The number of dandelions in a large park is recorded over the course of five months, as shown in the table below.

Month	Dandelions
1	12,500
2	2,500
3	500
4	100
5	20

Which of the following best describes the relationship between time and the number of dandelions during the five months?

A) Increasing linear
B) Decreasing linear
C) Exponential growth
D) Exponential decay

26

The number of subscribers, S, to a magazine increases by 21 percent each year. If the current number of subscribers to the magazine is 3,000, which of the following equations models the number of subscribers to the magazine h half years from now?

A) $S = 3,000(1.1)^h$
B) $S = 3,000(1.21)^h$
C) $S = 3,000(1.105)^h$
D) $S = 3,000(1.4641)^h$

Questions 27-28 refer to the following information.

The table below gives the distribution of weights, to the nearest pound, for 50 lobsters harvested off the coast of Maine and 50 lobsters harvested off the coast of Massachusetts.

Weight (pounds)	Maine	Massachusetts
1	20	30
2	20	15
3	8	5
4	2	0

27

What is the mean weight, in pounds, of all the harvested lobsters?

A) 1.34

B) 1.45

C) 1.67

D) 1.78

28

According to the data, which of the following accurately compares the median weight of the lobsters harvested off the coast of Maine with that of the lobsters harvested off the coast of Massachusetts?

A) The median weight of the lobsters from Maine is one pound less than that of the lobsters from Massachusetts.

B) The median weight of the lobsters from Maine is one pound more than that of the lobsters from Massachusetts.

C) The median weight of the lobsters from Maine is half a pound more than that of the lobsters from Massachusetts.

D) The median weight of the lobsters from Maine is the same as that of the lobsters from Massachusetts.

29

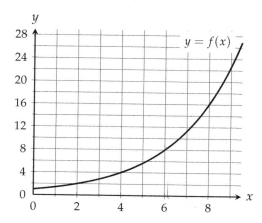

The graph of the function f is shown in the xy-plane above. If the function g (not shown) is defined by $g(x) = 20 - 2x$, for which of the following values of x does $f(x) = g(x)$?

A) 4

B) 5

C) 6

D) 8

30

If $a^4 - b^2 = 30$ and $a^2 + b = -5$, what is the value of $a^2 - b$?

A) -6

B) -2

C) 3

D) 6

31

The measures of the three angles of a triangle are $2y$, $3y$, and $60°$. What is the value of y ?

4 🖩 **4**

32

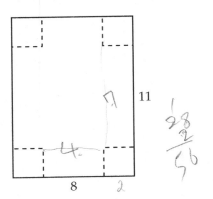

11

8

2

Squares of side length 2 are removed from the corners of an 8 by 11 piece of paper shown above by cutting along the dashed lines. The sides of the paper are then folded up to create a rectangular box with an open top. How many cubes of side length 1 are needed to completely fill this box?

33

A food manufacturer fills containers of seasoning with various spices, pepper, and salt. The amount of pepper p, in milligrams, used in the seasoning can be modeled by the equation $p = \dfrac{10 + 3s}{4}$, where s is the amount of salt, in milligrams, in the seasoning. According to the model, how many milligrams of pepper are added for every 1 milligram increase in the amount of salt?

34

$$y = x^2 - 6x + 9$$
$$y = x + 3$$

A solution to the system of equations above is (x, y). What is one possible value of $x + y$?

35

Number of Vacations each Year

	0	1	2+	Total
Doctor		45		100
Lawyer	35	40	20	95
Total		85		195

The incomplete table above shows the results of a survey that asked a group of doctors and lawyers how many vacations they take each year. If a doctor from the surveyed group is chosen at random, the probability that the doctor takes at least 1 vacation each year is $\dfrac{4}{5}$.

How many people from the surveyed group take at least 2 vacations each year?

36

$$y \le \frac{1}{2}x - 5$$

$$y \ge 3x - 20$$

In the xy-plane, a point with coordinates (h, k) lies in the solution set of the system of inequalities above. What is the maximum possible value of h ?

$3x-20 \le y \le \frac{1}{2}x-5$

$6.$

sold n

$150n$: total

$100 + \frac{36}{n} = 1$ necklace cost.

$150n - (100 + \frac{36}{n})n = 564$
36

$150n - 100n + 36$

$50n = 600$
$n = 12$

$11. \quad 12.$

Questions 37-38 refer to the following information.

$$C = 100 + \frac{36}{n}$$

A boutique shop is selling handmade necklaces. The cost per necklace C can be determined by the equation above, where n is the number of necklaces made.

37

What is the total cost of making 6 necklaces?

636

38

If the shop sells each necklace for $150, how many necklaces should be made so that the shop makes a total profit of $564 after all of them are sold?

$714 = 100 + \frac{36}{n}$
$914 = 100n + 36$

$12.$

$\frac{564 + 150n}{1} = \frac{100n + 36}{n}$

$250n =$

$150n - 5$

3

Practice Test 3

Math Test --- No Calculator

25 Minutes, 20 Questions

Reference

$A = \pi r^2$
$C = 2\pi r$

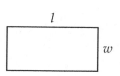

$A = lw$

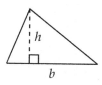

$A = \frac{1}{2}bh$

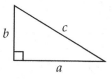

$c^2 = a^2 + b^2$

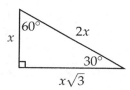

$x\sqrt{3}$

Special Right Triangles

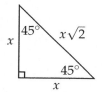

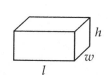

$V = lwh$

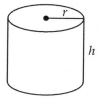

$V = \pi r^2 h$

$V = \frac{4}{3}\pi r^3$

$V = \frac{1}{3}\pi r^2 h$

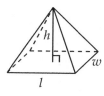

$V = \frac{1}{3}lwh$

There are 360 degrees of arc in a circle.
There are 2π radians of arc in a circle.
The sum of the measures of the angles of a triangle, in degrees, is 180.

3 **3**

1

$$0 < \left| \frac{5}{x} \right| < 1$$

Which of the following values of x satisfies the inequality above?

A) -8

B) -3

C) 2

D) 3

2

If $c = \dfrac{ab}{d}$ and $d \neq 0$, then $\dfrac{1}{ab} =$

A) $c + d$

B) cd

C) $\dfrac{1}{cd}$

D) $\dfrac{c}{d}$

3

If $x^2 < 25$, which of the following must be true?

A) $0 < x < 5$

B) $-5 < x < 0$

C) $-5 < x < 5$

D) $x < 5$

4

$$2x(x - y)(x + y)$$

Which of the following is equivalent to the expression above?

A) $4x^3 - 2xy^2$

B) $2x^3 + 2xy^2$

C) $2x^3 - 2xy^2$

D) $2x^3 - 4xy + 2xy^2$

5

The total amount of water w, in gallons, left in a tank can be modeled by the equation $w = 300 - 5t$, where t is the number of hours since the tank started leaking. Which of the following is the best interpretation of the number 5 in the equation?

A) The tank is empty after 5 hours.

B) The tank loses 5 gallons of water each hour.

C) The tank continues to lose water until 5 gallons are left.

D) Each hour, the tank loses 5 less gallons of water than it did the previous hour.

6

In the xy-plane, the line with equation $3x + 4y = 6$ is perpendicular to the line with equation $y = mx + b$, where m and b are constants. What is the value of m ?

A) $-\dfrac{4}{3}$

B) $-\dfrac{3}{4}$

C) $\dfrac{3}{4}$

D) $\dfrac{4}{3}$

3 **3**

7

The function f is defined by $f(x) = (x - 1)^2$. Which of the following is the graph of $y = f(x) + 1$ in the xy-plane?

A)

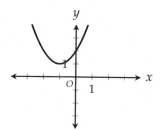

B)

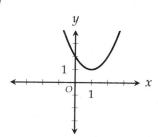

C)

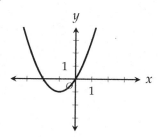

D)

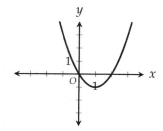

8

A car has a gas mileage of 32 miles per gallon when it travels at an average speed of 65 miles per hour. If the car travels for t hours at 65 miles per hour, which of the following expressions represents the amount of gas, in gallons, the car has consumed?

A) $\dfrac{32}{65t}$

B) $\dfrac{65}{32t}$

C) $\dfrac{32t}{65}$

D) $\dfrac{65t}{32}$

9

$$x^2 - x = 4$$

What are the solutions x to the quadratic equation above?

A) $\dfrac{-1 \pm \sqrt{15}}{2}$

B) $\dfrac{1 \pm \sqrt{15}}{2}$

C) $\dfrac{-1 \pm \sqrt{17}}{2}$

D) $\dfrac{1 \pm \sqrt{17}}{2}$

10

If $y^8 = m$ and $y^9 = \dfrac{2}{3}$, what is the value of y in terms of m ?

A) $\dfrac{2}{3}m$

B) $\dfrac{2}{3m}$

C) $\dfrac{3}{2}m$

D) $\dfrac{3}{2m}$

3 **3**

11

Mitch typically works 40 hours each week stocking shelves at a retail store. He stocks 8 shelves per hour. This week, he would like to earn $180 more by working overtime. If Mitch gets paid $15 per hour, which of the following equations can he use to solve for s, the additional number of shelves he should stock this week?

A) $\dfrac{8}{15}s = 180$

B) $\dfrac{15}{8}s = 180$

C) $\dfrac{8}{15}s = 780$

D) $\dfrac{15}{8}s = 780$

12

If a line contains the points $(0,0)$ and $(12,16)$, then the line will also contain which of the following points?

A) $(2,3)$

B) $(3,2)$

C) $(3,4)$

D) $(4,3)$

13

$$3x + ky = 8$$
$$x + 4y = -1$$

If (x,y) is a solution to the system of equations above and k is a constant, what is y in terms of k ?

A) $\dfrac{5}{k-12}$

B) $\dfrac{11}{k-12}$

C) $\dfrac{7}{k-4}$

D) $\dfrac{9}{k-4}$

14

$$\sin x = \cos y$$

In the equation above, x and y are measured in radians. Which of the following could be x in terms of y ?

A) $\dfrac{\pi}{2} - y$

B) $\dfrac{\pi}{2} + y$

C) $y - \dfrac{\pi}{2}$

D) $\pi - y$

15

A coffee company requires that the amount of caffeine in one large cup of coffee be less than 280 milligrams. A barista at the company wants to mix a signature blend of coffee from two types of coffee beans: Arabica and Robusta. An ounce of Arabica beans contains 40 milligrams of caffeine and an ounce of Robusta beans contains 60 milligrams of caffeine. If the barista's signature blend contains twice as many Arabica beans as Robusta beans, which inequality shows the acceptable amount a, in ounces, of Arabica beans for one large cup of the blend?

A) $0 < a < 1\dfrac{3}{4}$

B) $0 < a < 2$

C) $0 < a < 3\dfrac{1}{2}$

D) $0 < a < 4$

16

$$b(2a + 3)(2 + 5a)$$

What is the value of the coefficient of the ab term when the expression above is expanded and the like terms are combined?

17

If $(x + 3)(x - 3) = 91$, what is the value of x^2 ?

18

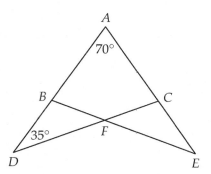

In the figure above, $\overline{BE}$ and $\overline{CD}$ intersect at point F, $AB = AC$, and $AD = AE$. What is the measure, in degrees, of $\angle BFD$? (Disregard the degree symbol when gridding your answer.)

19

$$f(x) = ax^3 + b$$

In the function f defined above, a and b are constants. If $f(-1) = 4$ and $f(1) = 10$, what is the value of b ?

20

$$\frac{x}{y + 2} = 2$$

$$3(y - 5) - x = -16$$

If (x, y) is the solution to the system of equations above, what is the value of x ?

4 📱 **4**

Math Test --- Calculator
55 Minutes, 38 Questions

Reference

$A = \pi r^2$
$C = 2\pi r$

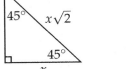

$A = lw$

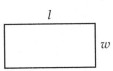

$A = \dfrac{1}{2}bh$

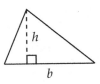

$c^2 = a^2 + b^2$

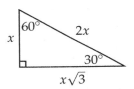

Special Right Triangles

$V = lwh$

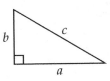

$V = \pi r^2 h$

$V = \dfrac{4}{3}\pi r^3$

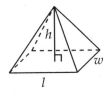

$V = \dfrac{1}{3}\pi r^2 h$

$V = \dfrac{1}{3}lwh$

There are 360 degrees of arc in a circle.
There are 2π radians of arc in a circle.
The sum of the measures of the angles of a triangle, in degrees, is 180.

1

$$\frac{2}{3}t + m = 40$$

A tennis player uses the formula above to estimate the tension t, in pounds, in his racquet strings after m tennis matches. Which of the following expresses t in terms of m?

$t = (40 - m)\frac{3}{2}$

A) $t = -\frac{3}{2}(40 - m)$

B) $t = -\frac{3}{2}(40) - m$

C) $t = \frac{3}{2}(40 - m)$

D) $t = \frac{3}{2}(40) - m$

2

$$a(3 - a) + 2(a + 5)$$

Which of the following is equivalent to the expression above?

A) $-a^2 + 5a + 5$

B) $-a^2 + 5a + 10$

C) $4a + 5$

D) $4a + 10$

$3a - a^2 + 2a + 10$

$-a^2 + 5a + 10$

3

At Lynnfield High School, the ratio of sophomores to juniors is 3:8 and the ratio of seniors to juniors is 7:5. If there are 120 juniors at the school, how many more seniors than sophomores are there?

A) 45

B) 90

C) 123

D) 168

$s:j = 3:8$

$s\theta j = 7:5$

4

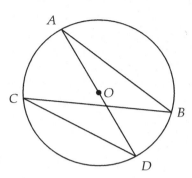

The circle above has center O. Which of the following line segments from the figure above is greatest in length?

A) $\overline{AB}$

B) $\overline{AD}$

C) $\overline{BC}$

D) It cannot be determined from the information given.

5

Jerry used a total of 258 nails to assemble two office desks. The first office desk required 62 fewer nails than the second office desk. How many nails did the first office desk require?

A) 88

B) 98

C) 150

D) 160

$x \quad\quad x - 62$

62

$2x - 62 = 258$

$2x = 320$

$x = 160$

$\frac{62}{98}$

6

Jones climbed a mountain at a speed of 1 kilometer per hour and came down at a speed of 2 kilometers per hour. Which of the following could be the graph of his distance from the bottom of the mountain as a function of time?

A)

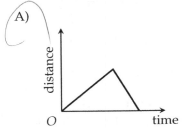

B)

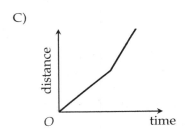

C)

distance / time

D)

distance / time

7

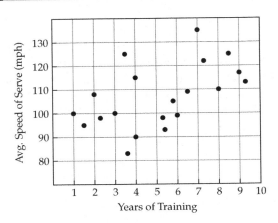

The average speed of serve and number of years of training were recorded for 20 tennis players and plotted in the grid above. Which of the following statements is supported by the plotted data?

A) The player with the least number of years of training had the slowest serve.

B) The player with the highest number of years of training had the fastest serve.

C) More than half of the players had a serve exceeding 110 miles per hour.

D) More than half of the players had more than 5 years of training.

8

At a kitchen equipment store, the price of pots is $14 and the price of pans is $10. If Amy spends more than $100 but less than $150 to buy 3 pots and x pans, which of the following is NOT a possible value of x?

A) 6
B) 8
C) 10
D) 12

9

$$y = x^2 + 10x + 16$$

The equation above represents a parabola in the xy-plane. Which of the following equivalent forms of the equation displays the minimum value of y as a constant or coefficient?

A) $y = (x + 8)(x + 2)$

B) $y - 16 = x(x + 10)$

C) $y = (x + 5)^2 - 9$

D) $y = (x - 5)^2 + 9$

▼

Questions 10-11 refer to the following information.

The Number of Magazine Subscribers and the Average Number of Advertisements per Issue

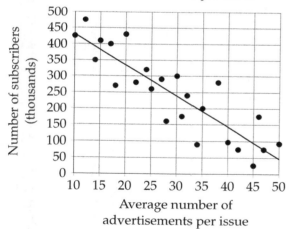

Average number of advertisements per issue

The scatterplot above shows the number of subscribers, in thousands, and the average number of advertisements per issue for each of 24 magazines. The line of best fit for the data is also shown.

10

Which of the following statements about the relationship between the average number of advertisements per issue and the number of subscribers is true?

A) As the average number of advertisements per issue increases, the number of subscribers tends to decrease.

B) As the average number of advertisements per issue increases, the number of subscribers tends to increase.

C) As the average number of advertisements per issue increases, the number of subscribers tends to stay the same.

D) As the average number of advertisements per issue decreases, the number of subscribers tends to decrease.

11

The line of best fit passes through the point $(55, -1)$. Based on this information, which of the following is an appropriate conclusion?

A) There are no magazines that have an average of more than 54 advertisements per issue.

B) A magazine that has an average of more than 54 advertisements per issue does not need to sell any subscriptions.

C) If a magazine had an average of more than 54 advertisements per issue, the magazine would not have any subscribers.

D) The line of best fit should not be used to predict the number of subscribers for magazines that have a large average number of advertisements per issue.

▲

4 🖩 **4**

12

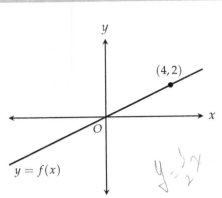

$y = f(x)$

(4, 2)

In the xy-plane above, a point (not shown) with coordinates $(t, t + 5)$ lies on the line represented by $y = f(x)$. What is the value of t ?

A) -10

B) $-\dfrac{5}{2}$

C) 5

D) $\dfrac{5}{2}$

13

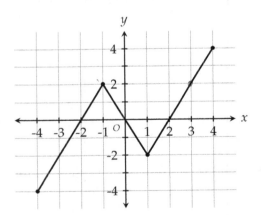

The function f is graphed in the xy-plane above. If $f(c) = f(3)$, which of the following could be the value of c ?

A) -3

B) -2

C) -1

D) 2

14

During a chemistry experiment, the kinetic energy of an object increased at a constant rate of 1,700 joules per second. Which of the following is closest to the total rise in kinetic energy of the object, in calories, over the course of 8 seconds during the experiment?
(Note: 1,000 calories = 4,187 joules)

A) 400

B) 3,250

C) 8,750

D) 57,000

15

The table below shows the final exam scores of 5 students who took history class and chemistry class together.

Final Exam Scores

Student	History class	Chemistry class
Lia	91	98
May	82	85
Mina	93	82
Sori	79	95
Ara	87	82

Let m_1 and r_1 be the median and range, respectively, of the students' final exam scores for history class, and let m_2 and r_2 be the median and range, respectively, of the students' final exam scores for chemistry class. Which of the following is true?

A) $m_1 < m_2$ and $r_1 < r_2$

B) $m_1 < m_2$ and $r_1 > r_2$

C) $m_1 > m_2$ and $r_1 < r_2$

D) $m_1 > m_2$ and $r_1 > r_2$

16

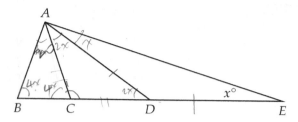

In the figure above, $\angle BAC = 20°$ and $AB = AC$. If triangles ACD and ADE are isosceles, what is the value of x ?

A) 10

B) 15

C) 20

D) 25

17

Lucy placed an order for custom wallets and keychains. Each wallet cost $12 and each keychain cost $8. If Lucy spent a total of $160 on the 18 items in her order, how many keychains did she order?

A) 4

B) 6

C) 12

D) 14

18

A glass block in the shape of a right rectangular prism measures 10 inches by 15 inches by 20 inches. A sculptor removes 880 cubic inches of glass from the block to form a right circular cylinder. If the height of the cylinder is 8 inches, what is the radius of the base of the cylinder, rounded to the nearest tenth of an inch?

A) 3.4

B) 7.8

C) 9.2

D) 11.6

19

If $y > 0$ and $\dfrac{y^b}{y^{\frac{1}{2}}} = \dfrac{1}{y^2}$, what is the value of b ?

A) $-\dfrac{3}{2}$

B) $-\dfrac{5}{2}$

C) $\dfrac{3}{2}$

D) $\dfrac{5}{2}$

20

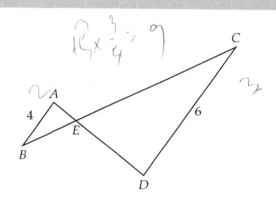

Note: Figure not drawn to scale.

In the figure above, $\overline{AB}$ is parallel to $\overline{CD}$. If $BC = 15$, what is the length of EC ?

A) 6

B) 7

C) 8

D) 9

| 4 | **| 4 |**

21

Tom buys a pack of baseball cards everyday. Each pack contains 7 cards but he gives away the two least valuable ones to his brother. Which of the following best describes the relationship between time (in days) and the total number of baseball cards in Tom's collection?

A) Increasing linear

B) Decreasing linear

C) Exponential growth

D) Exponential decay

▼

Questions 22-23 refer to the following information.

A survey of 250 randomly selected office workers in Boston and Chicago was conducted to gather data on workplace eating habits. The data are shown in the table below.

	Bring lunch to work	Do not bring lunch to work	Total
Boston	44	66	110
Chicago	35	105	140
Total	79	171	250

22

What fraction of those surveyed work in Boston?

A) $\dfrac{2}{5}$

B) $\dfrac{3}{5}$

C) $\dfrac{11}{14}$

D) $\dfrac{11}{25}$

23

Based on the results of the survey, how many times more likely is it for an office worker in Boston to bring lunch to work than it is for an office worker in Chicago to bring lunch to work? (Round the answer to the nearest hundredth.)

A) 0.63

B) 1.26

C) 1.60

D) 2.00

▲

24

A parking meter charges $0.25 for the first 30 minutes and $0.10 for every additional 5 minutes. If Megan is charged $1.35 for parking at this specific meter, how many minutes did she park for?

A) 70

B) 75

C) 80

D) 85

25

Which of the following is an equation of a circle in the xy-plane with center $(3, -1)$ and a radius of 4?

A) $(x-3)^2 + (y+1)^2 = 4$

B) $(x-3)^2 + (y+1)^2 = 16$

C) $(x+1)^2 + (y-3)^2 = 4$

D) $(x+3)^2 + (y-1)^2 = 16$

26

A gym wanted to evaluate the extent to which a new exercise class would appeal to all its members. The gym held a members-only trial class for those interested in attending, and the attendees were surveyed about their experience afterwards. The results showed that of the 60 members who attended, 75 percent would sign up for the class if it became available. Which of the following statements about the gym's survey results is true?

A) They are flawed because the trial class did not include people who are not members of the gym.

B) They are flawed because the attendees of the trial class were not randomly selected members of the gym.

C) They show that approximately 75 percent of the members of the gym would sign up for the new exercise class if it became available.

D) They show that approximately 45 members of the gym would sign up for the new exercise class if it became available.

Questions 27-28 refer to the following information.

Jane is performing an experiment in which she combines potassium and water to produce potassium hydroxide. The amount of water w, in milliliters, needed to create a chemical reaction between potassium and water can be modeled by the equation $w = 1.6a + 10$, where a is the amount of potassium hydroxide, in grams, Jane wishes to produce from the reaction.

27

According to the model, what is the meaning of the 1.6 in the equation?

A) An additional 1.6 milliliters of water is needed to react with one additional gram of potassium.

B) An additional 1.6 milliliters of water is needed to produce one more gram of potassium hydroxide.

C) One gram of potassium hydroxide can be produced by reacting 1.6 milliliters of water with potassium.

D) One additional milliliter of water is needed to produce 1.6 more grams of potassium hydroxide.

28

According to the model, how much more potassium hydroxide, in grams, is produced for each additional milliliter of water used in the reaction?

A) 0.6

B) 0.625

C) 0.875

D) 1.6

4 🖩 **4**

29

$$\frac{\sqrt{2x^2 - 14}}{a} = 3$$

If $x > 0$ and $a = 2$ in the equation above, what is the value of x ?

A) 4
B) 5
C) 6
D) 7

(handwritten: $\sqrt{2x^2-14} = 6$; $2x^2-14 = 36$; $2x^2 = 50$; $x^2 = 25$)

30

Tammy picks three sides of a rectangle and adds their lengths to get 140 cm. Gladys picks three sides of the same rectangle and adds their lengths to get 100 cm. What is the perimeter of the rectangle in cm?

A) 120
B) 140
C) 150
D) 160

(handwritten work: $2y+x=140$; $2x+y=100$; $2x+4y=200$; $3y=180$; $y=60$; $x=20$)

31

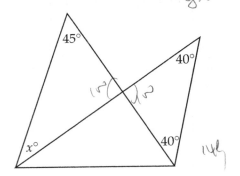

Note: Figure not drawn to scale.

In the figure above, what is the value of x ?

(handwritten: 35)

32

A technology company finds that 11 out of every 600 emails sent through its servers are lost. At this rate, how many emails are lost if 42,000 emails are sent through its servers?

(handwritten: 770)

33

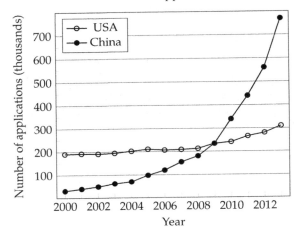

Patent Applications

The graph above shows the annual number of patent applications in the U.S. and in China from 2000 to 2012. In which year did the U.S. and China have the same number of patent applications?

(handwritten: 2009)

50

34

For all $x \geq 3$, $f(x) = \dfrac{\sqrt{x-3}}{2}$. If $f(n) = 3$, what is the value of n ?

$\dfrac{\sqrt{n-3}}{2} = 3$ $n-3=36$

$\sqrt{n-3} = 6$ $n = 33$

39

35

If $-4k + 12 \geq -24$, what is the maximum possible value of $3k$?

$-4k \geq -36$

$k \geq 9$

27

36

When $3x^2 + x + 2$ is divided by $x - 1$, the result can be expressed as $ax + b + \dfrac{c}{x - 1}$, where $a, b,$ and c are constants. What is the value of $a + b + c$?

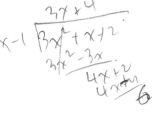

5 13

Questions 37-38 refer to the following information.

Juan's restaurant serves burritos during lunch and dinner. On a typical day, 25 percent more burritos are sold during lunch than during dinner. If x represents the number of burritos sold during lunch, the total number of burritos sold on a typical day can be represented by the expression ax, where a is a constant.

37

$x = $ lunch

What is the value of a in the expression?

$13 \cdot 1.25 = x$

$0 = \dfrac{100}{125} x$

$\dfrac{225}{125} =$ 1.8

38

If the restaurant typically sells 360 burritos during dinner, how many burritos does the restaurant typically sell during lunch?

$360 \times 1.25 =$

450

4

Practice Test 4

Math Test --- No Calculator

25 Minutes, 20 Questions

Reference

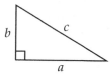

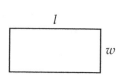

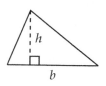

$$A = \pi r^2$$
$$C = 2\pi r$$

$$A = lw$$

$$A = \frac{1}{2}bh$$

$$c^2 = a^2 + b^2$$

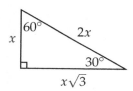

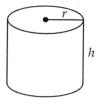

Special Right Triangles

$$V = lwh$$

$$V = \pi r^2 h$$

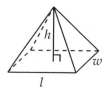

$$V = \frac{4}{3}\pi r^3$$

$$V = \frac{1}{3}\pi r^2 h$$

$$V = \frac{1}{3}lwh$$

There are 360 degrees of arc in a circle.
There are 2π radians of arc in a circle.
The sum of the measures of the angles of a triangle, in degrees, is 180.

3 **3**

1

If $3x - 6 = -6 + 3x$, which of the following must be true for this equation?

A) The equation is true only if $x = 0$.

B) The equation is true only if $x = 1$.

C) The equation is true only if $x = 2$.

D) The equation is true for any value of x.

2

Kevin has collected m coins. Ellie has collected half as many as Kevin, but 5 more than Robert. In terms of m, how many coins has Robert collected?

A) $2m - 5$

B) $\dfrac{m}{2} + 5$

C) $2m + 5$

D) $\dfrac{m}{2} - 5$

3

$$y = 40 + 10t$$

A teacher gives her class a test. After grading the tests, she finds that the model above can be used to predict a student's score y on the test in terms of the number of hours t the student spent studying for the test. Based on the model, by how much would one additional hour of studying increase a student's score on the test?

A) 4

B) 10

C) 20

D) 40

4

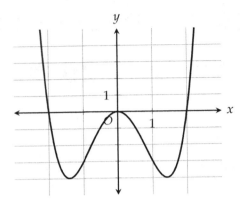

Which of the following could be the function g, as shown above?

A) $g(x) = x^2(x + 2)^2$

B) $g(x) = x^3(x - 2)$

C) $g(x) = x^2(x + 2)(x - 2)$

D) $g(x) = (x + 2)^2(x - 2)^2$

5

$$-2x - y = -9$$
$$5x - 2y = 18$$

Which of the following ordered pairs (x, y) fulfills the system of equations above?

A) $(-4, 1)$

B) $(2, 5)$

C) $(3, 3)$

D) $(4, 1)$

6

Which of the following is equivalent to $(\sqrt{a} - 2\sqrt{b})^2$ for all positive values of a and b ?

A) $a - 4b$

B) $a + 4b$

C) $a - 2\sqrt{ab} + 4b$

D) $a - 4\sqrt{ab} + 4b$

3 **3**

7

In which of the following figures is the slope of line shown closest to $-\dfrac{1}{2}$?

A)

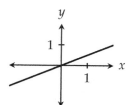

B)

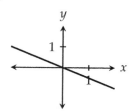

C)

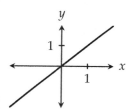

D)

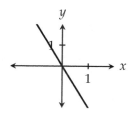

8

$$(x+6)^2 + (y-4)^2 = 100$$

The equation above defines a circle in the xy-plane. The circle intercepts the y-axis at $(0, 12)$ and $(0, c)$. What is the value of c ?

A) -16

B) -8

C) -4

D) 2

9

$$k^2 x^{2a} = x^{2a+2}$$

In the equation above, k, x, and a are positive integers greater than 1. What is the value of $x - k$?

A) -1

B) 0

C) 1

D) 2

10

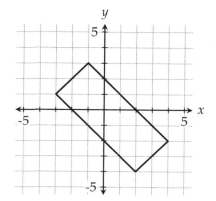

What is the area, in square units, of the rectangle shown in the xy-plane above?

A) 10

B) $10\sqrt{2}$

C) 16

D) 20

3 **3**

11

What is the value of $\sin 30° - \cos 60°$?

A) 0

B) $\dfrac{1 - \sqrt{3}}{2}$

C) $\dfrac{\sqrt{2} - 1}{2}$

D) $\dfrac{\sqrt{3} - 1}{2}$

12

The graph of the equation $y = 2x - b$ passes through the point $(2b, -9)$. What is the value of b ?

A) -6

B) -3

C) 3

D) 6

13

$$\frac{2i + 1}{3i - 2}$$

If the expression above is written in the form $a + bi$, where a and b are constants, what is the value of b ?

A) $-\dfrac{4}{13}$

B) $\dfrac{4}{13}$

C) $-\dfrac{7}{13}$

D) $\dfrac{7}{13}$

14

$$x + 2y < 11$$
$$y > 3$$

In the xy-plane, which of the following consists of the x-coordinates of all the solutions to the system of inequalities above?

A) $x < 4$

B) $x < 5$

C) $x < 7$

D) $x < 17$

15

$$x = 1 - 2y$$
$$4y = x^2 + 3$$

How many ordered pairs (x, y) in the xy-plane are solutions to the system of equations above?

A) 0

B) 1

C) 2

D) Infinitely many

16

If $\dfrac{1}{a + 2b} = 5$, then what is the value of $a + 2b$?

17

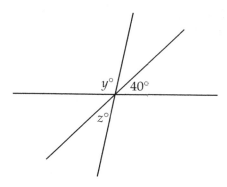

Note: Figure not drawn to scale.

Three lines intersect in the figure above. What is the value of $y + z$?

18

If $c + d = -5$ and $c - d = -12$, then what is the value of $c^2 - d^2$?

19

$$\frac{3}{2x} - \frac{2}{3x} = \frac{5}{3}$$

If $x \neq 0$, for what value of x is the equation above true?

20

$$7(2.5x - 1.5) = 12(0.5x - 0.3)$$

What is the solution to the equation above?

| 4 | 🖩 **| 4 |**

Math Test --- Calculator

55 Minutes, 38 Questions

Reference

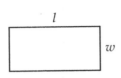

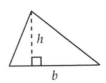

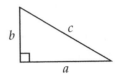

$A = \pi r^2$
$C = 2\pi r$

$A = lw$

$A = \frac{1}{2}bh$

$c^2 = a^2 + b^2$

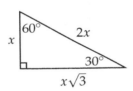

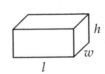

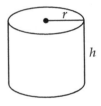

Special Right Triangles

$V = lwh$

$V = \pi r^2 h$

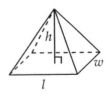

$V = \frac{4}{3}\pi r^3$

$V = \frac{1}{3}\pi r^2 h$

$V = \frac{1}{3}lwh$

There are 360 degrees of arc in a circle.
There are 2π radians of arc in a circle.
The sum of the measures of the angles of a triangle, in degrees, is 180.

4 **4**

1

When a certain gas tank is 70% empty, it contains 12 gallons. How many gallons can a full tank hold?

A) 30

B) 36

C) 40

D) 42

2

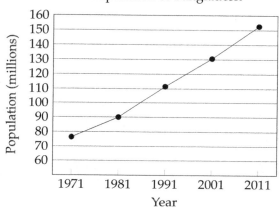

Population of Bangladesh

According to the graph above, which of the following is closest to the increase in the population of Bangladesh from 1971 to 2001?

A) 21 million

B) 54 million

C) 62 million

D) 75 million

3

Which scatterplot shows a positive association that is not linear?

A)

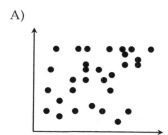

B)

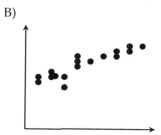

C)

D)

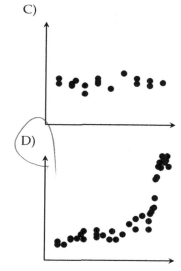

4

The table below shows the daily programming breakdown in hours at three different radio stations.

Station	Music	Commercials	News
WROK	18	5	1
WPOP	16	5	3
KJAZ	15	4	5

Approximately what percentage of the day does WPOP spend on commercials?

A) 12.5%

B) 18.3%

C) 20.8%

D) 66.7%

5

If $10xy - 3y + 6 = 41 + 2y$, what is the value of $2xy - y$?

A) 5

B) 6

C) 7

D) 15

Questions 6-7 refer to the following information.

Lawyers John and Will review legal documents. John charges an initial consultation fee and then $50 for each hour of legal review. Will does not charge a consultation fee but charges $75 for each hour of legal review. The graph below shows the two lawyers' wages, where h is the number of hours worked and y is the total wage in dollars.

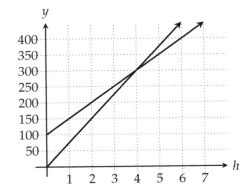

6

How much does John charge for his initial consultation?

A) $100

B) $200

C) $300

D) $400

7

Which of the following inequalities gives all the values of h for which it is less expensive to hire John than it is to hire Will for legal review?

A) $h \geq 0$

B) $h > 4$

C) $0 \leq h < 4$

D) $h > 300$

8

The table below summarizes the meal choices made by a group of students ordering lunch at a cafeteria. Each student in the group ordered one sandwich and one drink.

		Sandwich	
		Hot	Cold
Drink	Hot	27	30
	Cold	51	42

What percentage of the students in the group chose to have a cold sandwich?

A) 38%

B) 48%

C) 52%

D) 62%

9

If $\dfrac{2a+3b}{a-b} = \dfrac{3}{4}$, then $\dfrac{a}{b}$?

A) -3

B) $-\dfrac{1}{3}$

C) $\dfrac{1}{3}$

D) 3

$8a + 12b = 3a - 3b$

$5a = -15b$

$\dfrac{5a}{b} = -15$

10

If $a = 2x^3y^2 - 3x^2y^3$ and $b = -3x^3y^2 + 2x^2y^3$, what is $a + b$ in terms of x and y ?

A) $x^3y^2 + x^2y^3$

B) $x^3y^2 - x^2y^3$

C) $-x^3y^2 - x^2y^3$

D) $-x^3y^2 + x^2y^3$

$-x^3y^2 - x^2y^3$

11

$$4y < x - 5$$
$$x \le 2 - y$$

$4y - 5 < x$

Which ordered pair (x, y) satisfies the system of inequalities shown above?

A) $(-4, 2)$

B) $(-1, -3)$

C) $(3, 6)$

D) $(7, -2)$

$4y - 5 < x \le 2 - y$

12

A budget committee wanted to determine whether teachers in a school district would adopt electronic whiteboards if they were installed in classrooms. The committee surveyed a sample of 200 computer science teachers in the district and found that 180 of those sampled were in favor of adopting electronic whiteboards. Which of the following statements must be true?

A) The survey results are biased because the sample size is not large enough.

B) Approximately 90 percent of all teachers in the school district are in favor of adopting electronic whiteboards.

C) The survey results may not accurately reflect the opinions of all teachers in the school district.

D) Of all computer science teachers in the school district, 90 percent are in favor of adopting electronic whiteboards.

13

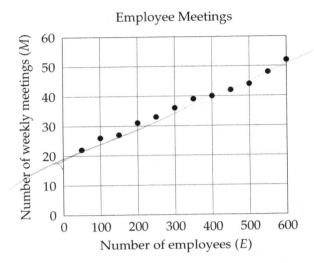

Employee Meetings

The scatterplot above shows the number of employees E and the number of weekly meetings M at 7 companies selected at random. Which of the following equations best models the relationship between E and M ?

A) $M = 0.05E + 20$

B) $M = 0.1E + 16$

C) $M = 0.5E + 18$

D) $M = 5E + 25$

▼

Questions 14-15 refer to the following information.

$$R(Q) = 20Q$$
$$C(Q) = 14Q + 114$$

The total revenue generated by a particular product and the total cost of producing it are both functions of the quantity of products sold. The function $R(Q)$ gives the total revenue when the quantity sold is Q units. The function $C(Q)$ gives the total cost when the quantity sold is Q units.

14

How will the total cost change if the quantity of units sold is decreased by 5?

A)   The total cost will decrease by $70.

B)   The total cost will increase by $70.

C)   The total cost will decrease by $44.

D)   The total cost will increase by $60.

15

At what quantity of units sold will the total revenue generated by the product equal the total cost of producing it?

A)   17

B)   18

C)   19

D)   20

▲

16

Jane receives $2.75 each month for each square foot of an apartment that she rents out. If the apartment has an area of 500 square feet, how much rent, in dollars, would Jane receive from a tenant who occupies the entire area for one year?

A)   16,500

B)   17,250

C)   18,375

D)   19,750

4 🖩 **4**

17

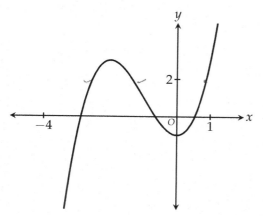

The graph of the function f in the xy-plane is shown above. For how many values of x in the portion of the graph shown above does $f(x) = 2$?

A) None

B) One

C) Two

D) Three

18

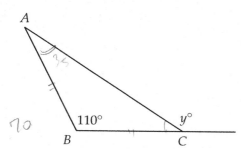

Note: Figure not drawn to scale.

In the figure above, $AB = BC$ and $\angle ABC = 110°$. What is the value of y?

A) 125

B) 130

C) 135

D) 145

19

A rectangle has a perimeter of 110 cm. The width of the rectangle is 35 cm more than its length. What is the area of the rectangle in square centimeters?

A) 200

B) 332

C) 450

D) 564

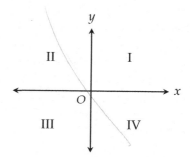

20

In the figure above, which quadrants contain the points (x, y) that satisfy the condition $\dfrac{2x}{y} = -1$?

A) II only

B) II and IV only

C) I and III only

D) I, II, III, and IV

21

If $f(4) = -2$, which of the following CANNOT be the definition of f?

A) $f(x) = x - 6$

B) $f(x) = x^2 - 4x - 2$

C) $f(x) = -3x + 14$

D) $f(x) = -2(x - 3)^2$

22

The mean tire pressure of the cars at Dealer A is equal to the mean tire pressure of the cars at Dealer B. However, while the standard deviation of the tire pressures of the cars at Dealer A is 2.5 psi (pounds per square inch), the standard deviation of the tire pressures of the cars at Dealer B is 1.2 psi. Which of the following statements must be true?

A) The mean tire pressure of the cars at Dealer A is 1.3 psi less than the mean tire pressure of the cars at Dealer B.

B) The median tire pressure of the cars at Dealer A is 1.3 psi less than the median tire pressure of the cars at Dealer B.

C) The median tire pressure of the cars at Dealer A is 1.3 psi greater than the median tire pressure of the cars at Dealer B.

D) The tire pressures of the cars at Dealer A are more variable than the tire pressures of the cars at Dealer B.

23

The base of a cylinder has a circumference of 5π. The height of the cylinder is 4. What is the volume of the cylinder?

A) 20π

B) 25π

C) 40π

D) 50π

Questions 24-25 refer to the following information.

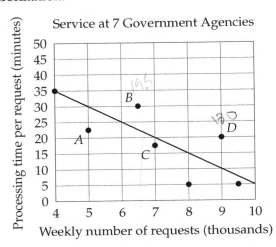

The scatterplot above shows the weekly number of requests received at 7 different government agencies and their processing time per request. The line of best fit is also shown.

24

How many of the 7 government agencies have a processing time per request that differs by more than 5 minutes from that predicted by the line of best fit?

A) 3

B) 4

C) 5

D) 6

25

Of the labeled points, which represents the government agency that spends the most time processing all of its requests each week?

A) *A*

B) *B*

C) *C*

D) *D*

26

Alfred's favorite drink is 2 parts lime juice to 5 parts raspberry soda. Jenny's favorite drink is 1 part lime juice to 4 parts raspberry soda. If Jenny has a bottle containing 21 ounces of Alfred's favorite drink, how many ounces of raspberry soda should she add to it to get her favorite drink?

A) 6

B) 7

C) 8

D) 9

27

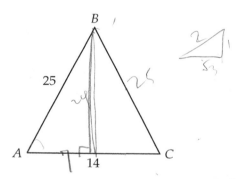

In the triangle above, $AB = BC$. What is the value of $\sin A$?

A) 0.28

B) 0.56

C) 0.84

D) 0.96

28

Price	Quantity demanded
$320	93,600
$360	84,200

A clothing company sells its flagship winter jacket all year round. The table above shows the quantity demanded when the price of the jacket is $320 and when it is $360. Assuming the quantity demanded decreases at a constant rate with respect to price, which of the following linear functions Q best models the quantity demanded when the price of the jacket is p dollars?

A) $Q(p) = 93,600 - 235p$

B) $Q(p) = 93,600 - 260p$

C) $Q(p) = 93,600 - 235(p - 320)$

D) $Q(p) = 93,600 - 260(p - 320)$

29

Anna opens a bank account with an initial deposit of $1,000. The bank account will earn 3 percent interest compounded annually for the first 5 years, after which it will earn 7 percent interest compounded annually. Which of the following expressions represents the total amount in the account after t years, where $t > 5$?

A) $1,000(1.03)^5(1.07)^t$

B) $1,000(1.03)^{t-5}(1.07)^t$

C) $1,000(1.03)^5(1.07)^{t-5}$

D) $1,000(1.03)^5(1.07)^{t+5}$

4 🖩 **4**

30

Solution A is 60% acid and solution B is 40% acid. Solving which of the following systems of equations gives the number of gallons of solution A, a, and the number of gallons of solution B, b, that should be mixed together to produce 100 gallons of a solution that is 55% acid?

A) $a + b = 100$
     $0.6a + 0.4b = 0.55$

B) $a + b = 55$
     $0.6a + 0.4b = 100$

C) $a + b = 100$
     $0.6a + 0.4b = 55$

D) $a + b = 100$
     $0.4a + 0.6b = 0.55$

31

Mary runs around a circular track with a radius of 25 meters. If she runs at 75 meters per minute, how many minutes will it take her to run one lap around the track, rounded to the nearest integer?

100π

$\frac{4}{n}$

32

Note: Figure not drawn to scale.

In the figure above, $AC = CD$. What is the length of $\overline{BC}$?

$3x-4 = 2x+6$
$x = 10$

6

33

$$(x - a)(x - a - b) = 0$$

In the quadratic equation above, a and b are constants greater than zero. If 3 and 8 are two solutions to the equation, what is the value of b ?

5

34

In the xy-plane, the line represented by $2y - 3x = 5$ is the same as the line represented by $8y - ax = 20$, where a is a constant. What is the value of a ?

12

35

Let the function f be defined by $f(x) = x^2 - x + 3$. If $f(m + 1) = 5$ and $m > 0$, what is the value of m ?

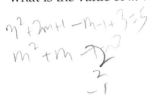

$m^2 + m \quad$
$\frac{2}{-1}$

1

36

A city planner is determining the layout of rectangular parking spaces along a street. The parking spaces are to be placed side by side in a single row until they form an area with a total width of 630 feet. Each parking space must have equal dimensions and a width between 17 and 20 feet. If the planner wants the total number of parking spaces along the street to be a multiple of 6, how wide must each parking space be, in feet?

---▼---

Questions 37-38 refer to the following information.

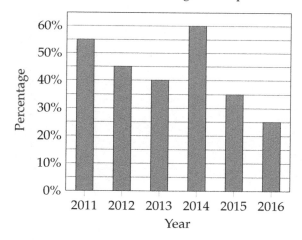

Students living on campus

The graph above shows the percentage of students living on campus each year from 2011 to 2016 for a certain university.

37

In 2013, university meal plans were purchased by 80% of the students living on campus and 25% of the students not living on campus. What percentage of all the students at the university purchased a meal plan in 2013? (Disregard the % when gridding your answer.)

38

In 2015, there were 18,000 students in total at the university. In 2016, there were x more students at the university than in 2015. If the number of students living on campus each year was the same, what is the value of x ?

---▲---

5

Practice Test 5

Math Test --- No Calculator

25 Minutes, 20 Questions

Reference

$A = \pi r^2$
$C = 2\pi r$

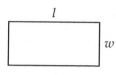

$A = lw$

$A = \frac{1}{2}bh$

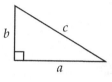

$c^2 = a^2 + b^2$

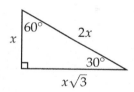

Special Right Triangles

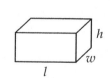

$V = lwh$

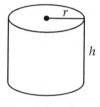

$V = \pi r^2 h$

$V = \frac{4}{3}\pi r^3$

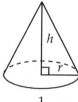

$V = \frac{1}{3}\pi r^2 h$

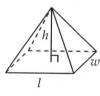

$V = \frac{1}{3}lwh$

There are 360 degrees of arc in a circle.
There are 2π radians of arc in a circle.
The sum of the measures of the angles of a triangle, in degrees, is 180.

3 **3**

1

Which of the following expressions is equivalent

to $\dfrac{\dfrac{x}{y}}{\dfrac{y}{z}}$?

A) $\dfrac{x}{z}$

B) $\dfrac{z}{x}$

C) $\dfrac{xz}{y^2}$

D) $\dfrac{y^2}{xz}$

2

A movie rental service charges \$15 as a monthly subscription fee and \$3 per movie rented. If Alex rents x movies per month from this service, which of the following expressions gives the total amount, in dollars, he spends on movie rentals in one year?

A) $12(18x)$

B) $15 + 12(3x)$

C) $12(15) + 3x$

D) $12(15 + 3x)$

3

If $\dfrac{x^{a^2} \cdot x^{b^2}}{x^{2ab}} = x^{25}$, $x > 1$, which of the following could be the value of $a - b$?

A) 3

B) 4

C) 5

D) 6

4

$$v = 100 + 25h$$

The daily number of visitors v to a store that is open for h hours each day can be modeled by the equation above, where $h \geq 1$. According to the model, how many more daily visitors can the store expect if it were open for two more hours each day?

A) 25

B) 50

C) 100

D) 200

5

If $mb < 0$, then the line whose equation is $y = mx + b$ cannot contain which of the following points?

A) $(-1, 0)$

B) $(0, 1)$

C) $(1, 0)$

D) $(0, -1)$

6

$$-3x + 2y = 5$$
$$-9x + 6y = 18$$

The system of equations above has how many solutions (x, y) ?

A) Zero

B) One

C) Two

D) More than two

3 **3**

7

If $\dfrac{x + x}{x \cdot x \cdot x \cdot n} = 1$, where $n \neq 0$, then $n =$

A) $\dfrac{1}{x^2}$

B) $\dfrac{2}{x^2}$

C) $\dfrac{x^2}{2}$

D) $2x^2$

8

Which of the following functions has a graph in the xy-plane that does not cross the x-axis?

A) $f(x) = 1 - x^2$

B) $f(x) = |x - 1|$

C) $f(x) = (x - 1)^2 + 1$

D) $f(x) = x^3 - 1$

9

Which of the following is equivalent to

$\left(\dfrac{1}{xy}\right)(2x + 2y)$?

A) $\dfrac{1}{x} + \dfrac{1}{y}$

B) $\dfrac{2}{x} + \dfrac{2}{y}$

C) $\dfrac{2}{x} + \dfrac{2}{xy} + \dfrac{2}{y}$

D) $2x^2y + 2xy^2$

10

$$\frac{1}{3}x + \frac{1}{6}y = 5$$

$$\frac{3}{5}x + \frac{1}{5}y = -4$$

Which of the following ordered pairs (x, y) fulfills the system of equations above?

A) $(-50, 130)$

B) $(2, 26)$

C) $(5, 20)$

D) $(20, -10)$

11

A car dealer has a budget of \$12,000 to advertise on television and on radio. A television ad costs \$800 and a radio ad costs \$300. The dealer wants to run no more than 24 radio ads. The total number of ads must be at least 3 times the number of television ads. Which of the following systems of inequalities represents the conditions described if x is the number of television ads and y is the number of radio ads?

A) $800x + 300y \geq 12,000$
$$y \geq 24$$
$$x + y \leq 3x$$

B) $800x + 300y \geq 12,000$
$$y \geq 24$$
$$x + y \leq 3y$$

C) $800x + 300y \leq 12,000$
$$y \leq 24$$
$$x + y \geq 3x$$

D) $800x + 300y \leq 12,000$
$$y \leq 24$$
$$x + y \geq 3y$$

12

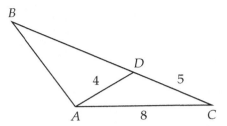

In the figure above, the measure of $\angle ABC$ is equal to the measure of $\angle CAD$. What is the value of $\dfrac{AB}{BC}$?

A) $\dfrac{1}{2}$

B) $\dfrac{4}{5}$

C) $\dfrac{5}{4}$

D) $\dfrac{5}{8}$

13

$$\frac{4i}{i-1}$$

Which of the following is equivalent to the expression above? (Note: $i = \sqrt{-1}$)

A) $-2 + 2i$

B) $-2 - 2i$

C) $2 + 2i$

D) $2 - 2i$

14

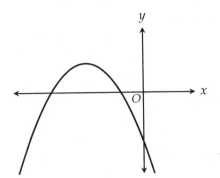

A parabola, defined by $y = a(x - b)^2 + c$, is graphed in the xy-plane above. Which of the following is true about the parabola with equation $y = c(x + a)(x + b)$?

A) The graph opens upward and has two negative x-intercepts.

B) The graph opens upward and has two positive x-intercepts.

C) The graph opens downward and has two negative x-intercepts.

D) The graph opens downward and has two positive x-intercepts.

15

$$p(x) = (3x^2 - 5)(x + k) - 20$$

In the polynomial $p(x)$ defined above, k is a constant. If x is a factor of $p(x)$, what is the value of k ?

A) -6

B) -4

C) 2

D) 4

16

Matt collects rare baseball cards. Each pack of baseball cards he buys contains 12 cards, two of which are rare. He currently has 40 rare cards. If his goal is to have 100 rare baseball cards, how many more packs of baseball cards will he have to buy?

17

If f is a function defined by $f(x) = \dfrac{2x - 5}{6}$, for what value of x is $f(x) = \dfrac{1}{2}$?

18

If $\dfrac{3c}{d} = 4$, what is the value of $\dfrac{60d}{c}$?

19

$$y = x^2 - 10x + k$$

In the equation above, k is a constant. If the equation represents a parabola in the xy-plane that is tangent to the x-axis, what is the value of k ?

20

What is one possible solution to the equation $\dfrac{22}{x + 3} - \dfrac{6}{x - 2} = 1$?

4 4

Math Test --- Calculator

55 Minutes, 38 Questions

Reference

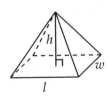

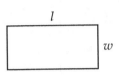

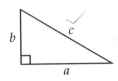

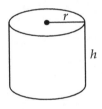

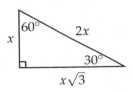

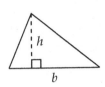

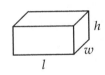

$A = \pi r^2$
$C = 2\pi r$

$A = lw$

$A = \frac{1}{2}bh$

$c^2 = a^2 + b^2$

Special Right Triangles

$V = lwh$

$V = \pi r^2 h$

$V = \frac{4}{3}\pi r^3$

$V = \frac{1}{3}\pi r^2 h$

$V = \frac{1}{3}lwh$

There are 360 degrees of arc in a circle.
There are 2π radians of arc in a circle.
The sum of the measures of the angles of a triangle, in degrees, is 180.

4 **4**

1

Anita is moving back to Mexico and exchanges 400 U.S. dollars for 6,650 Mexican pesos. Based on this information, which of the following is closest to the number of pesos one U.S. dollar is worth?

A) 15.83

B) 15.97

C) 16.24

D) 16.63

2

A bottle contains x ounces of soda. After Harry drinks from it, there are y ounces left. In terms of x and y, what percent of the bottle did Harry consume?

A) $\dfrac{x}{100(x-y)}\%$

B) $\dfrac{100(x-y)}{x}\%$

C) $\dfrac{100y}{x}\%$

D) $\dfrac{y}{100x}\%$

3

If $\dfrac{x-a}{5} = 12$ and $a = 10$, what is the value of x ?

A) 40

B) 50

C) 60

D) 70

4

A car has an estimated initial value of $65,000. Once the car is sold, its value decreases at a constant rate of $2,300 per year. Which of the following equations best approximates the value V, in dollars, of the car t years after it is sold, for $0 \le t \le 28$?

A) $V = 65,000 + 2,800t$

B) $V = 65,000 - 2,800t$

C) $V = 65,000 + 2,300t$

D) $V = 65,000 - 2,300t$

5

In the xy-plane, how many times does the graph of $f(x) = (x-3)(x-1)(x+2)^2$ intersect the x-axis?

A) 2

B) 3

C) 4

D) 5

4 **4**

Questions 6-7 refer to the following information.

Value of Painting A

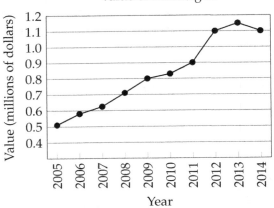

The line graph above shows the dollar value of a piece of artwork, Painting A, from 2005 to 2014.

6

According to the graph, what was the greatest change (in absolute value) in the value of the painting between two consecutive years?

A) $20,000

B) $100,000

C) $200,000

D) $650,000

7

What was the average rate of change in the value of Painting A from 2009 to 2014?

A) $20,000 per year

B) $30,000 per year

C) $50,000 per year

D) $60,000 per year

8

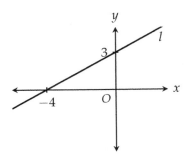

The graph of the line l is shown in the xy-plane above. The y-intercept of line l is 3 and the x-intercept is -4. If line m is perpendicular to line l, what is the slope of line m ?

A) $-\dfrac{4}{3}$

B) $-\dfrac{3}{4}$

C) $-\dfrac{1}{2}$

D) $\dfrac{3}{4}$

9

At a retail store, a salesperson can choose between two salary options. The first option is a monthly salary of $2,800. The second option is a monthly salary of $1,500 and a $12 commission on each dress shirt sold. Which of the following inequalities gives the number of dress shirts x that must be sold in a month for the salary offered by the second option to exceed the one offered by the first?

A) $x < 108$

B) $x \geq 108$

C) $x > 109$

D) $x \geq 109$

10

Town	Number of coffee shops
A	14
B	2
C	11
D	9
E	13
F	12
G	10

The table above shows the number of coffee shops in seven different towns. Removing which of the following towns from the data would bring the mean number of coffee shops and the median number of coffee shops for the six remaining towns closest together in value?

A) Town A

B) Town B

C) Town C

D) Town D

11

A store owner increases the price of a pillow by 35 percent, but a customer uses a coupon to buy the pillow at 35 percent off the already increased price. If the original price of the pillow was p dollars, which of the following represents the final price in terms of p ?

A) $(1.35)(0.65)p$

B) $(1.35)(1.65)p$

C) $(0.35)(1.65)p$

D) $1.35p - 0.35p$

Questions 12-13 refer to the following information.

A student studying agriculture performed an experiment in which a group of randomly selected seed potatoes was grown with fertilizer and another group was grown without fertilizer. The table below shows a summary of the weights for the 720 potatoes that were harvested.

Weight	With fertilizer	Without fertilizer
At least 6 ounces	236	138
Less than 6 ounces	159	187

12

If one of the harvested potatoes is chosen at random, which of the following is closest to the probability that the potato was grown without fertilizer and weighs less than 6 ounces?

A) 0.19

B) 0.22

C) 0.26

D) 0.58

13

What is the difference, to the nearest thousandth, between the proportion of potatoes grown with fertilizer that weigh at least 6 ounces and the proportion of potatoes grown without fertilizer that weigh at least 6 ounces?

A) 0.022

B) 0.136

C) 0.173

D) 0.262

4 **4**

14

A coal-processing plant can process 90 tons of coal per <u>minute</u>. Three trucks can deliver 135 tons of coal per <u>hour</u>. What is the minimum number of trucks necessary to keep up with the plant?

A) 40

B) 80

C) 100

D) 120

15

Which of the following is an equation of a circle in the xy-plane with center $(2, -3)$ and a circumference of 20π ?

A) $(x + 2)^2 + (y - 3)^2 = 20$

B) $(x - 2)^2 + (y + 3)^2 = 20$

C) $(x - 2)^2 + (y + 3)^2 = 100$

D) $(x + 2)^2 + (y - 3)^2 = 400$

16

$$f(x) = x^3 + 2$$

$$g(x) = 2x$$

The functions f and g are defined above. If $f(b) = 29$, what is the value of $g(b)$?

A) 4

B) 6

C) 8

D) 10

17

$$-4x^2y + 3x^2y^2$$

$$2xy^2 - 5x^2y^2$$

What is the sum of the two polynomials above?

A) $-4x^2y + 2xy^2 - 2x^2y^2$

B) $-4x^2y + 2xy^2 + 3x^2y^2$

C) $-2x^2y - 2x^2y^2$

D) $-2x^3y^3 - 2x^4y^4$

18

Researchers are attempting to model the growth of the recovering hawksbill turtle population in East Africa. They estimate the population to be 200 in the first year. In the second year, they record a population of 600 turtles. How much greater would the estimated population be in the third year if the turtle population growth were exponential rather than linear?

A) 800

B) 1000

C) 1200

D) 1800

Questions 19-20 refer to the following information.

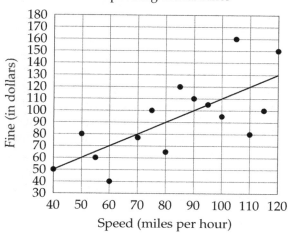

The scatterplot above shows the relationship between the speed of the driver and the amount of the fine, in dollars, for 15 speeding tickets issued by a local police department. The line of best fit is also shown.

19

Based on the line of best fit, what is the predicted fine, in dollars, for a driver speeding at 90 miles per hour?

A) 70

B) 80

C) 90

D) 100

20

Which of the following is the best interpretation of the slope of the line of best fit in the context of this problem?

A) The estimated fine increase, in dollars, for every mile per hour over the speed limit

B) The estimated fine increase, in dollars, for every 10 miles per hour over the speed limit

C) The estimated increase in the speed of the driver, in miles per hour, for every one dollar increase in the fine

D) The estimated increase in the speed of the driver, in miles per hour, for every 10 dollar increase in the fine

21

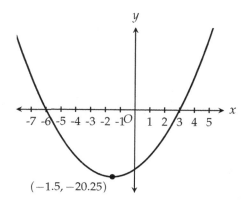

A parabola is shown in the xy-plane above. Which of the following equations correctly represents the parabola by displaying the x-intercepts of the parabola as constants or coefficients?

A) $y = (x + 1.5)^2 - 20.25$

B) $y = (x - 1.5)^2 - 20.25$

C) $y = (x + 6)(x - 3)$

D) $y = (x - 6)(x + 3)$

| 4 **4 |**

22

$$\frac{1}{10}(11x - 5) = 3x - 1.9x - 5$$

Which of the following statements describes the equation above?

A) $x = 0$ is the only solution.

B) $x = 10$ is the only solution.

C) There are infinitely many solutions.

D) There are no solutions.

23

Jake has a bank account that earns 5 percent interest compounded annually. After 8 years, he has a total of $4,000 in the account. Which of the following represents the value of his initial deposit?

A) $\dfrac{4,000}{(0.95)^8}$

B) $\dfrac{4,000}{(1.05)^8}$

C) $4,000(0.95)^8$

D) $4,000 - 4,000(.05)(8)$

24

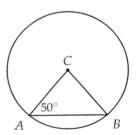

In the figure above, A and B are points on the circle C. If the area of the circle is 54π, what is the area of the sector formed by central angle ACB ?

A) 10π

B) 12π

C) 14π

D) 16π

25

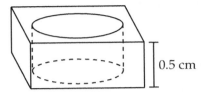

The figure above shows a metal ring with two square faces and a thickness of 0.5 cm. The square faces have a side length of 2.5 cm and the circular hole has a diameter of 2 cm. Which of the following is closest to the volume, in cubic centimeters, of the metal used to form the ring?

A) 1.07

B) 1.55

C) 2.14

D) 3.11

26

In the xy-plane, line l passes through $(0, 0)$ and is perpendicular to the line $3x + y = c$, where c is a constant. If the two lines intersect at the point $(k, k - 4)$, what is the value of k ?

A) 4

B) 6

C) 8

D) 10

4   **4**

27

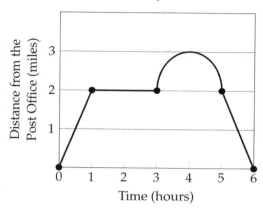

Delivery Route

Pat delivers packages for the post office. The graph above shows his distance from the post office during his delivery route. Which portion of the graph represents the times when Pat is driving in a circle around the post office?

A) The portion from 0 hours to 1 hour

B) The portion from 1 hour to 3 hours

C) The portion from 3 hours to 5 hours

D) The portion from 5 hours to 6 hours

28

John and Nick are assigned different data entry jobs. John can enter 40 records every hour and Nick can enter 50 records every hour. After working for 48 minutes, John and Nick each have 120 records left to enter. Which of the following will be the difference in their job completion times, in <u>minutes</u>?

A) 12

B) 24

C) 36

D) 48

29

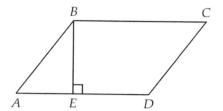

In the figure above, $ABCD$ is a parallelogram. If $\sin \angle ABE = n$, which of the following expresses $\cos \angle C$ in terms of n ?

A) n

B) $\dfrac{1}{n}$

C) $\sqrt{1 - n^2}$

D) $\dfrac{n}{\sqrt{1 + n^2}}$

30

If $3n - 8 < x < n$, which of the following must be true?

  I. $n - x < 0$
  II. $n < 4$
  III. $2x < 4n - 8$

A) I and II only

B) II only

C) II and III only

D) I, II, and III

31

Martin took a random sample of fast food orders at a local restaurant and found that 30 percent of the orders in the sample included fries. Out of 550 orders at the same restaurant, what would be the estimated number of orders that do NOT include fries?

4 🖩 **4**

32

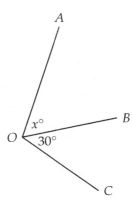

Note: Figure not drawn to scale.

In the figure above, the measure of $\angle AOB$ is $\frac{2}{5}$ the measure of $\angle AOC$. What is the value of x ?

33

$$\frac{4}{5} - 3\left(\frac{1}{2} + x\right) = \frac{3}{10} - 4x$$

What is the solution to the equation above?

34

$$y = \frac{1}{2}x^2 - 3x$$

$$y = 2x$$

If the ordered pairs $(0,0)$ and (a,b) satisfy the system of equations above, what is the value of b ?

35

There are 50 questions on a quiz given to a class of students. Only 20% of the class answered all the questions on the quiz. Of the remaining students, half answered two-fifths of the questions and the other half answered three-fifths. What was the average number of questions answered on this quiz?

36

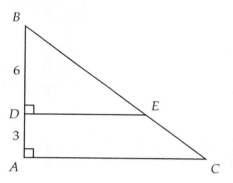

In the figure above, $AD = 3$, $BD = 6$, and $BC = 15$. What is the area of trapezoid $ADEC$?

Questions 37-38 refer to the following information.

Years of Experience	Commission rate
1	0.05
2	0.075
3	0.12
4	0.15
5	0.18
6 or more	0.20

The chart above shows the commission structure for the salespeople at a given company. Each salesperson's monthly salary can be calculated by using the formula $S = 2,400 + cx$, where S is the monthly salary, in dollars, c is the commission rate, and x is the salesperson's sales, in dollars, for the given month.

37

Becky, a salesperson with 3 years of experience, brings in $5,000 in sales in January. In dollars, what is Becky's salary in January?

38

A salesperson with 1 year of experience earns $4,500 in salary during one month. He would have earned $9,960 in salary during that same month if he had how many more years of experience?

6

Practice Test 6

Math Test --- No Calculator

25 Minutes, 20 Questions

Reference

$A = \pi r^2$
$C = 2\pi r$

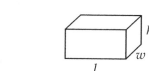

$A = lw$

$A = \frac{1}{2}bh$

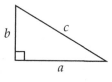

$c^2 = a^2 + b^2$

 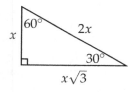

$x\sqrt{3}$

Special Right Triangles

x

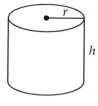

$V = lwh$

$V = \pi r^2 h$

$V = \frac{4}{3}\pi r^3$

$V = \frac{1}{3}\pi r^2 h$

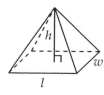

$V = \frac{1}{3}lwh$

There are 360 degrees of arc in a circle.
There are 2π radians of arc in a circle.
The sum of the measures of the angles of a triangle, in degrees, is 180.

3 **3**

1

If $3y \cdot 4y = \dfrac{3}{7} \cdot \dfrac{4}{7}$ and $y > 0$, what is the value of y ?

A) $\dfrac{1}{49}$

B) $\dfrac{1}{14}$

C) $\dfrac{1}{7}$

D) $\dfrac{2}{7}$

2

A grocery store uses crates to store a total of $36a$ apples and $24w$ watermelons. Each crate can be used to store either 12 apples or 6 watermelons. Which of the following expressions gives the total number of crates the grocery store uses to store apples and watermelons?

A) $3a + 4w$

B) $4a + 3w$

C) $\dfrac{1}{4a} + \dfrac{1}{3w}$

D) $\dfrac{1}{3a} + \dfrac{1}{4w}$

3

If the ratio of m to n is 3 to 4, which of the following could be true?

A) $m = 0, n = \dfrac{3}{4}$

B) $m = 2, n = \dfrac{8}{3}$

C) $m = 9, n = 16$

D) $m = 12, n = 9$

4

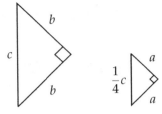

Note: Figure not drawn to scale.

Two right triangles are shown in the figure above. What is the value of b in terms of a ?

A) $2a$

B) $2a\sqrt{2}$

C) $4a$

D) $4a\sqrt{2}$

5

Jacob reads at a pace of 23 pages every 50 minutes. If a book contains a total of 740 pages, and Jacob has read for a total of t minutes, which of the following expresses the number of pages in the book he has yet to read?

A) $740 - 0.125t$

B) $740 - 0.46t$

C) $740 - 23t$

D) $740 - 27.6t$

6

If $f(x) = \sqrt{x} + 1$, what is $f(x^2 + 4)$ equal to?

A) $x + 3$

B) $x + 5$

C) $\sqrt{x^2 + 4} + 1$

D) $\sqrt{x^3 + 4x} + 1$

7

At a hospital, the average number of minutes a doctor spends with each patient can be modeled by the equation $y = 30 - 3x$, where x is the number of forms the doctor must fill out each day. In the context of this problem, what is the meaning of the number 3 in the equation?

A) One form takes a doctor an average of 3 minutes to fill out.

B) A doctor fills out an average of 3 forms for each patient.

C) A doctor decreases the time spent with each patient by 3 minutes for every form that must be filled out each day.

D) A doctor spends an average of 3 minutes with each patient.

8

The expression $\sqrt[4]{h^{8b}k^3}$, where $h > 0$ and $k > 0$, is equivalent to which of the following?

A) $h^{\frac{1}{2b}}k^{\frac{4}{3}}$

B) $h^{2b}k^{\frac{3}{4}}$

C) $h^{4b}k^{-1}$

D) $h^{4b}k^{\frac{3}{2}}$

9

If $\dfrac{2a + 2b}{3c + 3d} = 1$, what is the value of $\dfrac{3a + 3b}{4c + 4d}$?

A) $\dfrac{2}{3}$

B) $\dfrac{3}{4}$

C) $\dfrac{4}{3}$

D) $\dfrac{9}{8}$

10

At a fast food restaurant, a group of friends orders 5 tacos for x dollars each. The group also orders 7 burgers, each of which has a price double the price of a taco. If the restaurant applies a 5% tax to the total cost, which of the following represents the group's total bill, in dollars?

A) $19x + 0.05(12)$

B) $1.05(12x)$

C) $1.05(19x)$

D) $0.05(12x)$

11

Which ordered pair (x, y) satisfies the system of equations below?

$$5x + y = 9$$
$$10x - 7y = -18$$

A) $(-2, 19)$

B) $(1, 4)$

C) $(3, -6)$

D) $(5, -1)$

3 **3**

12

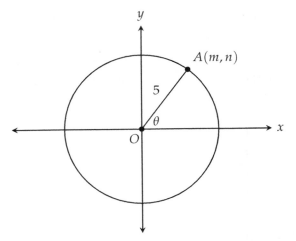

In the xy-plane above, a circle with radius 5 has its center at the origin. Point A lies on the circle and has coordinates (m, n). What is n in terms of θ ?

A) $5\sin\theta$

B) $5\cos\theta$

C) $\tan\theta$

D) $5(\sin\theta + \cos\theta)$

13

The expression $\dfrac{x+1}{x+2} - \dfrac{x-2}{x-1}$ is equivalent to which of the following?

A) $-\dfrac{5}{(x+2)(x-1)}$

B) $-\dfrac{1}{(x+2)(x-1)}$

C) $\dfrac{3}{(x+2)(x-1)}$

D) $\dfrac{2x^2+3}{(x+2)(x-1)}$

14

For a particular shipment, a farm uses a crate that weighs 12 pounds to hold 20 jars of jelly. Each jar of jelly weighs at least 0.8 pounds and no more than 2 pounds. What inequality gives all the possible values of w, the total weight, in pounds, of the shipment?

A) $16 \le w - 12 \le 40$

B) $16 \le w + 12 \le 40$

C) $38.8 \le w - 12 \le 40$

D) $38.8 \le w + 12 \le 40$

15

If $(mx + c)(nx + 3) = 12x^2 + 5x - 3$ for all values of x, where $m, n,$ and c are constants, what is the value of $m + n$?

A) 7

B) 8

C) 12

D) 13

16

A computer contains 2 memory cards. Each memory card gives 4 gigabytes of memory. How many gigabytes of memory will the computer have in total if 4 more memory cards are added?

3 **3**

17

If $c^{-3d} = \dfrac{1}{64}$ and c and d are positive integers, what is one possible value of d ?

18

$$(75x^2 - 20) - 10(6 + 7x^2)$$

The expression above can be written in the form $a(x + b)(x - b)$, where a and b are positive constants. What is the value of $a + b$?

19

$$5x + 16y = 36$$
$$cx + dy = 9$$

The system of equations above, where c and d are constants, has infinitely many solutions. What is the value of cd ?

20

A storage tank contains 7 liters of a 20% acid solution. How many liters of a 35% acid solution should be added to the tank so that the result is a 30% acid solution?

4   **4**

Math Test --- Calculator

55 Minutes, 38 Questions

Reference

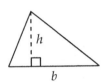

$$A = \pi r^2$$
$$C = 2\pi r$$

$$A = lw$$

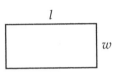

$$A = \frac{1}{2}bh$$

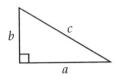

$$c^2 = a^2 + b^2$$

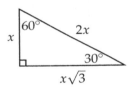

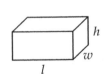

$$V = lwh$$

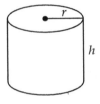

$$V = \pi r^2 h$$

Special Right Triangles

$$V = \frac{4}{3}\pi r^3$$

$$V = \frac{1}{3}\pi r^2 h$$

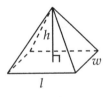

$$V = \frac{1}{3}lwh$$

There are 360 degrees of arc in a circle.
There are 2π radians of arc in a circle.
The sum of the measures of the angles of a triangle, in degrees, is 180.

4   **4**

1

Which scatterplot shows the weakest negative association between x and y ?

A)

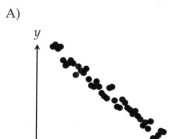

B)

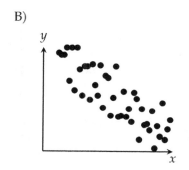

C)

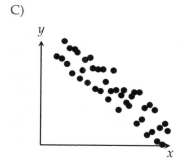

D)

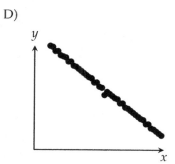

2

A 2-gallon jug is filled with a liquid solution consisting of 25% acetone and 75% water. How many <u>fluid ounces</u> of water does the jug contain? (1 gallon = 128 fluid ounces)

A) 64

B) 96

C) 128

D) 192

3

The table below shows the weight of the winning pumpkin at a local Halloween contest by year.

Year	Non-Organic	Organic
2010	398	261
2011	429	280
2012	447	292
2013	488	286
2014	473	317
2015	495	324

In 2012, the winning non-organic pumpkin was approximately what percent larger than the winning organic pumpkin?

A) 35%

B) 53%

C) 65%

D) 71%

| 4 | 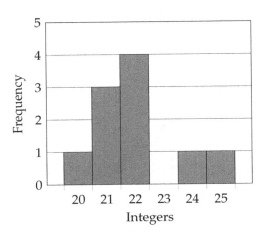 **| 4 |**

4

Number of Shots of Flu Vaccine

	No vaccine	1	2	Total
Contracted flu	6	8	6	20
Did not contract flu	24	28	36	88
Total	30	36	42	108

The table above was produced by a health clinic after it administered shots of flu vaccine to students at a school. Based on the table, what proportion of the students at the school received 2 shots of the vaccine and still contracted the flu?

A) $\frac{1}{18}$

B) $\frac{1}{7}$

C) $\frac{1}{6}$

D) $\frac{3}{10}$

5

$$3(2xy + xyz + yz) - (3xy + 5xyz - 2yz)$$

Which of the following expressions is equal to the one above?

A) $3xy + 8xyz + yz$

B) $3xy - 4xyz - yz$

C) $3xy - 2xyz + 5yz$

D) $3xy - 2xyz + 3yz$

6

The graph above shows the frequency distribution of a list of randomly generated integers between 20 and 26. What is the mean of the list of integers?

A) 21.5

B) 22

C) 22.5

D) 23

7

As part of her training, Margaret swims at a rate of 120 feet per minute at a local swimming pool. If one lap is equivalent to 160 feet, how many laps does she swim per hour?

A) 45

B) 60

C) 65

D) 80

4

4

8

Density of Liquid X

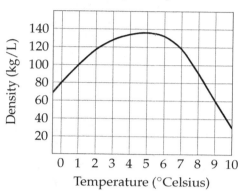

The graph above shows the density, in kilograms per liter, of Liquid X at different temperatures. Based on the graph, which of the following is closest to the mass, in kilograms, of 10 liters of Liquid X at 9 degrees Celsius?

A) 10

B) 100

C) 500

D) 1,000

9

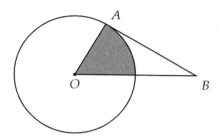

<u>Note:</u> Figure not drawn to scale.

In the figure above, the circle has center O and segment $\overline{AB}$ is tangent to the circle. If angle ABO measures $\dfrac{\pi}{10}$ radians and the area of the shaded sector is π, what is the area of the circle?

A) 5π

B) 6π

C) 8π

D) 9π

10

A person's maximum heart rate, in beats per minute, can be estimated by the expression $220 - x$, where x is the person's age in years for $20 \le x \le 70$. If it is generally recommended that at least 50% but not more than 80% of the maximum heart rate be reached during exercise, which of the following inequalities represents the target heart rate h, in beats per minute, for a 30-year-old?

A) $105 < h < 152$

B) $105 \le h \le 180$

C) $95 \le h \le 152$

D) $95 \le h \le 180$

4 **4**

11

A book has 50 more pages than another book. If the total number of pages in both books is 400, how many pages does the longer book have?

A) 150

B) 175

C) 200

D) 225

▼

Questions 12-14 refer to the following information.

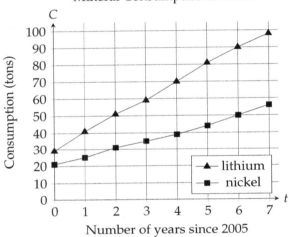

Mineral Consumption in Brazil

The graph above shows the consumption C, in tons, of lithium and nickel in Brazil t years after 2005.

12

Which of the following best approximates the combined total consumption, in tons, of lithium and nickel in Brazil in 2011?

A) 110

B) 125

C) 140

D) 155

13

The function $C(t) = at + b$ models the consumption, in tons, of nickel in Brazil from 2005 to 2012, where a and b are constants and t is the number of years since 2005. What does a represent in the function?

A) The predicted consumption, in tons, of nickel in Brazil in 2005

B) The predicted annual increase in the consumption, in tons, of nickel in Brazil from 2005 to 2012

C) The predicted total increase in the consumption, in tons, of nickel in Brazil from 2005 to 2012

D) The predicted consumption, in tons, of nickel in Brazil in 2012

14

During the period from 2005 to 2012, which of the following equations best models the annual difference d in the consumption, in tons, of lithium and the consumption, in tons, of nickel in Brazil t years after 2005?

A) $d = 10$

B) $d = 5t + 10$

C) $d = 8t + 25$

D) $d = 10t + 10$

▲

94

15

Time (months)	Number of ants
0	3,000
4	6,000
8	12,000
12	24,000

The table above gives the number of ants on an industrial ant farm over 12 months. Which of the following functions models the number of ants, $A(t)$, after t months?

A) $3,000t$

B) $3,000 + 750t$

C) $3,000 \cdot 2^t$

D) $3,000 \cdot 2^{\frac{t}{4}}$

16

If $3(a + b) = \dfrac{2}{3}$, what is the value of $\dfrac{a+b}{2}$?

A) $\dfrac{1}{18}$

B) $\dfrac{1}{9}$

C) $\dfrac{1}{6}$

D) $\dfrac{2}{9}$

17

$$2y + 3x = 5$$
$$2y - 3x = 5$$

Which of the following describes the graph of the system of equations above in the xy-plane?

A) A single line

B) Two parallel lines

C) Two perpendicular lines

D) Two distinct intersecting lines that are not perpendicular

18

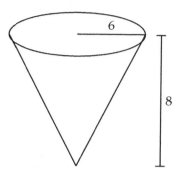

The figure above shows a paper cup in the shape of a right circular cone with a base radius of 6 and a height of 8. The cup is filled with water until its depth reaches half the height of the cone. What is the volume of the water in the cup?

A) 12π

B) 16π

C) 48π

D) 96π

19

A human resources officer surveyed a random sample of 200 employees at a company and asked each of them how he or she commutes to work. The officer found that 40 of those surveyed walk to work. Based on the results of the survey, which of the following statements must be true?

I. Of the 200 employees surveyed, 160 drive a car to work.

II. If a random sample of 400 employees at the company were surveyed, 80 of them would say that they walk to work.

III. The majority of the employees who were surveyed do not walk to work.

A) II only

B) III only

C) I and III only

D) I, II, and III

4 🖩 **4**

▼

Questions 20-21 refer to the following information.

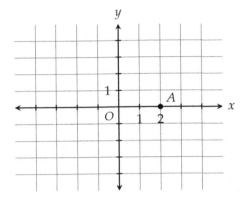

Point *B* (not shown) is located by starting at *A*, moving 2 units down and then moving 1 unit to the right. If a line is drawn through points *A* and *B*, what is the *y*-intercept of the line?

A) $\dfrac{1}{2}$

B) 1

C) 2

D) 4

21

Line *l* (not shown) contains point *A* and has a slope of 6. Which of the following points is on line *l* ?

A) $(1,6)$

B) $(2,6)$

C) $(3,6)$

D) $(6,1)$

▲

22

This year, a company consumed 30 percent fewer sheets of paper than it did last year. If the company used 270,000 sheets of paper this year, approximately how many sheets did it use last year?

A) 351,000

B) 362,000

C) 378,000

D) 386,000

23

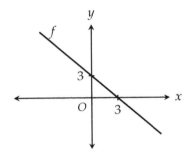

The function *f* is graphed in the *xy*-plane above. If the function *g* is defined by $g(x) = f(x) + 2$, what is the *x*-intercept of $g(x)$?

A) -1

B) 0

C) 1

D) 5

24

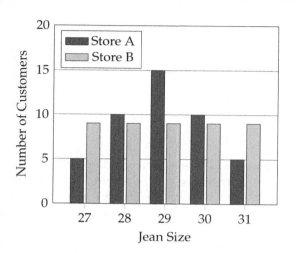

The bar chart above shows the distribution of jean sizes for 45 customers at Store A and 45 customers at Store B. Which of the following correctly compares the standard deviation of jean sizes for the customers at each of the stores?

A) The standard deviation of jean sizes for the customers at Store A is larger.

B) The standard deviation of jean sizes for the customers at Store B is larger.

C) The standard deviation of jean sizes for the customers at Store A and Store B is the same.

D) The relationship cannot be determined from the information given.

▼

Questions 25-26 refer to the following information.

For each of 20 job openings, the scatterplot below relates the number of applications to the time required to fill the opening. A quadratic function that best fits the data is modeled in the graph below.

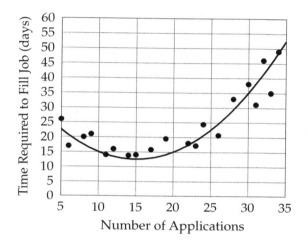

25

According to the best fit curve, which of the following best approximates the number of days required to fill a job for which there are 20 applications?

A) 6

B) 15

C) 18

D) 24

4 **4**

26

Which of the following is the best interpretation of the vertex of the best fit curve in this context?

A) The number of days required to fill a job for which there are 5 applications

B) The minimal number of applications required to fill a job within 15 days

C) The number of applications for a job that requires the least amount of time to fill

D) The number of applications for a job that requires 15 days to fill

---

27

The graph of the function f is the graph of the function g compressed horizontally by a factor of 2 and shifted to the right by 1. Which of the following correctly defines the function f ?

A) $f(x) = g(2x - 1)$

B) $f(x) = g(2x - 2)$

C) $f(x) = g\left(\dfrac{1}{2}x - \dfrac{1}{2}\right)$

D) $f(x) = g\left(\dfrac{1}{2}x - 1\right)$

28

Aaron's Math Test

Difficulty	Number of Questions	Average Rate of Completion (questions/minute)
Easy	28	7
Medium	42	3.5
Hard	30	2.4

Aaron will take a math test that contains 3 difficulty levels: easy, medium, and hard. The table above shows the number of questions and Aaron's average rate of completion, in questions per minute, for each difficulty level. If the teacher decides to replace all the medium-difficulty questions on the test with hard-difficulty questions, how many more minutes will Aaron take to finish the test than if the teacher hadn't replaced any of the questions?

A) 4

B) 5.5

C) 17.5

D) 30

29

At a school, there is one math teacher for every 10 students, one English teacher for every 15 students, and one science teacher for every 30 students. If the total number of math, science, and English teachers is k, how many students are there at the school, in terms of k ?

A) $3k$

B) $4k$

C) $5k$

D) $10k$

4 📱 **4**

30

$$y = (2x - 1)(2x - 11)$$

A parabola with vertex (a, b) in the xy-plane is represented by the equation above. What is the value of b ?

A) -25

B) 3

C) 6

D) 11

31

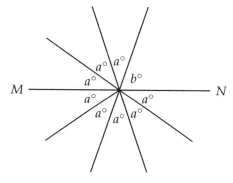

M ———— N

In the figure above, MN is a line. What is the value of b ?

32

Product reports suggest that 10 percent of all calculators require AAA type batteries and 25 percent of all alarm clocks require AAA type batteries. If there are 550 calculators and 440 alarm clocks in stock at a store, what is the estimated difference between the number of calculators that require AAA batteries and the number of alarm clocks that require AAA batteries?

33

If $f(x) = 3x - 1$ and $2f(b) = 28$, what is the value of $f(2b)$?

34

If $10 + \dfrac{6}{x} = 22$ and $x > 0$, what is the value of x ?

35

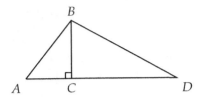

In $\triangle ABD$ above, $AB = 10$, $AC = 6$, and $CD = 8\sqrt{3}$. What is the length of $\overline{BD}$?

36

In the xy-plane, the graph of $y = x^2 - 7x + 9$ intersects the graph of $y = 9 - x$ at points $(0, 9)$ and (m, n). What is the value of m ?

37

If $9 \le -5x - 6 \le 34$, a is the greatest possible value of x, and b is the least possible value of x, what is the value of $a - b$?

38

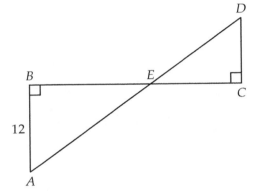

In the figure above, $\overline{AB}$ and $\overline{CD}$ are parallel and $\overline{AD}$ intersects $\overline{BC}$ at point E. If $\sin D = \dfrac{4}{5}$ and $AB = 12$, what is the length of $\overline{AE}$?

7

Practice Test 7

3 **3**

Math Test --- No Calculator

25 Minutes, 20 Questions

Reference

$A = \pi r^2$
$C = 2\pi r$

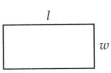

$A = lw$

$A = \frac{1}{2}bh$

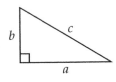

$c^2 = a^2 + b^2$

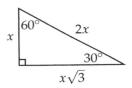

Special Right Triangles

$V = lwh$

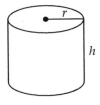

$V = \pi r^2 h$

$V = \frac{4}{3}\pi r^3$

$V = \frac{1}{3}\pi r^2 h$

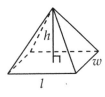

$V = \frac{1}{3}lwh$

There are 360 degrees of arc in a circle.
There are 2π radians of arc in a circle.
The sum of the measures of the angles of a triangle, in degrees, is 180.

3 **3**

1

Which of the following is equal to $\sqrt[3]{x^2} \cdot \sqrt{x^3}$?

A) x

B) $x^{\frac{9}{4}}$

C) $x^{\frac{13}{6}}$

D) x^3

2

To improve his health, James resolves to lose x pounds each month. If James weighs 230 pounds now, which of the following expressions represents his weight m months from now?

A) $mx - 230$

B) $230m - mx$

C) $230 + mx$

D) $230 - mx$

3

If $a = b + c$, which of the following must be equal to ab ?

A) $b^2 + c$

B) $b^2 - c$

C) $b^2 + bc$

D) $b^2 - bc$

4

$$y = 200 + 25x$$

An insurance company uses the equation above to calculate the monthly auto insurance premium y, in dollars, for a driver with x previous car accidents. What is the increase in the monthly insurance premium, in dollars, for each accident?

A) 8

B) 25

C) 75

D) 200

5

$$\frac{3x - 2}{12x^2}$$

Which of the following is equivalent to the expression above?

A) $-\dfrac{1}{2x}$

B) $\dfrac{x}{12}$

C) $\dfrac{1}{4x} - \dfrac{1}{6x^2}$

D) $\dfrac{x}{4} - \dfrac{x^2}{6}$

6

What is the equation of the line that is perpendicular to the y-axis and passes through the point $(3, 4)$?

A) $x = 3$

B) $x = 4$

C) $y = 3$

D) $y = 4$

7

Which of the following is equivalent to $(m + n + 1)(m + n - 1)$?

A) $m^2 + 2mn + n^2 - 1$

B) $m^2 - 2mn + n^2 - 1$

C) $m^2 - n^2 - 1$

D) $m^2 + 2m + n^2 + 2n - 1$

8

Colin bought a winter jacket for x dollars, but Jonas managed to find the same jacket at a 20 percent discount. If they both had to pay a sales tax of 10 percent on the final price, which of the following expressions represents the total amount, in dollars, Colin and Jonas spent on their jackets?

A) $(1.1)(1.8x)$

B) $(1.1)(1.2x)$

C) $(0.1)(1.8x)$

D) $(0.1)(1.2x)$

9

$$p = at^3 - bt + c$$

The equation above gives the population p, in thousands, of a certain species after t years. The species has a fertility rate of a, a death rate of b, and an initial population of c. Which of the following gives b in terms of p, a, t, and c ?

A) $\dfrac{p - at^3 - c}{t}$

B) $\dfrac{c + at^3 - p}{t}$

C) $\dfrac{p - at^3 + c}{t}$

D) $\dfrac{at^3 - c - p}{t}$

10

$$R = 16,000 + 7,000F$$

Jake sells his famous lobster rolls at his own restaurant and at several franchise locations. He uses the equation above to model his business finances, where F is the number of franchise locations and R is the total monthly revenue of the entire business. According to the model, what is the best interpretation of the 16,000 in the equation?

A) The monthly revenue generated by each franchise location

B) The total monthly revenue generated by all franchise locations

C) The monthly revenue generated by Jake's own restaurant

D) The number of lobster rolls the entire business sells each month

11

x	3	4	5	6	7
$f(x)$	-10	m	-2	2	n

The values in the table above define a linear function. What is the value of $m + n$?

A) -4

B) 0

C) 4

D) 8

3 **3**

12

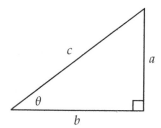

Given the right triangle above, which of the following is equal to a ?

A) $a\tan\theta$

B) $b\sin\theta$

C) $c\sin\theta$

D) $c\cos\theta$

13

At a summer school, there is at least one teacher for every 15 students. Before classes begin, each student receives 3 textbooks and each teacher receives 2 textbooks. The school has no more than 800 textbooks to distribute among its students and teachers. Let s represent the number of students and let t represent the number of teachers, where s and t are nonnegative integers. Which of the following systems of inequalities best represents this situation?

A) $2s + 3t \le 800$
    $t \ge 15s$

B) $3s + 2t \le 800$
    $t \ge 15s$

C) $3s + 2t \le 800$
    $s \ge 15t$

D) $3s + 2t \le 800$
    $s \le 15t$

14

$$x^2 + 3bx + 2b^2 = 0$$

In the quadratic equation above, b is a constant. What are the solutions x to the equation in terms of b ?

A) $-4b$ and $-2b$

B) $-\dfrac{3b}{2}$ and $\dfrac{b}{2}$

C) $-2b$ and $-b$

D) b and $2b$

15

A semicircle has a perimeter of P and a radius of r. Which of the following represents r in terms of P ?

A) $\dfrac{P}{\pi}$

B) $\dfrac{P}{2\pi}$

C) $\dfrac{P}{\pi + 2}$

D) $\dfrac{P}{2\pi + 2}$

16

A certain type of printer can print 50 pages in 3 minutes. How many pages can 4 printers of the same type print in 12 minutes?

3 **3**

17

$$2x - 3y = -1$$
$$-x + y = -1$$

According to the systems of equations above, what is the value of x ?

18

The angles of a triangle measure $\dfrac{\pi}{6}$ radians, $\dfrac{\pi}{2}$ radians, and $k\pi$ radians, where k is a constant. What is the value of k ?

19

The function f is defined by $f(x) = (x - 7)^2 + 9$. If $f(a - 2) = 25$, what is one possible value of a ?

20

$$p(x) = 4x^3 - kx + k$$

In the polynomial $p(x)$ defined above, k is a constant. If $x + 1$ is a factor of $p(x)$, what is the value of k ?

Math Test --- Calculator

55 Minutes, 38 Questions

Reference

$A = \pi r^2$
$C = 2\pi r$

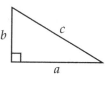

$A = lw$

$A = \dfrac{1}{2}bh$

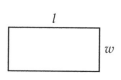

$c^2 = a^2 + b^2$

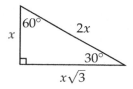

Special Right Triangles

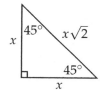

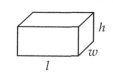

$V = lwh$

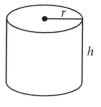

$V = \pi r^2 h$

$V = \dfrac{4}{3}\pi r^3$

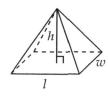

$V = \dfrac{1}{3}\pi r^2 h$

$V = \dfrac{1}{3}lwh$

There are 360 degrees of arc in a circle.
There are 2π radians of arc in a circle.
The sum of the measures of the angles of a triangle, in degrees, is 180.

4 **4**

1

Mon	3,830
Tue	2,960
Wed	2,435
Thu	2,605
Fri	3,860
Sat	5,695
Sun	6,230
Total	27,615

The table above shows the number of visitors to a museum over the course of one week. Based on the table, what is the mean number of visitors each day from Monday to Friday?

A) 3,138

B) 3,945

C) 4,326

D) 5,523

2

$$1 \text{ mile} = 5280 \text{ feet}$$

$$61 \text{ centimeters} = 2 \text{ feet}$$

Based on the information above, how many centimeters are equivalent to 3 miles?

A) 161,040

B) 322,080

C) 483,120

D) 644,160

3

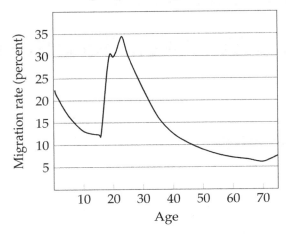

Age-Specific Migration Rates

The graph above shows how likely people of different ages are to migrate, or move away, from their original home. Which of the following is closest to the age at which the migration rate is highest?

A) 18

B) 20

C) 25

D) 30

4

Kevin surveyed a random sample of teachers in his district to determine whether new textbooks or new computers are a higher priority for schools. Of the 120 teachers surveyed, 37.5% think new computers are a higher priority. Based on this information, about how many of the 2,200 teachers in the district would be expected to think new textbooks are a higher priority?

A) 680

B) 825

C) 1,200

D) 1,375

5

Which of the following is equivalent to the expression $(1.4x + 2.5)^2 - (1.4x - 2.5)^2$?

A) 12.5

B) $7x$

C) $14x$

D) $14x + 12.5$

---▼---

Questions 6-7 refer to the following information.

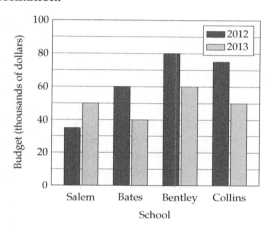

6

Which of the following schools had a budget in 2013 that was approximately $\frac{2}{3}$ of its budget in 2012?

I. Bates
II. Bentley
III. Collins

A) I only

B) I and III only

C) II and III only

D) I, II, and III

7

From 2012 to 2013, the total budget for all four schools decreased by approximately what percent?

A) 20%

B) 25%

C) 30%

D) 33%

---▲---

8

$$f(x) = \begin{cases} x+2 & \text{if } x \geq 0 \\ x-2 & \text{if } x < 0 \end{cases}$$

The function f is defined above. Which of the following CANNOT be $f(x)$ for any value of x ?

A) -6

B) -4

C) 1

D) 3

9

$$x^2 + (y-3)^2 = 25$$

The graph of the equation above in the xy-plane is a circle. At what points does the circle intersect the y-axis?

A) $(0, -2)$ and $(0, 8)$

B) $(0, -3)$ and $(0, 7)$

C) $(0, -8)$ and $(0, 2)$

D) $(0, -22)$ and $(0, 28)$

4 🖩 **4**

10

A house is losing a fourth of its value every year. Which of the following best describes the relationship between time (in years) and the value of the house?

A) Increasing linear

B) Decreasing linear

C) Exponential growth

D) Exponential decay

11

$$y = 2(x + 4)(3x - 18)$$

The equation above represents a parabola in the xy-plane. Which of the following equivalent equations displays the x- and y-coordinates of the vertex of the parabola as constants or coeffcients?

A) $y = 6(x + 4)(x - 6)$

B) $y = 6x^2 - 12x - 144$

C) $y = (2x + 8)(3x - 18)$

D) $y = 6(x - 1)^2 - 150$

12

A restaurant conducted a survey to determine what customers would think about a new sandwich menu item for lunch. During lunch time, the restaurant owner put the sandwich on the menu for 8 dollars and the first 40 customers to buy it were asked for their opinions. Which of the following factors makes it least likely that a reliable conclusion can be drawn about the opinions of all the restaurant's customers concerning the new sandwich menu item?

A) The sample size

B) The time the survey was given

C) The price of the sandwiches

D) The way the customers were selected for the survey

13

Sam makes a one-time deposit of $1,000 into an account that earns 4 percent interest compounded annually. Which of the following is closest to the total amount of interest earned in the account after 3 years?

A) $115

B) $120

C) $125

D) $130

14

James is traveling to France and needs to exchange 800 U.S. dollars for euros. He looks up the official exchange rate and sees that 1 euro is worth 1.40 U.S. dollars. However, the currency exchange station at the airport is offering 1 euro for 1.55 U.S. dollars. Approximately how many more euros would James have if he converts his money at the official exchange rate rather than at the one offered at the airport?

A) 50

B) 55

C) 60

D) 65

15

$$f(x) = x^2 - 3x$$
$$g(x) = 2x + 14$$

The functions f and g are defined above. For how many values of k is it true that $f(k) = g(k)$?

A) None

B) One

C) Two

D) More than two

4 **4**

16

At a toy store, two dolls and three toy cars cost 88 dollars. However, three dolls and two toy cars cost 62 dollars. How much does one doll and one toy car cost, in dollars?

A) 28

B) 30

C) 32

D) 34

17

The graph of the function f contains the points $(0,3)$, $(-2,7)$, and $(5,k)$. If the graph of f is a line, what must the value of k be?

A) -13

B) -7

C) 5

D) 8

18

An employment agency surveyed a random sample of 200 engineers working in Chicago and found that the mean annual salary of the engineers in the sample was $100,000 with an associated margin of error of $10,000. Which of the following conclusions is the most reasonable based on these data?

A) Most of the engineers working in Chicago earn exactly $100,000 in annual salary.

B) All engineers working in Chicago earn between $90,000 and $110,000 in annual salary.

C) It is unlikely that an engineer working in Chicago has an annual salary below $100,000.

D) The mean annual salary for all engineers working in Chicago is between $90,000 and $110,000.

▼

Questions 19-20 refer to the following information.

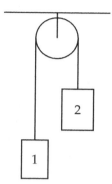

In the figure above, two objects are connected by a cord and hung over a pulley. The tension T, in newtons, in the cord can be found using the equation below.

$$T = \frac{2m_1m_2}{m_1 + m_2}g$$

where m_1 and m_2 are the masses of object 1 and object 2, respectively, in kilograms, and g is the acceleration due to Earth's gravity measured in $\dfrac{m}{sec^2}$.

19

Which of the following expresses g in terms of the other variables?

A) $\dfrac{T(m_1 + m_2)}{2m_1m_2}$

B) $\dfrac{2m_1m_2}{T(m_1 + m_2)}$

C) $\dfrac{2(m_1 + m_2)}{Tm_1m_2}$

D) $T(m_1 + m_2) - 2m_1m_2$

4   **4**

20

If the masses of both object 1 and object 2 were doubled, how would the tension in the cord be affected?

A) The tension would stay the same.

B) The tension would be halved.

C) The tension would be doubled.

D) The tension would be quadrupled (multipled by a factor of 4).

▲

21

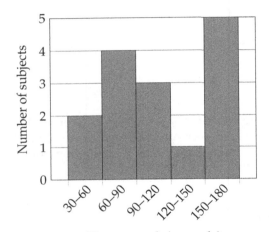

Time on task (seconds)

In an experiment, researchers recorded the time, in seconds, 15 subjects were able to remain focused on a difficult task. The results of the experiment are summarized in the table above. Which of the following could be the average time on task, in seconds, for the 15 subjects?

A) 68

B) 92

C) 123

D) 149

22

A function $f(x)$ has two properties:

$$f(a + b) = f(a) - b$$
$$f(2) = 10$$

What is the value of $f(5)$?

A) 5

B) 7

C) 9

D) 11

23

If $(x + y)^2 - (x - y)^2 = 60$ and x and y are positive integers, which of the following could be a value of $x + y$?

A) 6

B) 8

C) 10

D) 12

4 **4**

24

	Average Overtime Hours per Week				
	1-3	4-6	7-9	10+	Total
Marketing	6	7	5	6	24
Engineering	4	4	7	10	25
Accounting	1	15	18	3	37
Human Resources	2	5	4	3	14
Total	13	31	34	22	100

The table above shows the number of employees in different departments at a company, categorized by the average number of overtime hours they work. Which department at the company has the highest proportion of employees who work less than an average of 6 overtime hours per week?

A) Marketing

B) Engineering

C) Accounting

D) Human Resources

25

On a number line, the point with coordinate a is 8 units from the point with coordinate -5. Which of the following equations can be used to determine the two possible values of a ?

A) $|a - 5| = 8$

B) $|a + 5| = 8$

C) $|a - 8| = 5$

D) $|a + 8| = 5$

26

$$x^2 - y^2 = 48$$
$$x + y = 12$$

If (x, y) is the solution to the system of equations above, what is the value of xy ?

A) 28

B) 32

C) 45

D) 64

27

Derek has two pitchers containing equal amounts of water. He empties one of the pitchers by filling 8 medium glasses of water. He then empties the other by filling 6 large glasses of water. If each large glass holds 3 more ounces of water than a medium glass, how many ounces of water were in each pitcher originally?

A) 68

B) 72

C) 76

D) 80

4 **4**

Questions 28-29 refer to the following information.

Number of orders	Processing time t per order (minutes)
60	$1 \leq t \leq 5$
80	$6 \leq t \leq 12$

The table above summarizes the orders that need to be processed by a warehouse on a certain day.

28

If T represents the total number of <u>hours</u> needed to process all the orders in the table, which of the following inequalities gives the possible values of T ?

A) $8 \leq T \leq 16$

B) $8 \leq T \leq 21$

C) $9 \leq T \leq 16$

D) $9 \leq T \leq 21$

29

The warehouse finds that a new machine can cut the processing time of each order in half. If this new machine is used to process the orders in the table, which of the following CANNOT be the processing time of an order?

A) 1.2 minutes

B) 2.8 minutes

C) 3.6 minutes

D) 5.5 minutes

30

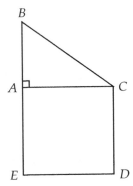

In the figure above, $ACDE$ is a square and ABC is a right triangle. If $AB = 3$ and $BC = 5$, what is the length of $\overline{BD}$ (not shown)?

A) $\sqrt{53}$

B) $\sqrt{62}$

C) 8

D) $\sqrt{65}$

31

If $a = \dfrac{2}{3b}$ and $ax = \dfrac{5}{6b}$ for $b \neq 0$, what is the value of x ?

32

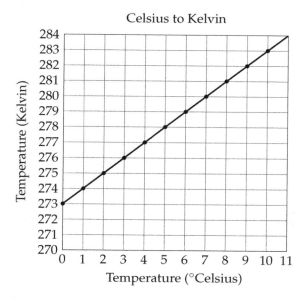

Celsius to Kelvin

In a class lab report, a student mistakenly calculates 279 kelvin to be equal to 2 degrees Celsius. Based on the graph above, by how many degrees Celsius is the correct result greater than what the student calculated?

33

$$l = \frac{7}{4}(a+5)$$

A biologist uses the model above to estimate the length l of a garden snake, in inches, based on the snake's age a, in months. According to the model, by how many inches in length does a garden snake grow over 5 months?

34

A furniture store offers a free chair for every four chairs that a customer purchases. The price of each chair is $12. If Alice spends a total of $108 on chairs, how many chairs did she receive altogether?

35

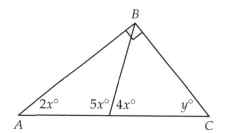

Note: Figure not drawn to scale.

In right triangle ABC above, what is the value of y?

36

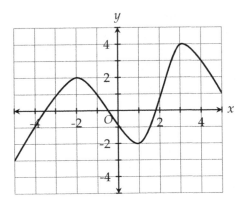

What is the difference between the minimum and maximum values of the function graphed in the xy-plane above, for $-5 \leq x \leq 5$?

▼

Questions 37-38 refer to the following information.

To determine which external hard drive to buy, Brandon analyzed 8 randomly selected devices compatible with his computer. For each device, he recorded the storage capacity, in terabytes, and the price, in dollars. The results are shown, along with the line of best fit, in the scatterplot below.

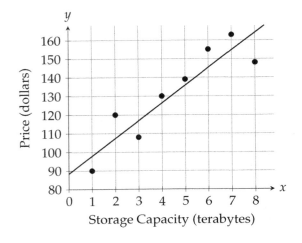

37

Brandon decides he will choose from only those hard drive devices for which there is no other device that has both greater storage capacity and lower price. According to the scatterplot, how many devices will Brandon choose from?

38

One of Brandon's friends finds another compatible hard drive device that is being sold for 120 dollars. If the price of the device is more than that predicted by the line of best fit, what is the greatest storage capacity, in terabytes, the device could have? (Assume the storage capacities of hard drive devices come in whole numbers of terabytes.)

▲

8

Practice Test 8

Math Test --- No Calculator
25 Minutes, 20 Questions

Reference

$A = \pi r^2$
$C = 2\pi r$

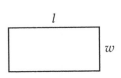

$A = lw$

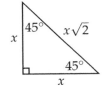

$A = \frac{1}{2}bh$

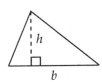

$c^2 = a^2 + b^2$

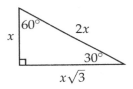

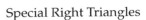

Special Right Triangles

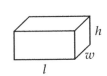

$V = lwh$

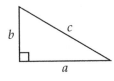

$V = \pi r^2 h$

$V = \frac{4}{3}\pi r^3$

$V = \frac{1}{3}\pi r^2 h$

$V = \frac{1}{3}lwh$

There are 360 degrees of arc in a circle.
There are 2π radians of arc in a circle.
The sum of the measures of the angles of a triangle, in degrees, is 180.

3 **3**

1

If $x > 0$ and $9x^2 = 40$, which of the following is equivalent to the value of x ?

A) $\left(\dfrac{40}{9}\right)^2$

B) $\dfrac{\sqrt{40}}{9}$

C) $\sqrt{\dfrac{9}{40}}$

D) $\sqrt{\dfrac{40}{9}}$

2

Which of the following is equal to $\sqrt[3]{b^{\frac{1}{2}}}$?

A) $b^{\frac{1}{6}}$

B) $b^{\frac{2}{3}}$

C) $b^{\frac{3}{2}}$

D) b^6

3

Line k has a negative slope and passes through the origin. If line m is perpendicular to line k, which of the following must be true?

A) Line m passes through the origin.

B) Line m does not pass through the origin.

C) Line m has a positive slope.

D) Line m has a negative slope.

4

$$y = 500 - 4x$$

A manager operates a retail store that sells shirts. She uses the equation above to model the number of shirts left in inventory each day after x coupons for the shirts have been given out to customers. What does the number 500 in the equation mean?

A) The store starts each day with 500 shirts in inventory.

B) Each day, an average of 500 shirts are sold to customers using coupons.

C) It takes 500 coupons to sell all the shirts left in inventory.

D) There are 500 shirts left in inventory on days when no coupons are given out.

5

If $|x + 3| < 2$, which of the following could be the value of $|x|$?

A) 1

B) 4

C) 6

D) 10

6

$$(a + b)^2 - (a - b)^2$$

The expression above is equivalent to which of the following?

A) $2ab$

B) $4ab$

C) $4ab + 2b^2$

D) $2a^2 + 2b^2$

7

If $f(x + 1) = 3x + 2$, the function f could be defined by which of the following?

A) $f(x) = 3x - 2$

B) $f(x) = 3x - 1$

C) $f(x) = 3x + 1$

D) $f(x) = 3x + 5$

8

The total price of x pens is 4 dollars and the total price of y notebooks is 6 dollars. Which of the following expresses the total cost of 9 pens and 7 notebooks, in dollars?

A) $9\left(\dfrac{x}{4}\right) + 7\left(\dfrac{y}{6}\right)$

B) $9\left(\dfrac{4}{x}\right) + 7\left(\dfrac{6}{y}\right)$

C) $7\left(\dfrac{x}{4}\right) + 9\left(\dfrac{y}{6}\right)$

D) $7\left(\dfrac{4}{x}\right) + 9\left(\dfrac{6}{y}\right)$

9

For every transaction made, an electronic payment system charges $0.30 plus 2% of the amount of the transaction. If the system charges $5.00 for a transaction, which of the following equations gives the amount a, in dollars, of the transaction?

A) $a = \dfrac{5}{0.02} - 0.30$

B) $a = \dfrac{5}{2} - 0.30$

C) $a = \dfrac{5 - 0.30}{0.02}$

D) $a = \dfrac{5 - 0.30}{2}$

10

If $m = \dfrac{1}{\sqrt{n}}$, where $m > 0$ and $n > 0$, what is n in terms of m?

A) $n = \dfrac{1}{\sqrt{m}}$

B) $n = \dfrac{1}{m}$

C) $n = \dfrac{1}{m^2}$

D) $n = m^2$

11

$$f(x) = \frac{3}{8}\left(\frac{1}{2}x + 4k\right) + 50$$

During a fundraiser, a charity group decides to sell bracelets at a country fair. The number of bracelets the group sells can be modeled by the function f above, where k is a constant and x is the number of people who attend the fair for $600 \leq x \leq 1,500$. The group predicts it will sell 320 bracelets if 800 people attend the fair. What is the value of k?

A) 60

B) 80

C) 120

D) 180

3 **3**

12

Sarah is writing a book that will have an introduction and 12 chapters. Each chapter must be at least 9 pages long and no more than 15 pages long. Sarah has already determined that the introduction will be 10 pages long. Which of the following inequalities represents all possible values of the total number of pages x the book will have?

A) $72 \leq x - 10 \leq 135$

B) $72 \leq x + 10 \leq 135$

C) $108 \leq x - 10 \leq 180$

D) $108 \leq x + 10 \leq 180$

13

If $\sqrt{4 + \sqrt{x}} = 1 + \sqrt{3}$, what is the value of x ?

A) 0

B) 2

C) 6

D) 12

14

$$y = 3x - 1$$
$$y = (x + 1)^2$$

The system of equations above has how many solutions?

A) 0

B) 1

C) 2

D) Infinitely many

15

The expression $\dfrac{2x^2 - 5x}{2x - 1}$ is equivalent to which of the following?

A) $x - 3 - \dfrac{3}{2x - 1}$

B) $x - 3 + \dfrac{3}{2x - 1}$

C) $x - 2 - \dfrac{2}{2x - 1}$

D) $x - 2 + \dfrac{2}{2x - 1}$

16

Maria's English teacher has noticed that Maria is behind in her reading. To catch up, Maria is assigned to read k pages each day, where k is a constant. After 7 days, her teacher sees that she is on page 120. After 11 days, Maria is on page 196. What is the value of k ?

17

$$-4x - 15y = -17$$
$$-x + 5y = -13$$

If (x, y) is the solution to the system of equations above, what is the value of x ?

3   **3**

18

The expression $\dfrac{3x + 7}{5} - \dfrac{1 - 2x}{5}$ is how much more than x ?

19

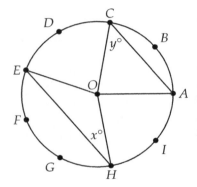

In the circle above, point O is the center and points A through I divide the circumference into 9 arcs of equal length. What is the value of $x + y$?

20

A country consists of a mainland and 9 outlying islands. If the mainland's population is 6 times the average population of each island, then the mainland's population is what fraction of the total population of the country?

Math Test --- Calculator

55 Minutes, 38 Questions

Reference

$A = \pi r^2$
$C = 2\pi r$

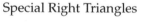

$A = lw$

$A = \dfrac{1}{2}bh$

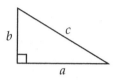

$c^2 = a^2 + b^2$

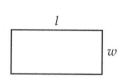

Special Right Triangles

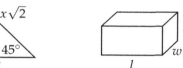

$V = lwh$

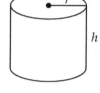

$V = \pi r^2 h$

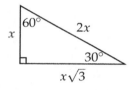

$V = \dfrac{4}{3}\pi r^3$

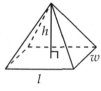

$V = \dfrac{1}{3}\pi r^2 h$

$V = \dfrac{1}{3}lwh$

There are 360 degrees of arc in a circle.
There are 2π radians of arc in a circle.
The sum of the measures of the angles of a triangle, in degrees, is 180.

4 **4**

1

$$(-2a^2 + 5) - (3 - 8a^2)$$

Which of the following expressions is equivalent to the one shown above?

A) $6a^2 - 2$

B) $6a^2 + 2$

C) $-10a^2 + 2$

D) $-10a^2 + 8$

2

$$v = 550 - 9.8t$$

The equation above gives the velocity v of a ball t seconds after it is thrown vertically upwards with an initial velocity of 550 meters per second. After approximately how many seconds will the ball stop and start to drop back to the ground?

A) 47.8

B) 51.4

C) 55.5

D) 56.1

3

$$\frac{y}{x} = 90$$

The total number of glass bottles y that can be sorted by an automatic inspection machine in x hours is given by the equation above. In the equation, what does the number 90 represent?

A) The number of hours it takes to sort each glass bottle

B) The number of different glass bottle types

C) The number of glass bottles that can be sorted in one hour

D) The number of automatic inspection machines

4

Year	Seal population
2000	350
2001	342
2002	348
2003	357
2004	345
2005	
2006	355

The incomplete table above shows the seal population in an Arctic region from 2000 to 2006. Which of the following is a reasonable approximation of the seal population in the same region in 2005?

A) 35

B) 350

C) 3,500

D) 350,000

5

The table below shows the number of vowels and consonants in 4 different languages.

Language	Vowels	Consonants	Total
Danish	32	20	52
German	17	25	42
Greek	5	18	23
Portuguese	14	23	37

Based on the table, vowels make up approximately 38% of the alphabet in which language?

A) Danish

B) German

C) Greek

D) Portuguese

6

Jonas walks 10 miles in 2.5 hours. How long will it take him to walk 25 miles?

A) 6 hours and 15 minutes

B) 6 hours and 20 minutes

C) 6 hours and 30 minutes

D) 6 hours and 45 minutes

▼

Questions 7-8 refer to the following information.

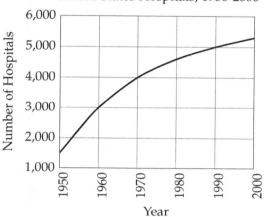

United States Hospitals, 1950-2000

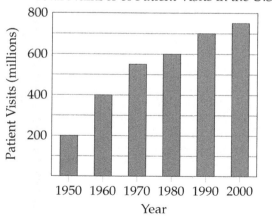

Total Number of Patient Visits in the U.S.

7

Which of the following is NOT a valid conclusion from the information shown in the graphs?

A) From 1960 to 1990, the number of hospitals increased by approximately 2,000.

B) From 1950 to 2000, the number of hospitals increased.

C) In 1970, there were about 550 million patient visits.

D) From 1950 to 1960, the number of patient visits increased by approximately 50%.

8

According to the graphs, which of the following best approximates the average number of patient visits per hospital in 1990?

A) 120,000

B) 130,000

C) 140,000

D) 150,000

▲

9

At the start of the semester, Andrew could swim a mile in 16 minutes. At the end of the semester, he could swim a mile in 12 minutes. What is the percent decrease (to the nearest percent) in his time from the start to the end of the semester?

A) 20%

B) 25%

C) 33%

D) 40%

4 📱 **4**

10

	Chicken over rice	Lamb over rice	Total
Lunch	72	36	108
Dinner	204	108	312
Total	276	144	420

The table above shows the distribution of meals ordered from a food truck during lunch and dinner. Based on the data, what proportion of the lamb over rice orders came during dinner time?

A) $\dfrac{1}{4}$

B) $\dfrac{9}{35}$

C) $\dfrac{9}{26}$

D) $\dfrac{3}{4}$

11

A box in the shape of a right rectangular prism has a length of 80 inches. The ratio of the length of the box to the width is 3:2. The ratio of the width to the height is 4:9. What is the height, in inches, of the box?

A) $53\dfrac{1}{3}$

B) 80

C) 120

D) 270

12

Amy charges $60 per hour for freelance design work and earns a minimum of $3,600 every 2 weeks. The number of hours she works each week depends on the job. If x represents the number of hours Amy works each week over a 2-week period, which of the following inequalities gives all possible values of x ?

A) $x \le 30$

B) $x \ge 30$

C) $x \le 60$

D) $x \ge 60$

13

		Actual		
Forecast		Rain	No rain	Total
Rain		75	20	95
No rain		50	220	270
Total		125	240	365

A weather station summarizes the accuracy of its daily rain forecasts for the past year (365 days) in the table above. What fraction of the station's daily rain forecasts last year were correct?

A) $\dfrac{15}{73}$

B) $\dfrac{3}{5}$

C) $\dfrac{15}{19}$

D) $\dfrac{59}{73}$

4 **4**

Questions 14-15 refer to the following information.

A kitchen renovation company charges $120 per square foot for the first 50 square feet and then $200 per square foot thereafter.

14

Which of the following expressions gives the company's charge, in dollars, for renovating a kitchen with an area of $k + 75$ square feet?

A) $10,000 + 120k$

B) $11,000 + 200k$

C) $21,000 + 200k$

D) $5,000 + 320k$

15

Which of the following graphs could show the relationship between the area of the kitchen to be renovated and the company's charge?

A)

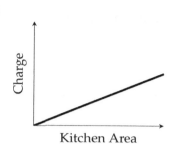

B)

C)

D)

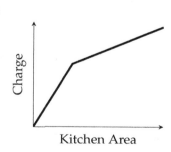

4 **4**

16

A filtration system removes 12.5 grams of lead for every 800 cubic meters of water that flows through it. Which of the following is closest to the number of grams of lead that are removed when 200,000 cubic feet of water flow through the system? (1 cubic meter = 35 cubic feet)

A) 89

B) 146

C) 452

D) 3,125

17

$$5x = 273 - 6y$$

$$y = \frac{4}{3}x$$

The equations above represent two lines that are graphed in the xy-plane. Which of the following is the y-coordinate of the point (x, y) at which the two lines intersect?

A) 15

B) 21

C) 24

D) 28

18

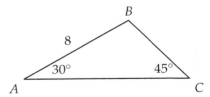

In the figure above, $\angle BAC = 30°$, $\angle BCA = 45°$, and $AB = 8$. What is the length of $\overline{BC}$?

A) 4

B) $4\sqrt{2}$

C) $4\sqrt{3}$

D) $8\sqrt{2}$

19

Breaths per minute				
7	8	10	12	14
18	18	18	19	20
21	21	22	23	24

The table above lists the resting breath rates (in breaths per minute) of 15 college-age students. If a student with a resting breath rate of 18 breaths per minute is added to the values listed, which of the following statistical measures of the data will change?

   I. Mean
   II. Median
   III. Range

A) I only

B) I and II only

C) II and III only

D) I, II, and III

20

$$y = x^2 - k$$

In the equation above, k is a constant. If the graph of the equation in the xy-plane is a parabola with x-intercepts of -4 and 4, what is the minimum value of y in terms of k ?

A) $-k$

B) $1 - k$

C) $4 - k$

D) $16 - k$

▼

Questions 21-22 refer to the following information.

From 1997 to 2010, a financial services company used banking data to determine the percentage of adults in the United States who had retirement savings. The scatterplot below shows y, the percentage of adults with retirement savings, plotted against x, the number of years since 1997. The line of best fit is also shown.

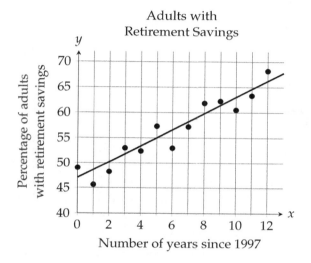

Adults with
Retirement Savings

21

Which of the following is closest to the equation of the line of best fit shown?

A) $y = \dfrac{5}{2}x$

B) $y = \dfrac{5}{2}x + 47$

C) $y = \dfrac{5}{3}x$

D) $y = \dfrac{5}{3}x + 47$

22

Which of the following is the best interpretation of the y-intercept of the line of best fit shown in the scatterplot?

A) The predicted number of adults with retirement savings in 1997

B) The actual number of adults with retirement savings in 1997

C) The predicted percentage of adults with retirement savings in 1997

D) The actual percentage of adults with retirement savings in 1997

▲

23

Of the following situations, which one would most likely begin an exponential growth of the number of greeting cards being sent?

A) Ann sends 3 greeting cards everyday to a different person.

B) Every month, thirty students send greeting cards to their penpals abroad who each agree to send one of their own back.

C) Jake sends greeting cards to 3 different friends, who all agree to send greeting cards to three of their friends who agree to do the same.

D) Caleb sends 3 greeting cards for every 2 greeting cards that he receives.

| 4 | 🖩 **| 4 |**

24

A company ships medium and large refrigerators by using trucks of two different sizes. A large truck can carry 4 medium refrigerators and 5 large refrigerators. A small truck can carry 3 medium refrigerators and 2 large refrigerators. If a is the number of large trucks and b is the number of small trucks, which of the following represents the number of trucks of each size necessary to deliver an order for 20 medium refrigerators and 30 large refrigerators?

A) $4a + 3b \geq 20$
$2a + 5b \geq 30$

B) $3a + 4b \leq 20$
$5a + 2b \leq 30$

C) $4a + 3b \geq 20$
$5a + 2b \geq 30$

D) $4a + 3b \geq 30$
$5a + 2b \geq 20$

25

In the xy-plane, the points $(a, 7)$ and $(b, 12)$ lie on the graph of $y = x^2 + 3$. What is the minimum possible value of $a + b$?

A) -5

B) -1

C) 1

D) 5

26

$$x^2 - 4x + y^2 + 6y = 12$$

The graph of the equation above in the xy-plane is a circle. What is the circumference of the circle?

A) 5π

B) 10π

C) 25π

D) 50π

27

In the xy-plane, the line with equation $y = ax + b$, where a and b are constants, intersects the line with equation $y = 2bx + a$ at the point $(3, 4)$. If $b \neq 0$, what is the value of $\frac{a}{b}$?

A) $\frac{2}{3}$

B) $\frac{3}{4}$

C) $\frac{5}{2}$

D) $\frac{7}{3}$

28

A medical research center selected a random sample of 500 patients suffering from disease X and found that the patients had a mean recovery time of 3.5 days and a margin of error of 1.25 days. Based on these results, which of the following is an appropriate conclusion?

A) The true mean recovery time of all patients suffering from disease X is 3.5 days.

B) The true mean recovery time of all patients suffering from disease X is likely between 2.25 days and 4.75 days.

C) All patients suffering from disease X take 3.5 days to recover.

D) All patients suffering from disease X take at least 2.25 days but no more than 4.75 days to recover.

29

For how many different positive integer values of m does $(mx - 10)^2 = 0$ have integer solutions?

A) None

B) Two

C) Four

D) Six

4

4

30

Which of the following graphs represents all x and y such that $-1 \leq x + y \leq 1$?

A)

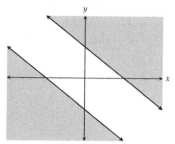

B)

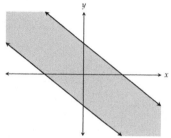

C)

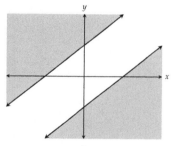

D)

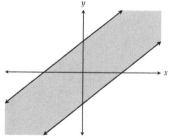

31

Traveling at an average speed of 40 miles per hour, a bus takes 3 hours to complete its morning route. At what average speed, in miles per hour, must the bus travel if it is to complete its morning route in 2.5 hours?

32

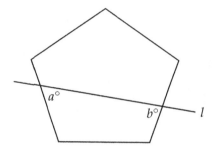

In the figure above, line l intersects a regular pentagon. What is the value of $a + b$?

4 **4**

33

$$\sin 24° = \cos(3k + 6)°$$

In the equation above, the angle measures are in degrees. If $0° < k < 90°$, what is the value of k ?

34

$$0.3x - 0.7y = 1$$
$$kx - 2.8y = 3$$

In the system of equations above, k is a constant. If the system has no solution, what is the value of k ?

35

The functions f and g are defined by $f(x) = x^2 + 2$ and $g(x) = 4x - 3$. If $a > 0$, for what value of a does $g(f(a)) = 41$?

36

A square and a rectangle have the same area. The length of the rectangle is 8 inches less than twice the side of the square. The width of the rectangle is 3 inches more than the side of the square. What is the area of the square?

▼

Questions 37-38 refer to the following information.

A wooden block with a mass of 0.8 kilograms is pressed against a coiled spring on a frictionless surface as shown in the figure below.

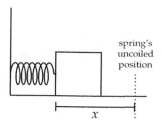

The potential energy P, in joules, of the spring is given by the formula

$$P = \frac{1}{2}kx^2$$

where x is the distance, in meters, the spring is displaced from its uncoiled position and k is a constant, in newtons per meter. When the spring is displaced 0.05 meters, it has a potential energy of 10 joules.

37

What is the potential energy, in joules, of the spring when it is displaced 0.08 meters?

38

The kinetic energy K, in joules, of an object is given by the formula $K = \frac{1}{2}mv^2$, where m is the mass of the object in kilograms and v is its velocity in meters per second. When the spring is uncoiled, all of its potential energy gets transferred to the wooden block as kinetic energy. What is the velocity of the block, in meters per second, immediately after the spring is uncoiled from a displaced position of 0.05 meters?

▲

9

Practice Test 9

Math Test --- No Calculator

25 Minutes, 20 Questions

Reference

$A = \pi r^2$
$C = 2\pi r$

$A = lw$

$A = \dfrac{1}{2}bh$

$c^2 = a^2 + b^2$

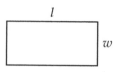
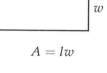

$V = lwh$

$V = \pi r^2 h$

Special Right Triangles

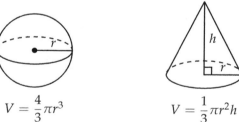
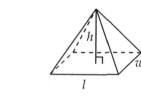

$V = \dfrac{4}{3}\pi r^3$

$V = \dfrac{1}{3}\pi r^2 h$

$V = \dfrac{1}{3}lwh$

There are 360 degrees of arc in a circle.
There are 2π radians of arc in a circle.
The sum of the measures of the angles of a triangle, in degrees, is 180.

3 **3**

1

If $4b = 7$, what is the value of $12b - 3$?

A) 18

B) 21

C) 24

D) 27

2

Which of the following is equivalent to the expression $\dfrac{2a^2b - 3ab^2 + ab}{ab}$?

A) $2a^2b - 3ab^2 + 1$

B) $2a^2b - 3b + ab$

C) $2a - 3ab^2 + ab$

D) $2a - 3b + 1$

3

John is a member of a recreational bowling league. His bowling scores from 2006 to 2015 can be modeled by the equation $p = 80.5 + 16.8t$, where t represents the number of years since he joined the league in 2006 and p represents the average number of points he scored per game. Which of the following is the best interpretation of the number 16.8 in the equation?

A) The total number of points John scored in 2006

B) The average number of points John scored per game in 2006

C) The yearly increase in the average number of points John scored per game

D) The average number of games John played each year

4

If $c^{-\frac{1}{3}} = x$, where $c > 0$ and $x > 0$, which of the following equations gives c in terms of x?

A) $c = -x^3$

B) $c = \sqrt[3]{x}$

C) $c = \dfrac{1}{\sqrt[3]{x}}$

D) $c = \dfrac{1}{x^3}$

5

An apartment complex charges tenants \$3.50 per 1,000 gallons of water used and \$12.00 for trash removal each month. Which of the following expressions represents a tenant's total monthly charges, in dollars, for g gallons of water used and trash removal?

A) $0.00035g + 12$

B) $0.0035g + 12$

C) $0.035g + 12$

D) $3.50g + 12$

6

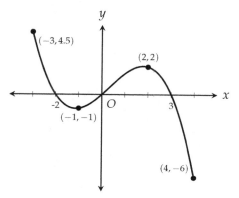

The function $y = f(x)$, defined for $-3 \le x \le 4$, is graphed in the xy-plane above. Which of the following gives all values of x for which $f(x)$ is negative?

A) $-3 \le x \le 4$

B) $-2 < x \le 4$

C) $-2 < x < 0$ and $3 < x \le 4$

D) $-3 \le x < -2$ and $0 < x < 3$

7

If $8a^2 = 3(a^2 + b)$ and $b \ne 0$, what is the value of $\dfrac{a^2}{b}$?

A) $\dfrac{1}{5}$

B) $\dfrac{3}{5}$

C) $\dfrac{5}{3}$

D) 5

8

A food vendor was hired to provide sandwich platters and seafood platters at an event with 300 attendees. Each sandwich platter served up to 9 people and each seafood platter served up to 6 people. The vendor was able to provide more than enough food for all the attendees with fewer than 40 platters. Which of the following systems of inequalities describes x, the possible number of sandwich platters, and y, the possible number of seafood platters, that the vendor provided at the event?

A) $x + y > 40$
   $9x + 6y > 300$

B) $x + y < 40$
   $9x + 6y < 300$

C) $x + y > 40$
   $9x + 6y < 300$

D) $x + y < 40$
   $9x + 6y > 300$

9

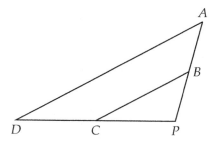

In the figure above, point B is the midpoint of $\overline{AP}$ and point C is the midpoint of $\overline{DP}$. If $AP = 8$, $DP = 12$, and $BC = 8$, what is the perimeter of quadrilateral $ABCD$?

A) 30

B) 34

C) 38

D) 44

3 **3**

10

A circle in the xy-plane passes through the point $(2,2)$ and has a radius of 5. Which of the following could be an equation of the circle?

A) $(x-1)^2 + y^2 = 5$

B) $(x+2)^2 + (y-5)^2 = 25$

C) $(x-2)^2 + (y-2)^2 = 25$

D) $(x-7)^2 + (y-7)^2 = 25$

11

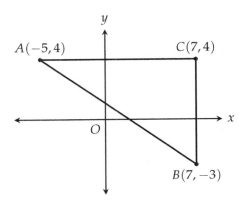

Right triangle ABC is shown in the xy-plane above. What is the value of $\tan A$?

A) $\dfrac{7}{12}$

B) $\dfrac{3}{4}$

C) $\dfrac{7}{9}$

D) $\dfrac{12}{7}$

12

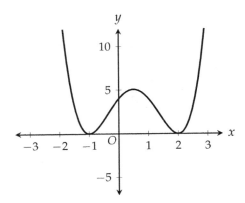

Which of the following could be the equation of the graph in the xy-plane above?

A) $y = -(x-2)^2(x+1)^2$

B) $y = (x-2)^2(x+1)^2$

C) $y = x(x-2)(x+1)$

D) $y = x^2(x-2)(x+1)$

13

Bob can finish painting a house in 4 days. Carl can finish painting a house in 6 days. Which of the following equations can be used to find the number of days d that Bob and Carl would need to finish painting one house working together?

A) $\dfrac{d}{4} + \dfrac{d}{6} = 1$

B) $\dfrac{4}{d} + \dfrac{6}{d} = 1$

C) $\dfrac{d}{4} + \dfrac{d}{6} = 12$

D) $\dfrac{4}{d} + \dfrac{6}{d} = 12$

3 **3**

14

If the expression $\frac{1}{4}x^2 + 3x + 9$ is rewritten in the form $\frac{1}{4}(x + a)^2$, where a is a positive constant, what is the value of a ?

A) $\frac{3}{2}$

B) 3

C) 6

D) $2\sqrt{3}$

15

$$-2x + 6y = 10$$
$$-3x + 9y = 18$$

How many solutions (x, y) are there to the system of equations above?

A) Zero

B) One

C) Two

D) More than two

16

For what value of k is $5 - \dfrac{6}{k} = -13$?

17

The graph of a line in the xy-plane passes through points $(0, 0)$ and $(1, 2)$. The graph of a second line passes through points $(1, 2)$ and $(k, 0)$. If the two lines are perpendicular, what is the value of k ?

18

$$x^2 + 2xy + y^2 = 25$$
$$x - y = 7$$

If (x, y) is a solution to the system of equations above, what is one possible value of x ?

19

In the xy-plane, the line defined by the equation $y = 3x - 5$ passes through the vertex of a parabola with x-intercepts of 3 and 15. What is the y-coordinate of the vertex of the parabola?

3 **3**

20

$$9x^3 - kx + 4$$

In the polynomial above, k is an integer. If $3x - 2$ is a factor of the polynomial, what is the value of k ?

Math Test --- Calculator

55 Minutes, 38 Questions

Reference

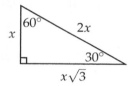

$A = \pi r^2$
$C = 2\pi r$

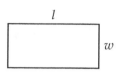

$A = lw$

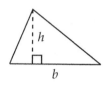

$A = \dfrac{1}{2}bh$

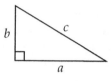

$c^2 = a^2 + b^2$

Special Right Triangles

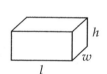

$V = lwh$

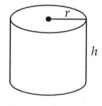

$V = \pi r^2 h$

$V = \dfrac{4}{3}\pi r^3$

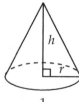

$V = \dfrac{1}{3}\pi r^2 h$

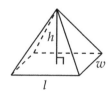

$V = \dfrac{1}{3}lwh$

There are 360 degrees of arc in a circle.
There are 2π radians of arc in a circle.
The sum of the measures of the angles of a triangle, in degrees, is 180.

4 📋 **4**

1

If an ant travels at a constant rate of 4 feet per minute, how many <u>inches</u> does it travel in a half hour?

A) 1,280

B) 1,440

C) 1,560

D) 1,720

2

Gillian scored an 84 on her midterm and a 94 on her final. Which of the following best approximates the percent increase in her score from her midterm to her final?

A) 10.6%

B) 11.9%

C) 12.1%

D) 15.5%

3

Jonathan can edit at least 15 essays per day but no more than 18 essays per day. Which of the following could be the total number of essays he edits in a week?

A) 98

B) 102

C) 112

D) 130

4

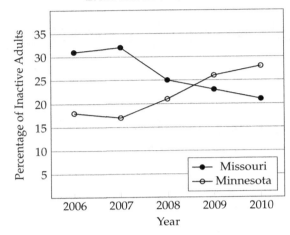

Physical Inactivity among Adults in MS and MN from 2006-2010

The graph above shows the percentage of physically inactive adults in Missouri and Minnesota from 2006 to 2010. Which of the following is a correct statement about the data above?

A) Minnesota had a higher percentage of physically inactive adults for none of the five years.

B) Minnesota had a higher percentage of physically inactive adults for two of the five years.

C) Minnesota had a higher percentage of physically inactive adults for three of the five years.

D) Minnesota had a higher percentage of physically inactive adults during all five years.

4 **4**

Questions 5-6 refer to the following information.

A ball starts from rest at the top of a ramp and rolls down, as illustrated by the figure above. The speed s, in meters per second, of the ball is given by the equation $s = \sqrt{\dfrac{3d}{4}}$, where d is the distance, in meters, the ball has traveled along the ramp.

5

If the speed of the ball is 6 meters per second when it reaches the bottom of the ramp, how long is the ramp, in meters?

A) 16

B) 27

C) 48

D) 64

6

Which of the following graphs best models the height of the ball as it rolls down the ramp?

A)

B)

C)

D)

4 🖩 **4**

7

A cable company surveyed a random sample of 400 subscribers to determine their favorite sport to watch. The results of the survey are shown in the table below.

Basketball	80
Baseball	70
Football	150
Hockey	40
Tennis	20
Other	40

The cable company has 2 million subscribers. Based on the survey data, which of the following is most likely to be an accurate statement?

A) Baseball is the favorite sport to watch for about 200,000 subscribers

B) Baseball is the favorite sport to watch for about 450,000 subscribers

C) Football is the favorite sport to watch for about 600,000 subscribers

D) Football is the favorite sport to watch for about 750,000 subscribers

8

During one season, a baseball player managed to hit 25 percent of the balls pitched at him. Of the balls he hit, 5 percent were home runs. Which of the following expresses the estimated number of home runs this player would hit if n balls were pitched at him?

A) $(0.25 + 0.05)n$

B) $(0.25)(.05)n$

C) $\dfrac{n}{(0.25)(.05)}$

D) $(1.25)(1.05)n$

9

Mike has $650 in his bank account and withdraws $16 at the end of each week. Kyle has $100 in his bank account and deposits $6 at the end of each week. After how many weeks will Mike and Kyle have the same amount of money in their bank accounts?

A) 17

B) 20

C) 22

D) 25

10

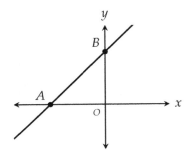

In the xy-plane above, the line $y = \dfrac{4}{3}x + 8$ crosses the x and y axes at points A and B respectively. What is the length of $\overline{AB}$?

A) 6

B) 8

C) 10

D) 12

4 ▤ **4**

▼

Questions 11-12 refer to the following information.

The table below shows some values of x and y.

x	1	2	3	4
y	$\dfrac{(0)(2)}{2}$	$\dfrac{(1)(3)}{4}$	$\dfrac{(2)(4)}{6}$	$\dfrac{(3)(5)}{8}$

11

Based on the relationship shown in the table, what is the value of y when x is equal to 5 ?

A) 1.8

B) 2

C) 2.4

D) 2.8

12

Which of the following equations describes the relationship between x and y in the table?

A) $y = \dfrac{2x - 2}{x + 1}$

B) $y = \dfrac{(x - 1)(x + 1)}{2x}$

C) $y = \dfrac{(x - 1)(3x - 1)}{2x}$

D) $y = \dfrac{(x - 1)(x + 1)}{2^x}$

▲

13

A bottle holds 5 cups of grape juice. If $\dfrac{2}{3}$ pound of grapes makes 2 cups of grape juice, how many bottles can be filled with the grape juice made from 30 pounds of grapes?

A) 8

B) 9

C) 18

D) 36

14

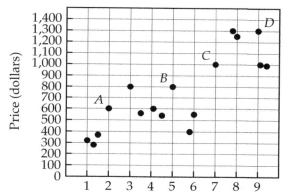

Flight Distance (thousands of miles)

A travel site summarized the flight distance and price for 17 flights in the scatterplot above. Of the labeled points, which represents the flight for which the ratio of flight distance to price is greatest?

A) A

B) B

C) C

D) D

4 ▦ **4**

▼

Questions 15-16 refer to the following information.

Star Rating	Number of movies
1	4
2	5
3	2
4	3
5	6

Twenty different movies were shown at a film festival and given a rating from 1 star (worst) to 5 stars (best). The results are summarized in the table above.

15

If one of the movies is chosen at random, what is the probability that the movie was given at least 3 stars?

A) 0.25

B) 0.35

C) 0.45

D) 0.55

16

What is the average star rating of the movies shown at the film festival?

A) 3.1

B) 3.3

C) 3.6

D) 4.2

▲

17

If $\dfrac{4}{2x-7} > 3$, which of the following could be a value of x?

A) 1

B) 2

C) 3

D) 4

18

At a pet store, puppies sell at one price and kittens sell at another. Jimmy pays $240 for 3 puppies and 2 kittens. Marissa pays $210 for 1 puppy and 5 kittens. What is the price of a puppy?

A) $30

B) $45

C) $60

D) $75

19

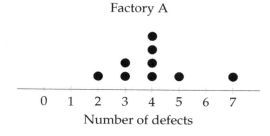

Factory A

Number of defects

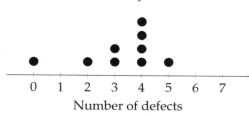

Factory B

Number of defects

A phone manufacturer is using two different factories to test a new product. The dotplots above show the number of defects in 9 products from each factory. Which of the following correctly compares the mean number of defects in the products from each factory?

A) The mean number of defects in the products from Factory A is greater.

B) The mean number of defects in the products from Factory B is greater.

C) The mean number of defects in the products from Factory A and Factory B is the same.

D) The relationship cannot be determined from the information given.

20

$$w = \frac{5}{7}(2a + 1)$$

Conservationists use the equation above to estimate the wing span w of an eagle, in inches, based on the eagle's age a, in years. According to the equation, an increase of 1 inch in the wingspan of an eagle takes how many years?

A) 0.7

B) 1.4

C) 2

D) 2.8

21

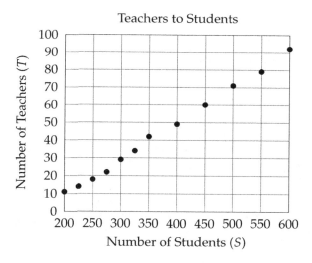

Teachers to Students

The scatterplot above shows the number of teachers T and the number of students S at 12 schools selected at random. Which of the following equations best models the relationship between T and S ?

A) $T = 0.15S - 20$

B) $T = 0.2S - 30$

C) $T = 0.2S + 11$

D) $T = 10S + 10$

4 🖩 **4**

22

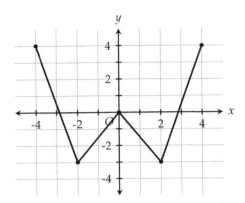

The complete function f is shown in the xy-plane above. If $f(x) = k$ has two solutions, which of the following could be the value of k ?

   I. -3
  II. 0
 III. 2.5

A) I and II only

B) III only

C) I and III only

D) I, II, and III

23

In a regular polygon with n sides, the degree measure of each interior angle is given by the expression $\dfrac{180(n - 2)}{n}$. Which of the following expressions gives the <u>radian</u> measure of each interior angle of the polygon?

A) $\dfrac{\pi(n - 2)}{n}$

B) $\dfrac{\pi(n - 2)}{2n}$

C) $\dfrac{\pi(n - 2)}{4n}$

D) $\dfrac{2\pi(n - 2)}{n}$

24

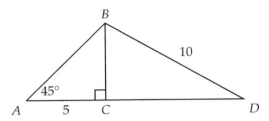

In $\triangle ABD$ above, $AC = 5$ and $BD = 10$. What is the length of $\overline{CD}$?

A) $5\sqrt{2}$

B) $5\sqrt{3}$

C) 6

D) $6\sqrt{2}$

25

Tickets to a concert are $40 for reserved seats and $15 for general admission seats. If a total of 1,200 tickets have been sold and x of them are for reserved seats, which of the following gives all possible values of x for which total ticket sales are at least $30,000?

A) $x \leq 480$

B) $x \geq 480$

C) $x \leq 520$

D) $x \geq 520$

26

Anne and her family took two camping trips to Site X. During the second trip, they all used a new mosquito repellent that advertises itself as the most effective in reducing mosquito bites. After the second trip, they all reported a lower number of mosquito bites than they had after the first trip. Which of the following is an appropriate conclusion?

A) The new mosquito repellent will cause a reduction in mosquito bites for any camper.

B) The new mosquito repellent will cause a reduction in mosquito bites for any camper at Site X.

C) The new mosquito repellent was the cause of the reduction in mosquito bites for Anne and her family during the second camping trip.

D) No conclusion about cause and effect can be made regarding the new mosquito repellent and its effectiveness in reducing mosquito bites.

27

2 pins on each side   3 pins on each side   4 pins on each side

In the figure above, pins are used to outline squares of different sizes. For example, a total of 4 pins are needed to outline a square with 2 pins on each side. Which of the following represents the total number of pins needed to outline a square with n pins on each side?

A) $2n + 2$

B) $4n - 4$

C) $4n$

D) n^2

28

$$\frac{x - y}{y} = x$$

If x is positive in the equation above, which of the following must be true?

A) $y > 1$

B) $0 < y < 1$

C) $-1 < y < 0$

D) $y < -1$

29

The function f is defined by $f(x) = \frac{1}{2}x + a$, where a is a constant. If $f(a) = 3$, what is the value of $f(8)$?

A) 6

B) 7

C) 8

D) 9

30

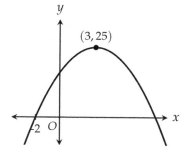

The graph of the equation $y = -x^2 + 6x + 16$ is a parabola with vertex $(3, 25)$ as shown in the xy-plane above. If one of the x-intercepts is at -2, which of the following equivalent forms of the equation shows the x-intercepts of the parabola as constants or coefficients?

A) $y = -2(x + 2)(x - 8)$

B) $y = -(x + 2)(x - 8)$

C) $y = (x + 2)(x - 8)$

D) $y = -(x - 3)^2 + 25$

4 **4**

31

A car is traveling along a highway at 80 miles per hour. Before it exits the highway and enters a residential area, it must slow down to meet the residential speed limit of 30 miles per hour. If it decelerates so that its speed drops by 2 miles per hour every second, how many seconds will it take the car to slow down to the residential speed limit?

32

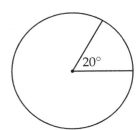

Note: Figure not drawn to scale.

To make a certain light fixture, a blacksmith cuts wedges from a 270-gram iron disk, as shown in the figure above. Each wedge forms a 20° angle at the center of the disk. If the weight of the disk is uniformly distributed, how many grams does each wedge weigh?

33

$$\frac{1}{2}(x - 2) + 6\left(\frac{1}{4}x + 1\right)$$

If the expression above is rewritten in the form $px + q$, where p and q are constants, what is the value of $p + q$?

34

$$\frac{1}{2}x^2 - 3y^2 = 55$$

$$x = -4y$$

If (x, y) is a solution to the system of equations above, what is the value of y^2?

35

A printer's input capacity is the maximum number of sheets of paper the printer can hold at one time. The table below gives the distribution of input capacities for a randomly selected group of printers.

Input Capacity (pages)	Frequency
200	3
300	x
400	5
500	5
600	10

If the median input capacity of these printers is 400 pages, what is the maximum possible value of x ?

36

A group of students leased a 900 square foot storage unit and distributed the space evenly among themselves. When 3 more students decided to join the lease, each of the students in the initial group gave up 25 square feet of space so that everyone on the lease would have an equal share of the storage unit. How many students were in the initial group?

Questions 37-38 refer to the following information.

The initial price of a computer is a dollars. For each month that passes by, the price is reduced to 10 percent less than the price for the previous month. Based on this information, the price P of the computer can be modeled by the equation

$$P = a(r)^n$$

where n is the number of months that have passed and r is a constant.

37

What is the value of r ?

38

The price of the computer decreases by n percent every 3 months. What is the value of n ?

10

Practice Test 10

Math Test --- No Calculator

25 Minutes, 20 Questions

Reference

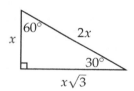

$A = \pi r^2$
$C = 2\pi r$

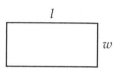

$A = lw$

$A = \frac{1}{2}bh$

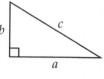

$c^2 = a^2 + b^2$

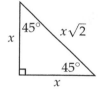

Special Right Triangles

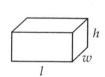

$V = lwh$

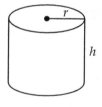

$V = \pi r^2 h$

$V = \frac{4}{3}\pi r^3$

$V = \frac{1}{3}\pi r^2 h$

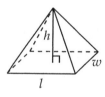

$V = \frac{1}{3}lwh$

There are 360 degrees of arc in a circle.
There are 2π radians of arc in a circle.
The sum of the measures of the angles of a triangle, in degrees, is 180.

3 **3**

1

If $y + \dfrac{3}{5} = \dfrac{27}{35}$, then what is the value of y ?

A) $-\dfrac{6}{35}$

B) $\dfrac{6}{35}$

C) $\dfrac{4}{5}$

D) $\dfrac{48}{35}$

2

At a bookstore, each magazine costs the same price. If 8 magazines cost d dollars, then which of the following expresses the number of magazines that can be purchased for 15 dollars?

A) $\dfrac{15d}{8}$

B) $\dfrac{d}{120}$

C) $\dfrac{120}{d}$

D) $\dfrac{8d}{15}$

3

Line m is graphed in the xy-plane. If an equation for line m is $6y + 2x = 5$, which of the following statements is true?

A) Line m has a slope of -3.

B) Line m has a slope of $\dfrac{1}{3}$.

C) The x-intercept of line m is $\dfrac{5}{2}$ and the y-intercept is $\dfrac{5}{6}$.

D) The x-intercept of line m is $\dfrac{5}{6}$ and the y-intercept is $\dfrac{5}{2}$.

4

If $3\sqrt{x^3} = \sqrt{72}$, what is the value of x ?

A) 2

B) 3

C) 4

D) 5

5

$$(x - c)^2 = x + 3$$

If $c = 3$, what is the solution set of the equation above?

A) $\{1\}$

B) $\{6\}$

C) $\{1, 6\}$

D) $\{-3, 1, 6\}$

6

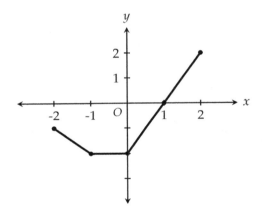

The graph of $f(x)$ is shown in the xy-plane above. If $f(a) = -2$, which of the following is a possible value of a ?

A) -1.5

B) -0.5

C) 1

D) 2

154

3 **3**

7

Anna writes checks from her checkbook to pay her business expenses. The number of checks c left in her checkbook after t weeks is given by the equation $c = 120 - 2t$. What is the meaning of the number 120 in the equation?

A) The number of checks Anna writes each week

B) The number of weeks it takes for Anna to write all the checks in her checkbook

C) The number of checks left in Anna's checkbook at the end of one week

D) The initial number of checks in Anna's checkbook

8

The property tax rate in a certain town increased from 0.014 in 1995 to 0.023 in 2003. If the relationship between property tax rate and year is linear, which of the following equations best models the property tax rate R in the town t years after 1995?

A) $R = \dfrac{9}{800}t + 0.014$

B) $R = \dfrac{9}{8,000}t + 0.014$

C) $R = \dfrac{11}{800}t + 0.014$

D) $R = \dfrac{11}{8,000}t + 0.014$

9

An online office supply store sells pens at p dollars per box and offers free shipping on orders of \$75 or more. If John decides to order new pens from this store, which of the following inequalities expresses the number of boxes n that he must purchase for the order to qualify for free shipping?

A) $n \le \dfrac{p}{75}$

B) $n \ge \dfrac{p}{75}$

C) $n \le \dfrac{75}{p}$

D) $n \ge \dfrac{75}{p}$

10

$$\frac{3(-h+3)+2}{4} = \frac{5-(1-2h)}{10}$$

In the equation above, what is the value of h ?

A) $\dfrac{43}{19}$

B) $\dfrac{47}{19}$

C) $\dfrac{47}{14}$

D) $\dfrac{47}{11}$

11

$$3x + 5y = 10$$
$$-x + y = 2$$

Which of the following ordered pairs (x, y) satisfies the system of equations above?

A) $(-2, 0)$

B) $(0, 2)$

C) $(2, 4)$

D) $(4, 6)$

12

Which of the following expressions is equivalent to $\left(\dfrac{1}{z-y}\right)\left(\dfrac{1}{y}-\dfrac{1}{z}\right)$?

A) $\dfrac{1}{yz}$

B) $\dfrac{1}{y^2z^2}$

C) $-\dfrac{1}{(y-z)^2}$

D) -1

13

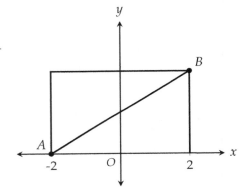

In the xy-plane above, line segment $\overline{AB}$ is the diagonal of a rectangle. If the area of the rectangle is 20, what is the slope of $\overline{AB}$?

A) 1.25

B) 1.5

C) 2.5

D) 5

14

In the xy-plane, the graph of a parabola has x-intercepts at -3 and 5. If the y-coordinate of the vertex of the parabola is 8, which of the following could be the equation of the parabola?

A) $y = -\dfrac{1}{2}(x+3)(x-5)$

B) $y = 2(x+3)(x-5)$

C) $y = -\dfrac{2}{3}(x-3)(x+5)$

D) $y = \dfrac{1}{4}(x-3)(x+5)$

15

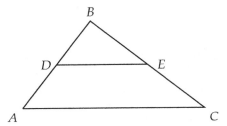

In the figure above, D is the midpoint of $\overline{AB}$ and E is the midpoint of $\overline{BC}$. The area of trapezoid $ADEC$ is how many times the area of triangle DBE ?

A) 2

B) 2.5

C) 3

D) 3.5

16

If $\dfrac{3}{x} = 12$, what is the value of $\dfrac{2}{x}$?

3 **3**

17

$$5x + 12 = \frac{10x + 3c}{2}$$

In the equation above, c is a constant. For what value of c will the equation have infinitely many solutions?

18

In a circle with center C and radius 6, minor arc $\overarc{AB}$ has a length of 4π. If the measure, in radians, of central angle ACB is written as $k\pi$, where k is a positive constant, what is the value of k ?

19

There are 50 tennis balls, 20 of which are blue, in a container. After x blue tennis balls are removed, 25% of the tennis balls in the container are blue. What is the value of x ?

20

$$x - y + 2 = 0$$
$$(x + 2)^2 - 7(x + 2) + 25 = 4y - 5$$

If (x, y) is a solution to the system of equations above, what is one possible value of x ?

4 **4**

Math Test --- Calculator

55 Minutes, 38 Questions

Reference

$A = \pi r^2$
$C = 2\pi r$

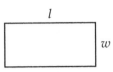

$A = lw$

$A = \frac{1}{2}bh$

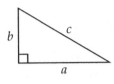

$c^2 = a^2 + b^2$

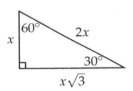

$x\sqrt{3}$

Special Right Triangles

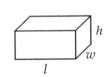

$V = lwh$

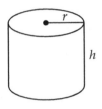

$V = \pi r^2 h$

$V = \frac{4}{3}\pi r^3$

$V = \frac{1}{3}\pi r^2 h$

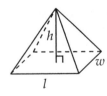

$V = \frac{1}{3}lwh$

There are 360 degrees of arc in a circle.
There are 2π radians of arc in a circle.
The sum of the measures of the angles of a triangle, in degrees, is 180.

4 📷 **4**

1

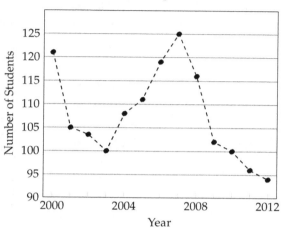

Summer Camp Enrollment

The graph above shows the number of students who enrolled in a summer math camp from 2000 to 2012. According to the graph, the student enrollment was the same in which of the following years?

A) 2000 and 2007
B) 2001 and 2004
C) 2002 and 2012
D) 2003 and 2010

2

In 2005, a toy manufacturer found that an estimated 4 out of every 15 dolls produced posed a safety hazard to young children. If the manufacturer produced 6 million dolls in 2005, which of the following is closest to the estimated number of dolls produced by the manufacturer in 2005 that do NOT pose a safety hazard?

A) 1.6 million
B) 4.4 million
C) 4.6 million
D) 4.8 million

3

Rachel discarded exactly 45 percent of the pens that she owned. Which of the following could be the total number of pens that she has left?

A) 22
B) 24
C) 26
D) 28

4

Which of the following expressions is NOT equal to 0 for some value of x ?

A) $(x+1)^2$
B) $\sqrt{x}+1$
C) $\sqrt{x+1}$
D) $|x+1|$

5

The number of criminal cases in a state district is recorded over the course of five years, as shown in the table below.

Year	Cases
1	450
2	400
3	350
4	300
5	250

Which of the following best describes the relationship between time and the number of cases during the five years?

A) Increasing linear
B) Decreasing linear
C) Exponential growth
D) Exponential decay

4 🖩 **4**

▼

Questions 6-7 refer to the following information.

Projected Sales for Toy X

Price of Toy X	Projected number of toys sold
$10	50,000
$20	40,000
$30	30,000
$40	30,000
$50	30,000

6

Based on the projections, how much more money would be received from sales of Toy X when the price is $40 than when the price is $20?

A) $100,000

B) $400,000

C) $600,000

D) $700,000

7

Based on the table, which of the following graphs best represents the relationship between the price of Toy X and the projected number of toys sold?

A)

B)

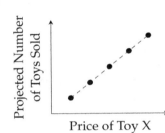

C)

D)

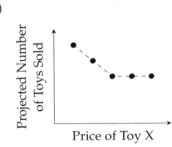

▲

4 [calculator icon] **4**

8

In a recent study comparing two high schools, a random sample of students from School A and a random sample of students from School B were surveyed. The results of the study indicated that 85% of the students from School A spend at least 3 hours each day reading, while 70% of the students from School B spend at least 3 hours each day reading. If the margin of error for both samples were the same, which of the following statements is best supported by the study's results?

A) Students from School A read more because School A has better teachers.

B) Students from School A read more because students from School A study harder.

C) There is evidence that students from School A read more than students from School B.

D) There is evidence that students from School A read more fiction novels than students from School B.

9

Oleg is deciding between renting and buying an apartment. The purchase price is $180,000. If he rents it, he will pay $1,100 in rent each month, in addition to monthly fees of $150 for utilities and parking. If x represents the number of months he stays in the apartment, what are all the values of x for which buying the apartment is less expensive than renting it?

A) $x < 144$

B) $x > 144$

C) $x < 164$

D) $x > 164$

10

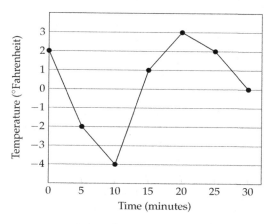

The graph above gives the inside temperature of a refrigerator as it is being adjusted over time. On which of the following intervals does the temperature change (in absolute value) by 5 degrees Fahrenheit?

A) 0 to 5 minutes

B) 5 to 10 minutes

C) 10 to 15 minutes

D) 20 to 25 minutes

11

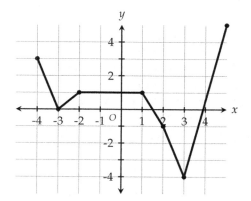

The graph above shows the function g. What is the value of $g(3)$?

A) -4

B) 0

C) 3

D) 4

4 📱 **4**

12

	Car	Train	Total
Late	20	15	35
On time			225
Total			260

A company decides to investigate whether the mode of transportation taken to work affects its employees' arrival to work. The results for a given day are shown in the incomplete table above. If there are 50 more employees at the company who commute by train than by car, what is the probability that an employee who was on time that day took the train?

A) $\dfrac{7}{13}$

B) $\dfrac{31}{52}$

C) $\dfrac{28}{45}$

D) $\dfrac{28}{31}$

13

An environmentalist studied a random sample of 30 rivers in China to determine whether there is a relationship between water pollution levels and the number of fish. She found significant evidence that water pollution levels are lower in rivers with large numbers of fish. Based on the results, which of the following conclusions is most appropriate?

A) For rivers in China, there is a negative association between water pollution levels and the number of fish.

B) For all rivers, there is a negative association between water pollution levels and the number of fish.

C) For rivers in China, an increase in water pollution levels causes a decrease in the number of fish.

D) For all rivers, an increase in water pollution levels causes a decrease in the number of fish.

14

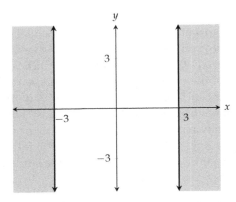

Which of the following inequalities is represented by the graph in the xy-plane above?

A) $|x| \le 3$

B) $|x| \ge 3$

C) $|y| \le 3$

D) $|y| \ge 3$

15

A chemical reaction between a block of sugar and sulfuric acid can be modeled by the equation $s = 27 - 3a$, where a is the amount of sulfuric acid, in milliliters, used in the reaction and s is the amount of sugar, in grams, left after the reaction. What does it mean for $(9, 0)$ to be a solution to this equation?

A) It takes 9 milliliters of sulfuric acid to react with 3 grams of sugar.

B) It takes 9 grams of sugar to react with 3 milliliters of sulfuric acid.

C) It takes 9 milliliters of sulfuric acid to react with 27 grams of sugar.

D) It takes 9 grams of sugar to react with 27 milliliters of sulfuric acid.

16

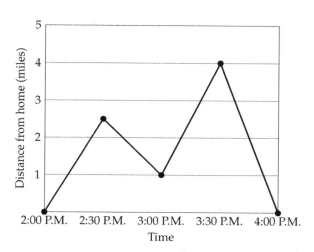

To run some errands, Amy travels back and forth along the straight road on which she lives. The graph above shows Amy's distance from home from 2:00 P.M. to 4:00 P.M. Based on the graph, when was Amy's average speed the greatest?

A) From 2:00 P.M. to 2:30 P.M.

B) From 2:30 P.M. to 3:00 P.M.

C) From 3:00 P.M. to 3:30 P.M.

D) From 3:30 P.M. to 4:00 P.M.

17

$$h = -6t^2 + 36t + 12$$

The height of a model rocket is modeled by the equation above, where h is the height of the rocket, in meters, and t is the number of seconds after launch. In which of the following equations do both the maximum height of the rocket and the number of seconds it takes the rocket to reach the maximum height appear as constants or coefficients?

A) $h = -6(t + 3)^2 + 42$

B) $h = -6(t - 3)^2 + 66$

C) $h = -6(t^2 - 6t - 2)$

D) $h = -6(t - 2)(t - 4) + 60$

Questions 18-19 refer to the following information.

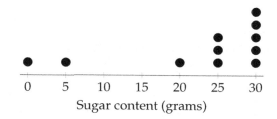

Sugar content (grams)

The dotplot above shows the sugar content (in grams) in each of the 11 most popular soft drinks in Japan.

18

What is the mode of the data set?

A) 0

B) 23

C) 25

D) 30

19

If the dots representing the two soft drinks with the lowest sugar content are removed from the dot plot, what will happen to the mean, median, and range of the new data set?

A) Only the mean will increase.

B) Only the mean and range will increase.

C) Only the mean and median will increase.

D) The mean, median, and range will increase.

4 **4**

20

A Belgian chocolate company sells milk chocolate bars for \$5 each and dark chocolate bars for \$7 each. Each milk chocolate bar costs \$2 to make and each dark chocolate bar costs \$5 to make. The company projects total sales to be at least \$5,000 and total costs to be at most \$2,800 for its chocolate bars this month. Which of the following systems of inequalities represents the possible number of milk chocolate bars m and dark chocolate bars d the company makes and sells to meet its projections?

A) $7m - 5d \geq 5,000$
$2d - 5m \leq 2,800$

B) $5m + 7d \geq 5,000$
$2m + 5d \geq 2,800$

C) $5m - 2m \geq 5,000$
$7d - 5d \leq 2,800$

D) $5m + 7d \geq 5,000$
$2m + 5d \leq 2,800$

21

A radioactive element decays over time, losing 8 percent of its mass every 5 years. If scientists have collected an initial 500 grams of this element, how much will be left, to the nearest gram, after 30 years?

A) 41
B) 258
C) 303
D) 330

22

$$P = \frac{1,500}{\sqrt{n}}$$

A hotel uses the formula above to determine the price P, in dollars, of a one-night reservation when there are n rooms available. If the price of a one-night reservation is greater than 350 dollars, what is the greatest number of rooms the hotel can have available?

A) 17
B) 18
C) 19
D) 20

23

$$x + ay = 5$$
$$2x + 6y = b$$

In the system of equations above, a and b are constants. If the system has one solution, which of the following could be the values of a and b ?

A) $a = 3, b = 10$
B) $a = 3, b = 12$
C) $a = 3, b = -4$
D) $a = 10, b = 3$

Questions 24-25 refer to the following information.

The table below shows the cost of a taxicab ride in 5 different cities. The base fare refers to a fixed fee that is charged regardless of the distance traveled.

City	Base Fare	Charge per $\frac{1}{4}$ of a mile traveled
A	None	$1.25
B	$1.50	$1.00
C	$2.00	$1.00
D	$2.50	$0.75
E	$3.00	$0.50

24

What is the total cost of riding a taxicab for $2\frac{1}{2}$ miles in City C?

A) $10.50

B) $11

C) $11.50

D) $12

25

For what distance traveled, in miles, would the total cost of a taxicab ride in City A equal the base fare of a taxicab ride in City E?

A) 0.6 miles

B) 0.8 miles

C) 1.2 miles

D) 2.4 miles

26

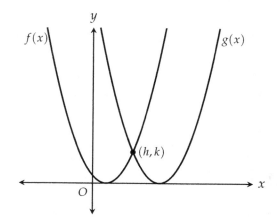

Functions $f(x) = x^2 - 2x + 1$ and $g(x) = x^2 - 10x + 25$ are graphed in the xy-plane above. If the graphs of f and g are tangent to the x-axis and intersect at the point (h, k), what is the value of $h + k$?

A) 3

B) 7

C) 13

D) 21

27

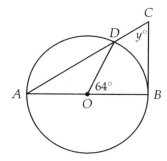

In the figure above, $\overline{BC}$ is tangent to a circle with center O and point D lies on $\overline{AC}$. What is the value of y ?

A) 54

B) 58

C) 62

D) 66

4 **4**

28

If $x - 2$ and $x + 1$ are both factors of the polynomial $p(x)$, which of the following could be $p(x)$?

A) $p(x) = x^3 - 2x^2 - 5x + 6$

B) $p(x) = x^3 - 4x^2 + x + 6$

C) $p(x) = x^3 - 6x^2 + 11x - 6$

D) $p(x) = x^3 - 7x - 6$

29

Two right circular cylinders A and B have the same volume. The radius of cylinder A is 20% longer than the radius of cylinder B. Which of the following statements correctly describes the relationship between the heights of the two cylinders?

A) The height of cylinder B is 14% greater than the height of cylinder A.

B) The height of cylinder B is 20% greater than the height of cylinder A.

C) The height of cylinder B is 24% greater than the height of cylinder A.

D) The height of cylinder B is 44% greater than the height of cylinder A.

30

In the xy-plane, the points $(c, 2d)$ and $(c + 3, 4d)$ lie on the line with equation $y = mx + b$, where m and b are nonzero constants. What is the value of $\dfrac{d}{m}$?

A) $\dfrac{2}{3}$

B) 1

C) $\dfrac{3}{2}$

D) 2

31

The difference between two numbers is 30. One of the numbers, x, is 20% less than the other number. What is the value of x ?

32

$$g(x) = \frac{1}{\sqrt{x + 10} - 9}$$

For what value of x is the function g above undefined?

4 **4**

33

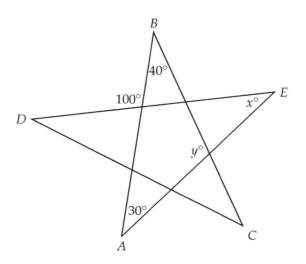

Note: Figure not drawn to scale.

In the figure above, AB, BC, CD, DE, and EA are line segments. What is the value of $x + y$?

34

Type	Bolts	Washers
Regular	18	12
Deluxe	40	25

The table above shows the contents of two types of assortment packs that a hardware store sells. Sam and Ali want to buy a number of the assortment packs so that they can split the contents according to each of their needs. Sam needs at least 540 bolts and Ali needs at least 400 washers. If they buy 10 regular assortment packs, what is the least number of deluxe assortment packs they can buy to satisfy their requirements?

35

Lianna plays a card game in which she gets 5 points for every red card she draws but loses 10 points for every black card she draws. By the end of the game, Lianna drew 7 times as many red cards as black cards for a final total of 75 points. How many red cards did she draw during the game?

36

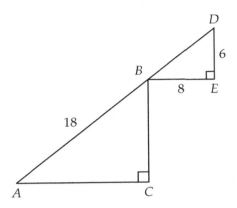

In the figure above, points A, B, and D lie on the same line. If $AB = 18$, $BE = 8$, and $DE = 6$, what is the value of $\sin A$?

Questions 37-38 refer to the following information.

The total resistance R, measured in ohms, of a parallel circuit with two resistors is given by

$$\frac{1}{R} = \frac{1}{R_1} + \frac{1}{R_2}$$

where R_1 and R_2 are the resistances, in ohms, of the first and second resistors, respectively.

37

What is the total resistance, in ohms, of a parallel circuit in which the first resistor has a resistance of 6 ohms and the second has a resistance of 4 ohms?

38

In a parallel circuit with two resistors, the first resistor has twice the resistance of the second. The total resistance of the circuit is what fraction of the resistance of the second resistor?

Practice Test 1 Answers

Question categories correspond to chapters in *The College Panda's SAT Math: The Advanced Guide and Workbook*. To estimate your score, visit *thecollegepanda.com/sat-score-calculator*

Section 3

1. $\boxed{A}$ Manipulating & Solving Equations
2. $\boxed{A}$ Expressions
3. $\boxed{C}$ Manipulating & Solving Equations
4. $\boxed{C}$ Exponents & Radicals
5. $\boxed{C}$ Triangles
6. $\boxed{D}$ Word Problems
7. $\boxed{C}$ Lines
8. $\boxed{C}$ Interpreting Linear Models
9. $\boxed{B}$ Complex Numbers
10. $\boxed{C}$ Quadratics
11. $\boxed{C}$ Rates
12. $\boxed{A}$ Lines
13. $\boxed{B}$ Expressions
14. $\boxed{D}$ More Equation Solving Strategies / Synthetic Division
15. $\boxed{B}$ Systems of Equations
16. $\boxed{21, 25, \text{ or } 29}$ Functions
17. $\boxed{35}$ Angles
18. $\boxed{7}$ Minimum & Maximum Word Problems
19. $\boxed{18}$ Functions
20. $\boxed{3}$ Manipulating & Solving Equations

Section 4

1. $\boxed{A}$ Constructing Models
2. $\boxed{C}$ Rates
3. $\boxed{A}$ Percent
4. $\boxed{D}$ Circles
5. $\boxed{D}$ Quadratics
6. $\boxed{A}$ Lines
7. $\boxed{B}$ Manipulating & Solving Equations
8. $\boxed{C}$ Probability
9. $\boxed{C}$ Percent
10. $\boxed{A}$ Inequalities
11. $\boxed{B}$ Circles
12. $\boxed{D}$ Reading Data
13. $\boxed{B}$ Reading Data
14. $\boxed{C}$ Manipulating & Solving Equations
15. $\boxed{C}$ Exponential vs. Linear Growth
16. $\boxed{B}$ Percent
17. $\boxed{A}$ Interpreting Linear Models
18. $\boxed{B}$ Manipulating & Solving Equations
19. $\boxed{B}$ Word Problems
20. $\boxed{A}$ Systems of Equations
21. $\boxed{B}$ Trigonometry
22. $\boxed{C}$ Statistics II

23. $\boxed{C}$ Rates
24. $\boxed{B}$ Reading Data
25. $\boxed{B}$ Functions
26. $\boxed{C}$ Statistics I
27. $\boxed{D}$ Triangles
28. $\boxed{D}$ Systems of Equations
29. $\boxed{D}$ Manipulating & Solving Equations
30. $\boxed{A}$ Manipulating & Solving Equations
31. $\boxed{88}$ Exponential vs. Linear Growth
32. $\boxed{25}$ Expressions
33. $\boxed{1 < x < 2}$ Functions
34. $\boxed{16}$ Rates
35. $\boxed{75}$ Word Problems
36. $\boxed{11}$ Inequalities
37. $\boxed{17}$ Statistics II
38. $\boxed{20}$ Statistics II

Practice Test 1 Answer Explanations

Section 3

1. $\boxed{A}$ $V = (3)^2 - 3(3) + 3 = 3$

2. $\boxed{A}$ $\dfrac{\frac{1}{x}}{x+3} = \dfrac{1}{x} \div (x+3) = \dfrac{1}{x} \times \dfrac{1}{x+3} = \dfrac{1}{x(x+3)}$

3. $\boxed{C}$ The equation is satisfied only when $x = 2, y = 3$, and $z = -4$. Therefore, $x + y + z = 2 + 3 + (-4) = 1$.

4. $\boxed{C}$

$$3^{x-3} = 3^3$$
$$x - 3 = 3$$
$$x = 6$$

Of course, guessing and checking from the answer choices is also a valid strategy in this question.

5. $\boxed{C}$ If $b > a$, then $AC > BC$, making answer (C) false.

6. $\boxed{D}$ If we let the width be w, then the length is $w - 9$. Since the perimeter is the sum of twice the width and twice the length,

$$2w + 2(w - 9) = p$$
$$2w + 2w - 18 = p$$
$$4w - 18 = p$$
$$4w = p + 18$$
$$w = \frac{p + 18}{4}$$

7. $\boxed{C}$ The two lines must have the same slope. Converting $2x + 3y = 6$ to slope-intercept form, we get $y = -\frac{2}{3} + 2$. Since $-\frac{2}{3}$ is the slope of this line, m must also be $-\frac{2}{3}$.

8. $\boxed{C}$ Because the slope is 1.5, 1.5 must be the cost associated with producing each cup of lemonade. The number 100, then, must be a cost not associated with each cup of lemonade. Instead, it is the initial cost of setting up the lemonade stand, when 0 cups of lemonade have been sold. Answer (D) is incorrect because the total cost increases as more lemonade gets sold; there is no maximum.

9. $\boxed{B}$ $(5 + 2i)(5 - 2i) = 25 - 10i + 10i - 4i^2 = 25 - 4i^2 = 25 + 4 = 29$

10. $\boxed{C}$ Only answer (C) results in a y-value of 0 both when $x = \frac{3}{5}$ and when $x = -\frac{1}{2}$.

11. $\boxed{C}$ It took him 20 minutes to drive $85 - 75 = 10$ miles, which means he drove 1 mile every 2 minutes. At 6:40 PM, he needed to drive an additional $140 - 85 = 55$ miles to get to the 140-mile point.

$$55 \text{ miles} \times \frac{2 \text{ minutes}}{1 \text{ mile}} = 110 \text{ minutes} = 1 \text{ hour and 50 minutes}$$

To get to the 140-mile point, he needed an additional 1 hour and 50 minutes beyond 6:40 PM, which turns out to be 8:30 PM.

170

12. $\boxed{A}$ The line with the lowest slope is k, because it has a negative slope. The next one up is j, because it's a flat line, meaning its slope is 0. Finally, $i < h$ because i is not as steep. The correct order is $k < j < i < h$.

13. $\boxed{B}$ The expression follows the $(a - b)^2 = a^2 - 2ab + b^2$ pattern, where $a = \dfrac{1}{m}$ and $b = \dfrac{1}{n}$. Therefore, the expression is equivalent to $\left(\dfrac{1}{m} - \dfrac{1}{n}\right)^2$.

14. $\boxed{D}$ Multiply both sides by $3x - 2$.

$$kx^2 + 14x - 20 = 5x(3x - 2) + 8(3x - 2) - 4$$
$$kx^2 + 14x - 20 = 15x^2 - 10x + 24x - 20$$

Without going any further, we can compare coefficients to see that $k = 15$.

15. $\boxed{B}$ The solutions to the system are the intersection points. Substituting the second equation into the first, we get

$$(y - 2)^2 + 3(y - 2) - 1 = y$$
$$(y^2 - 4y + 4) + 3y - 6 - 1 = y$$
$$y^2 - y - 3 = y$$
$$y^2 - 2y - 3 = 0$$
$$(y - 3)(y + 1) = 0$$

Therefore, the y-coordinates of the intersection points are 3 and -1. Only -1 is an answer choice.

16. $\boxed{21, 25, \text{ or } 29}$ The value of b is 4, 5, or 6. When $b = 4$, $g(2) = 4(2)^2 + 2(2) + 1 = 21$. Therefore, 21 is one possible answer. Other possible answers are 25, when $b = 5$, and 29, when $b = 6$.

17. $\boxed{35}$ The measure of $\angle ADB$ must be $180 - 80 = 100$. Using $\triangle ABD$,

$$x = 180 - 45 - 100 = 35$$

18. $\boxed{7}$ The two steps together require $5 + 3 = 8$ wooden boards and $9 + 6 = 15$ nails. The 70 wooden boards are enough for $70 \div 8 = 8.75 \Rightarrow 8$ bookshelves (we only want whole bookshelves). The 110 nails are enough for $110 \div 15 \approx 7.33 \Rightarrow 7$ bookshelves. Comparing these numbers, we can see that the nails are the limiting resource. Therefore, 7 is the maximum number of bookshelves Eric could put together.

19. $\boxed{18}$ $h = f(2) = 2^2 + 2 - 2 = 4$. Since $k = f(h)$, $k = f(4) = 4^2 + 4 - 2 = 18$.

20. $\boxed{3}$

$$x^3 - 3x^2 + 3x - 9 = 0$$
$$x^2(x - 3) + 3(x - 3) = 0$$
$$(x^2 + 3)(x - 3) = 0$$

Because $x^2 + 3$ is always positive, x must equal 3.

Section 4

1. $\boxed{A}$ Starting from home, Maya must start from the x-axis (a distance of 0 from home) and end up back at the x-axis. The only graphs that do that are (A) and (D). Because she stayed at the bookstore, the graph must also have a flat portion to represent her constant distance away from home during that time. Therefore, the answer is (A).

2. $\boxed{C}$ $3,700 \text{ tons} \times \dfrac{2,000 \text{ pounds}}{1 \text{ ton}} = 7,400,000 \text{ pounds} = 7.4 \times 10^6 \text{ pounds}$

3. $\boxed{A}$ Zach memorized $(1.30)a$ words. James memorized 10 percent more than that, $(1.10)(1.30)a$ words.

4. $\boxed{D}$ The circumference of the pizza is $2\pi r = 2\pi(10) = 20\pi \approx 62.83$

   We divide this value by 4 to get the maximum number of slices that can be cut out: $62.83 \div 4 \approx 15.7$

   Since the slices must be full slices, the answer is 15.

5. $\boxed{D}$ If there are x-intercepts at -5 and 3, then $(x+5)$ and $(x-3)$ must be factors the function. Multiplying these factors,
$$(x+5)(x-3) = x^2 + 2x - 15$$
   Matching the coefficients up, $b = 2$ and $c = -15$.

6. $\boxed{A}$ Draw any line and its reflection across the y-axis. They always intersect at the y-intercept b. Therefore, $(0, b)$ is the point at which the two lines intersect.

7. $\boxed{B}$

$$d = \frac{2}{3}f$$
$$20 = \frac{2}{3}f$$
$$30 = f$$

   So 20 meters requires 30 liters of fuel. Any amount of fuel greater than 30 results in a distance farther than 20 meters. In the table, there are only two rockets that burned more than 30 liters of fuel.

8. $\boxed{C}$

$$\frac{\text{Undergraduates at Southwest}}{\text{Students at either State or Southwest}} = \frac{19,443}{38,626 + 22,361} \approx 0.32$$

9. $\boxed{C}$ The second machine recycled $240(1.30) = 312$ plastic bottles and $180(0.9) = 162$ metal cans, a total of $312 + 162 = 474$ items. The first machine took in a total of $240 + 180 = 420$ items. Calculating the percent increase from the first to the second,

$$\frac{474 - 420}{420} \approx 0.13 = 13\%$$

10. $\boxed{A}$ If Ashley's estimate, a, is within 15 of the actual number, b, then $b - 15 \le a \le b + 15$. Subtracting b from each part of the inequality (like we might in a regular equation), we get $-15 \le a - b \le 15$. And this makes sense. The difference between Ashley's estimate and the actual number is at most 15 (positive or negative depending on whether Ashley's estimate is too high or too low).

11. $\boxed{B}$ The horizontal distance between the two points is 3. The vertical distance is 4. If you connect the two points, you can form a 3–4–5 right triangle. Therefore, the distance between the two points is 5. This distance is also the radius of the circle. The standard form of a circle with center (h, k) and radius r is $(x - h)^2 + (y - k)^2 = r^2$. So, the equation of the circle is $(x - 1)^2 + (y - 2)^2 = 25$.

12. $\boxed{D}$ John reached his maximum speed 50 meters into the race, which is $\dfrac{50}{100} = 50\%$ of the 100-meter-dash.

13. $\boxed{B}$ The graph goes up and then stays at the same level. The best description of this is that John accelerated to his maximum speed and then held that speed for the rest of the race.

14. $\boxed{C}$ Plugging in, $\dfrac{10}{5} = \dfrac{k}{3}$, which yields $k = 6$. Using the same equation, we can cross multiply.

$$\frac{2}{5} = \frac{6}{y}$$
$$2y = 30$$
$$y = 15$$

15. $\boxed{C}$ Going up by 200% every hour means tripling every hour, which means this is exponential growth.

16. $\boxed{B}$ Calculating the percent decrease for footballs,

$$\frac{3,060 - 3,600}{3,600} = -0.15 = 15\% \text{ decrease}$$

Calculating the number of basketballs produced,

$$2,200(1 - 0.15) = 2,200(0.85) = 1,870$$

17. $\boxed{A}$ The expression bd represents the total number of boxes received. Since the equation gives the total number of books in the warehouse, 100 must be the number of books in each box.

18. $\boxed{B}$ Combine like terms and square both sides.

$$\sqrt{x} = 3\sqrt{y}$$
$$x = 9y$$

19. $\boxed{B}$ If Fred has x pineapples, then Richard has $7x$ and Nathan has $3x$.

$$7x = 3x + 32$$
$$4x = 32$$
$$x = 8$$

20. $\boxed{A}$ The total number of shots he took is $x + y$, which turns out to be 30. He scored $2x$ points from 2-pointers and $3x$ points from 3-pointers. The total number of points he scored is $2x + 3y = 68$.

21. $\boxed{B}$ In relation to angle B, $\dfrac{c}{b} = \dfrac{\text{adjacent}}{\text{opposite}}$. This is the reciprocal of $\tan B$, $\dfrac{1}{\tan B}$.

22. $\boxed{C}$ Based on the design on the study (random sampling and random assignment), we can conclude a cause and effect relationship: low lighting is likely to cause a decrease in reading speed. However, we can't say that this is true for every single person (like answer (B) does). Nor can we guess the effect of high lighting on reading speed when the study didn't involve high lighting (answer (D)). We also can't jump to the conclusion that low lighting harms the eyes (answer (A)).

23. $\boxed{C}$ The total distance traveled by the train on the given trip is $80 \times 8 = 640$. At a speed of 120 miles per hour, the same trip would take $640 \div 120 = 5\frac{1}{3}$ hours, or 5 hours and 20 minutes (a third of an hour is 20 minutes).

24. $\boxed{B}$ According to the graph, the aquarium uses about 600 joules per hour when the outside temperature is 25° C. That's a total of $600 \times 3 = 1,800$ joules over 3 hours.

25. $\boxed{B}$ The strategy here is to use a point from the graph. When $x = 0$, $E \approx 4,700$. Plugging this point into the model equation,

$$4,700 = a(0 - 20)^2 + 300$$
$$4,700 = 400a + 300$$
$$4,400 = 400a$$
$$a = 11$$

We can be pretty confident $a = 11$ is the answer, but it's worth noting that in these types of questions, it's always a good idea to test more than one point on the graph for confirmation.

26. $\boxed{C}$ The mode is 3 because that's the outcome that occurred with the highest frequency. The median is the average of the 20th and 21st outcomes when the outcomes are put in order. The 1's, 2's, and 3's amount to the first $4 + 2 + 12 = 18$ outcomes. Continuing to count up in the table, the 20th and 21st outcomes are "4" and "4", which means the median is $\frac{4+4}{2} = 4$. Finally, the mean is the sum of all the outcomes divided by the total number of outcomes: $\frac{1 \times 4 + 2 \times 2 + 3 \times 12 + 4 \times 10 + 5 \times 4 + 6 \times 8}{40} = \frac{152}{40} = 3.8$. Therefore, mode < mean < median.

27. $\boxed{D}$ $\triangle ADE$ is a 30–60–90 triangle,

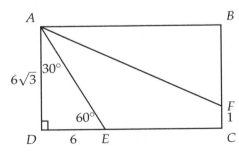

$AD = 6\sqrt{3}$ and $BF = 6\sqrt{3} - 1$.

28. $\boxed{D}$ Simplifying the second equation gives $x - 3y = 4$, which is the same as the first equation. Therefore, there are infinitely many solutions (more than two).

29. $\boxed{D}$

$$f_{obs} = f_s \left(\frac{v_w}{v_w - v_a} \right)$$

$$f_{obs}(v_w - v_a) = f_s v_w$$

$$f_{obs}v_w - f_{obs}v_a = f_s v_w$$

$$f_{obs}v_w - f_s v_w = f_{obs}v_a$$

$$\frac{f_{obs}v_w - f_s v_w}{f_{obs}} = v_a$$

30. $\boxed{A}$

$$f_{obs} = f_s \left(\frac{v_w}{v_w - v_a} \right)$$

$$500 = f_s \left(\frac{340}{340 - 22} \right)$$

$$500 \left(\frac{340 - 22}{340} \right) = f_s \approx 468$$

31. $\boxed{88}$ Work back each day by doubling the value. So on March 5th, the stock was worth $2.75(2) = \$5.50$. On March 4th, the stock was worth $2.75(2)(2) = \$11$. On March 3rd, the stock was worth $2.75(2)(2)(2) = \$22$. See the pattern? On March 2nd, the stock was worth $2.75(2)^4 = \$44$. Finally, on March 1st, the stock was worth $2.75(2)^5 = \$88$.

32. $\boxed{25}$ Since $(3x + 2y)^2 = 9x^2 + 12xy + 4y^2$, $9 + 12 + 4 = 25$.

33. $\boxed{1 < x < 2}$ Taking the square root of a negative number would make the function undefined. So we are looking for an x such that $(x - 1)(x - 2) < 0$. You can use trial and error or the x-intercepts of 1 and 2 to see that this only happens when $1 < x < 2$.

34. $\boxed{16}$

$$12 \text{ pounds} \times \frac{16 \text{ ounces}}{1 \text{ pound}} \times \frac{2/3 \text{ pizza}}{8 \text{ ounces}} = 16 \text{ pizzas}$$

35. $\boxed{75}$ There are a total of $180 - 60 = 120$ students in the beginner and advanced classes. If we let the number of students in the beginner class be x, then the number of students in the advanced class is $\frac{3}{5}x$. Setting up an equation,

$$x + \frac{3}{5}x = 120$$

$$5x + 3x = 600$$

$$8x = 600$$

$$x = 75$$

36. $\boxed{11}$ Graphing these two inequalities in the xy-plane, we see that the minimum possible value of x occurs at the intersection of the two lines.

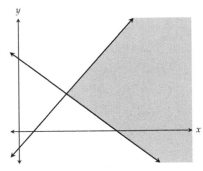

Solving for the intersection by setting the two equations equal to each other,

$$3x - 10 = -2x + 45$$
$$5x = 55$$
$$x = 11$$

37. $\boxed{17}$ At a temperature of 80° Fahrenheit, the line of best fit gives a chirp rate of 17 chirps per second.

38. $\boxed{20}$ The data point farthest from the line of best fit is the one furthest to the right, at a temperature of about 88° Fahrenheit. The chirp rate represented by this point is 20 chirps per second.

Practice Test 2 Answers

Question categories correspond to chapters in *The College Panda's SAT Math: The Advanced Guide and Workbook*. To estimate your score, visit *thecollegepanda.com/sat-score-calculator*

Section 3

1. $\boxed{D}$ Expressions
2. $\boxed{B}$ Constructing Models
3. $\boxed{C}$ Manipulating & Solving Equations
4. $\boxed{D}$ Triangles
5. $\boxed{C}$ Word Problems
6. $\boxed{D}$ Quadratics
7. $\boxed{D}$ Functions
8. $\boxed{A}$ Systems of Equations
9. $\boxed{B}$ Constructing Models
10. $\boxed{B}$ Lines
11. $\boxed{C}$ Circles
12. $\boxed{C}$ More Equation Solving Strategies
13. $\boxed{D}$ Triangles
14. $\boxed{D}$ Exponents & Radicals
15. $\boxed{D}$ Inequalities
16. $\boxed{9}$ Manipulating & Solving Equations
17. $\boxed{27}$ Minimum & Maximum Word Problems
18. $\boxed{5}$ Functions
19. $\boxed{19}$ Expressions
20. $\boxed{8}$ Quadratics

Section 4

1. $\boxed{D}$ Rates
2. $\boxed{C}$ Circles
3. $\boxed{B}$ Manipulating & Solving Equations
4. $\boxed{B}$ Reading Data
5. $\boxed{B}$ Uncategorized
6. $\boxed{B}$ Percent
7. $\boxed{A}$ Constructing Models
8. $\boxed{D}$ Statistics II
9. $\boxed{B}$ Statistics II
10. $\boxed{D}$ Functions
11. $\boxed{D}$ Percent
12. $\boxed{D}$ Rates
13. $\boxed{A}$ Constructing Models
14. $\boxed{C}$ Reading Data
15. $\boxed{D}$ Interpreting Linear Models
16. $\boxed{B}$ Lines
17. $\boxed{B}$ Triangles
18. $\boxed{A}$ Inequalities
19. $\boxed{B}$ Expressions
20. $\boxed{A}$ Manipulating & Solving Equations
21. $\boxed{C}$ Lines
22. $\boxed{C}$ Percent
23. $\boxed{A}$ Quadratics

24. $\boxed{B}$ Manipulating & Solving Equations
25. $\boxed{D}$ Exponential vs. Linear Growth
26. $\boxed{A}$ Percent
27. $\boxed{C}$ Statistics I
28. $\boxed{B}$ Statistics I
29. $\boxed{C}$ Functions
30. $\boxed{A}$ Expressions / Manipulating & Solving Equations
31. $\boxed{24}$ Angles
32. $\boxed{56}$ Volume
33. $\boxed{.75}$ Interpreting Linear Models
34. $\boxed{5 \text{ or } 15}$ Systems of Equations
35. $\boxed{55}$ Probability
36. $\boxed{6}$ Inequalities
37. $\boxed{636}$ Manipulating & Solving Equations
38. $\boxed{12}$ Word Problems

Practice Test 2 Answer Explanations

Section 3

1. $\boxed{D}$ Distributing,

$$ab(c+d) = abc + abd$$

(D) is not equivalent because it's missing an a in the second term.

2. $\boxed{B}$ The adults spent $10x$ on tickets and $4(6) = 24$ dollars on popcorn. That's a total of $10x + 24$, where x is the number of adults.

3. $\boxed{C}$ x cannot be 0 because anything multiplied by 0 is 0. It doesn't matter what y is.

4. $\boxed{D}$ Since $AB = AC$, $b = c$. So $b = 50$, and $a = 180 - b - c = 180 - 50 - 50 = 80$.

5. $\boxed{C}$ From the information,

$$x = \frac{1}{2}y$$
$$y = 2x$$

6. $\boxed{D}$ Sum $= -\dfrac{b}{a} = -\dfrac{-6}{2} = 3.$

7. $\boxed{D}$

$$g(1) = (1)^2 + 3 = 4$$
$$f(4) = 2(4)^3 - 1 = 128 - 1 = 127$$

8. $\boxed{A}$ For the system to have no solution, the coefficients should be able to match but the constants on the right hand side shouldn't. Looking at the y's, we need to multiply the first equation by $\dfrac{7}{4}$ to get the coefficients to match. Doing so yields

$$\frac{7}{4}a = 5$$

Solving for a, we get $a = \dfrac{20}{7}$.

9. $\boxed{B}$ There are 8 30-minute segments in 4 hours so Janice read $8x$ pages. There are 20 15-minute segments in 5 hours so Kim read $20y$ pages. Altogether, they read $8x + 20y$ pages.

10. $\boxed{B}$ Line l has a negative slope. If n is perpendicular to l, then n must have a positive slope, meaning $m > 0$.

11. $\boxed{C}$ Since the ratio of the lengths of $\overset{\frown}{AB}$ to $\overset{\frown}{BC}$ is 2:3, the ratio of their respective central angles must also be 2:3. Therefore, the ratio of x to the measure of $\angle BOC$ is 2:3, which means x is $\dfrac{2}{2+3} = \dfrac{2}{5}$ of $\angle AOC$. Since $\angle AOC$ is a diagonal of the rectangle, it's a straight line measuring $180°$. As a result, $x = \dfrac{2}{5} \times 180 = 72°$.

12. $\boxed{C}$ Expand the right side:

$$x^2 + kx + 9 = x^2 + 2ax + a^2$$

Comparing both sides, we see that

$$9 = a^2 \text{ and } k = 2a$$

Therefore, $a = 3$ and $k = 2 \cdot 3 = 6$

13. $\boxed{D}$ Let the height of $\triangle ABC$ be h. Since the area of $\triangle ABC$ is 75,

$$\frac{1}{2}(AC)h = 75$$

$$\frac{1}{2}(30)h = 75$$

$$15h = 75$$

$$h = 5$$

Since $\triangle ABD$ also has height h, its area is $\frac{1}{2}(8)(5) = 20$. Now we can find the area of $\triangle BDC$ by subtracting the area of $\triangle ABD$ from the area of $\triangle ABC$: $75 - 20 = 55$.

14. $\boxed{D}$

$$27^{81} = 3^x$$

$$(3^3)^{81} = 3^x$$

$$3^{3 \cdot 81} = 3^x$$

$$243 = x$$

15. $\boxed{D}$ Since Fabiano needs to order at least 16 printer cartridges, $b + c \geq 16$. The total cost of the black and white cartridges will be $25b$ and the total cost of the color cartridges will be $35c$. To stay within budget, $25b \leq 300$ and $35c \leq 400$. Notice that $0 \leq 25b + 35c \leq 700$ is true but does NOT represent the situation the same way. For example, Fabiano could buy 16 color cartridges ($c = 16$) and no black and white cartridges under this inequality, but in reality, that would put him over-budget for the color cartridges and should not be a possibility.

16. $\boxed{9}$ Multiply everything by 6.

$$\frac{1}{2}x - \frac{1}{3}x = 1 + \frac{1}{2}$$

$$3x - 2x = 6 + 3$$

$$x = 9$$

17. $\boxed{27}$ The 120 food pellets are enough for $120 \div 8 = 15$ full meals. The 63 pieces of shrimp are enough for $63 \div 5 = 12.6 \Rightarrow 12$ full meals. Therefore, the turtle will be able to have $15 + 12 = 27$ more full meals before the supply runs out.

18. $\boxed{5}$ If $g(m) = 6$, then from the table, m must be 3 since $g(3) = 6$. Finally, $f(m) = f(3) = 5$.

19. $\boxed{19}$ For both fractions to have the common denominator of $x(x-3)^2$, we need to multiply the top and bottom of the second fraction by $(x-3)$.

$$\frac{3x+10}{x(x-3)^2} - \frac{3(x-3)}{x(x-3)^2} = \frac{3x+10-3(x-3)}{x(x-3)^2} = \frac{3x+10-3x+9}{x(x-3)^2} = \frac{19}{x(x-3)^2}$$

20. $\boxed{8}$ The sum of the solutions is $-\dfrac{b}{a} = -\dfrac{-5}{1} = 5$. If the other solution is x, then

$$x + (-3) = 5$$
$$x = 8$$

Section 4

1. $\boxed{D}$ $7 \text{ windows} \times \dfrac{5 \text{ hours}}{4 \text{ windows}} = 8.75 \text{ hours} = 8 \text{ hours and } 45 \text{ minutes}$

2. $\boxed{C}$ $\pi r^2 = \dfrac{\pi}{4} \longrightarrow r^2 = \dfrac{1}{4} \longrightarrow r = \dfrac{1}{2}$

   The diameter is twice the radius: $d = 2\left(\dfrac{1}{2}\right) = 1$

3. $\boxed{B}$ The best way to do this is to test out each answer choice:

   A) $3600 - 400(5) + 20(5)^2 = 2100$

   B) $3600 - 400(10) + 20(10)^2 = 1600$

   C) $3600 - 400(15) + 20(15)^2 = 2100$

   D) $3600 - 400(20) + 20(20)^2 = 3600$

   Choice (B) is clearly the lowest.

4. $\boxed{B}$ The question is asking for the biggest difference between the x-value and the y-value among the points. Point A has a difference of $3 - 1 = 2$. Point B has a difference of $7 - 2 = 5$. Point C has a difference of $9 - 5 = 4$. Point D has a difference of $8 - 4 = 4$. Point B has the largest difference.

5. $\boxed{B}$ If the perimeter of one face is $2k$, then each side must be $\dfrac{2k}{4} = \dfrac{k}{2}$. The area of each face is then $\left(\dfrac{k}{2}\right)^2 = \dfrac{k^2}{4}$. Since a cube has 6 faces, the surface area is $6 \times \dfrac{k^2}{4} = \dfrac{3}{2}k^2$.

6. $\boxed{B}$ Let $Z = 100$. Then $Y = 0.30 \times 100 = 30$ and $X = 0.20 \times 30 = 6$. X is $\dfrac{6}{100} = 6\%$ of Z.

7. $\boxed{A}$ The total amount of data the cable can transfer over k seconds is $8k^2$ megabytes. The average data transfer speed is then $\dfrac{8k^2}{k} = 8k$ megabytes per second.

8. $\boxed{D}$ The line of best fit has a negative slope (high to low). This means that forests that have lower mean spring temperatures tend to have higher sparrow densities. Notice that the scatterplot deals with sparrow density, NOT sparrow population.

9. $\boxed{B}$ At 20 along the x-axis, the line of best fit gives a y-value closest to 17. It's not 18 since the line of best fit intersects the grid line below the midpoint of 15 and 20 (below 17.5).

10. $\boxed{D}$ At $x = 1$, f is at 1 and g is at 3. Since g is 2 greater than f at $x = 1$, it's possible that g is $f + 2$.

11. $\boxed{D}$ If Roger won 25% of the matches, then Rafael won 75% of the matches. Let x be the total number of matches they played against each other. Since 75% is $\dfrac{3}{4}$,

$$\frac{3}{4}x = 18$$
$$x = 24$$

Therefore, Roger won $\dfrac{1}{4}(24) = 6$ matches. Another way to get this answer is to realize that 75% is three times 25%, so Rafael must have won 3 times as many matches: $18 \div 3 = 6$.

12. $\boxed{D}$

$$120^\circ \cancel{F} \times \frac{1^\circ \cancel{C}}{33.8^\circ \cancel{F}} \times \frac{1 \cancel{\text{calorie}}}{1^\circ \cancel{C}} \times \frac{4.184 \text{ joules}}{1 \cancel{\text{calorie}}} \approx 14.85 \text{ joules}$$

13. $\boxed{A}$ When the course is discounted by d dollars, the enrollment increases by $\dfrac{9}{200}d = \dfrac{45}{1,000}d = 0.045d$. Since 150 is the starting enrollment when there is no discount, $E = 150 + 0.045d$.

14. $\boxed{C}$ Alicia's speed was 0 from 3 hours to 4 hours, which means she started her nap after 3 hours of driving.

15. $\boxed{D}$ The f-intercept is the number of flowers that blossom when $b = 0$, when there are no bees in the garden.

16. $\boxed{B}$ The y-intercept is 28. The line goes up 4 units for every 2 units to the right, so the slope is $4/2 = 2$. Using $y = mx + b$ form, the equation of the line is $f = 28 + 2b$.

17. $\boxed{B}$ $\triangle ABC$ is similar to $\triangle DEC$. Therefore,

$$\frac{3}{9} = \frac{DE}{18}$$

Cross multiplying,

$$9(DE) = 54$$
$$DE = 6$$

18. $\boxed{A}$ The total number of computers after t months is $200 + 8t$.

$$600 \le 200 + 8t \le 700$$

Subtract by 200 and then divide by 8.

$$400 \le 8t \le 500$$
$$50 \le t \le 62.5$$

Because t is an integer, $50 \le t \le 62$.

19. $\boxed{B}$

$$3(x^2 - 5x + 2) - (3x^3 + 4x^2 - 6) = 3x^2 - 15x + 6 - 3x^3 - 4x^2 + 6$$
$$= -3x^3 - x^2 - 15x + 12$$

20. $\boxed{A}$ First, multiply both sides by $(x-2)$ to get rid of the fraction. Then simplify and square root both sides.

$$\frac{9}{x-2} = 3(x-2)$$
$$9 = 3(x-2)^2$$
$$3 = (x-2)^2$$
$$\pm\sqrt{3} = x-2$$

Of the answer choices, only $\sqrt{3}$ is a possible value for $x-2$.

21. $\boxed{C}$ Because it has a slope of $-\dfrac{5}{4}$, line l goes down 5 units for every 4 units to the right. Therefore, the y-intercept is 5. The base of the triangle is 4 and the height is 5.

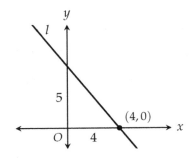

The area of the triangle is $\dfrac{1}{2}(4)(5) = 10$

22. $\boxed{C}$ Let last year's price be x. Then

$$p = 1.20x$$
$$p = \frac{6}{5}x$$
$$\frac{5}{6}p = x$$

23. $\boxed{A}$ Complete the square. Divide the middle term by 2 to get -1 and square that result to get 1. We put the -1 inside the parentheses with x and subtract the 1 at the end.

$$y = (x-1)^2 - 3 - 1$$
$$y = (x-1)^2 - 4$$

24. $\boxed{B}$

$$8 = 2\pi\sqrt{\frac{L}{9.8}}$$

$$\frac{8}{2\pi} = \sqrt{\frac{L}{9.8}}$$

$$\frac{64}{4\pi^2} = \frac{L}{9.8}$$

$$\frac{64}{4\pi^2} \cdot 9.8 = L \approx 15.9$$

25. $\boxed{D}$ Each month, the number of dandelions is one-fifth of what it was the previous month. This is exponential decay.

26. $\boxed{A}$ Let t be the number of years that pass. Then

$$S = 3,000(1.21)^t$$

Since $h = 2t$ (there are 2 half years for every 1 year), $t = \dfrac{h}{2}$. Substituting this into the equation above,

$$S = 3,000(1.21)^{\frac{h}{2}}$$

$$S = 3,000(1.21^{\frac{1}{2}})^h$$

$$S = 3,000(\sqrt{1.21})^h$$

$$S = 3,000(1.1)^h$$

27. $\boxed{C}$

$$\frac{1 \times (20 + 30) + 2 \times (20 + 15) + 3 \times (8 + 5) + 4 \times (2 + 0)}{20 + 30 + 20 + 15 + 8 + 5 + 2} = \frac{167}{100} = 1.67$$

28. $\boxed{B}$ The median for both Maine and Massachusetts is the average weight of the 25th and 26th lobsters. In Maine, the median is 2 pounds. In Massachusetts, the median is 1 pound.

29. $\boxed{C}$ The question is asking where f and g intersect. If we graph $g(x)$ ourselves, we can see that the intersection occurs at $x = 6$. Just be careful when plotting g because the scales for the x-axis and y-axis are different.

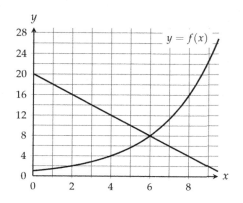

30. $\boxed{A}$ Since $x^2 - y^2 = (x+y)(x-y)$, we can factor $a^4 - b^2$ into $(a^2 + b)(a^2 - b)$. Then we can substitute in $a^2 + b = -5$.

$$(a^2 + b)(a^2 - b) = 30$$
$$-5(a^2 - b) = 30$$
$$a^2 - b = -6$$

31. $\boxed{24}$ The angles of a triangle sum to 180.

$$2y + 3y + 60 = 180$$
$$5y = 120$$
$$y = 24$$

32. $\boxed{56}$ The box has a length of $8 - 2 - 2 = 4$, a width of $11 - 2 - 2 = 7$, and a height of 2.

$$V = lwh = 4(7)(2) = 56$$

33. $\boxed{.75}$ Putting the equation into $y = mx + b$ form, $p = \frac{3}{4}s + \frac{10}{4}$. We see that the slope is $\frac{3}{4}$, or 0.75, which means 0.75 milligrams of pepper are added for every 1 milligram increase in the amount of salt.

34. $\boxed{5 \text{ or } 15}$ Substitute the second equation into the first.

$$x + 3 = x^2 - 6x + 9$$
$$0 = x^2 - 7x + 6$$
$$0 = (x - 6)(x - 1)$$

Therefore, the x-coordinates of the solutions are 1 and 6. When $x = 1$, $y = 1 + 3 = 4$. When $x = 6$, $y = 6 + 3 = 9$. Therefore, the possible values of $x + y$ are $1 + 4 = 5$ or $6 + 9 = 15$.

35. $\boxed{55}$ Let x be the number of doctors who take at least 2 vacations each year.

$$\frac{45 + x}{100} = \frac{4}{5}$$

Cross multiplying,

$$225 + 5x = 400$$
$$5x = 175$$
$$x = 35$$

The number of people from the surveyed group who take at least 2 vacations each year is $35 + 20 = 55$.

36. [6] Graphing the two inequalities in the xy-plane, we see that the maximum possible value of x occurs at the intersection of the two lines.

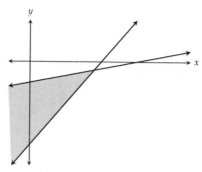

Solving for the intersection by setting the two equations equal to each other,

$$\frac{1}{2}x - 5 = 3x - 20$$
$$x - 10 = 6x - 40$$
$$-5x = -30$$
$$x = 6$$

37. [636] The cost per necklace is $C = 100 + \dfrac{36}{6} = 106$. So the total cost is $106 \times 6 = 636$.

38. [12] Let x be the number of necklaces that should be made. In selling the necklaces, the shop earns $150x$ and incurs a total cost of $x\left(100 + \dfrac{36}{x}\right)$. The total earnings minus the total cost should give \$564:

$$150x - x\left(100 + \frac{36}{x}\right) = 564$$
$$50x - 36 = 564$$
$$50x = 600$$
$$x = 12$$

Practice Test 3 Answers

Question categories correspond to chapters in *The College Panda's SAT Math: The Advanced Guide and Workbook.* To estimate your score, visit *thecollegepanda.com/sat-score-calculator*

Section 3

1. $\boxed{A}$ Absolute Value
2. $\boxed{C}$ Manipulating & Solving Equations
3. $\boxed{C}$ Inequalities
4. $\boxed{C}$ Expressions
5. $\boxed{B}$ Interpreting Linear Models
6. $\boxed{D}$ Lines
7. $\boxed{B}$ Functions
8. $\boxed{D}$ Rates
9. $\boxed{D}$ Quadratics
10. $\boxed{B}$ Exponents & Radicals
11. $\boxed{B}$ Word Problems
12. $\boxed{C}$ Lines
13. $\boxed{B}$ Systems of Equations
14. $\boxed{A}$ Trigonometry
15. $\boxed{D}$ Inequalities
16. $\boxed{19}$ Expressions
17. $\boxed{100}$ Manipulating & Solving Equations
18. $\boxed{40}$ Triangles
19. $\boxed{7}$ Functions
20. $\boxed{10}$ Systems of Equations

Section 4

1. $\boxed{C}$ Manipulating & Solving Equations
2. $\boxed{B}$ Expressions
3. $\boxed{C}$ Ratio & Proportion
4. $\boxed{B}$ Circles
5. $\boxed{B}$ Word Problems
6. $\boxed{A}$ Constructing Models
7. $\boxed{D}$ Reading Data
8. $\boxed{D}$ Minimum & Maximum Word Problems
9. $\boxed{C}$ Quadratics
10. $\boxed{A}$ Statistics II
11. $\boxed{D}$ Statistics II
12. $\boxed{A}$ Lines
13. $\boxed{C}$ Functions
14. $\boxed{B}$ Rates
15. $\boxed{C}$ Statistics I
16. $\boxed{C}$ Triangles
17. $\boxed{D}$ Systems of Equations
18. $\boxed{C}$ Volume
19. $\boxed{A}$ Exponents & Radicals
20. $\boxed{D}$ Triangles
21. $\boxed{A}$ Exponential vs. Linear Growth
22. $\boxed{D}$ Probability
23. $\boxed{C}$ Probability
24. $\boxed{D}$ Rates
25. $\boxed{B}$ Circles
26. $\boxed{B}$ Statistics II
27. $\boxed{B}$ Interpreting Linear Models
28. $\boxed{B}$ Interpreting Linear Models
29. $\boxed{B}$ Manipulating & Solving Equations
30. $\boxed{D}$ Systems of Equations
31. $\boxed{35}$ Angles
32. $\boxed{770}$ Rates
33. $\boxed{2009}$ Reading Data
34. $\boxed{39}$ Functions
35. $\boxed{27}$ Inequalities
36. $\boxed{13}$ Synthetic Division
37. $\boxed{1.8}$ Percent
38. $\boxed{450}$ Percent

Practice Test 3 Answer Explanations

Section 3

1. $\boxed{A}$ When $x = -8$, $\left|\dfrac{5}{-8}\right| = \dfrac{5}{8}$, which is between 0 and 1. None of the other answer choices work.

2. $\boxed{C}$ Multiplying both sides by d gives us
$$cd = ab$$
Then $\dfrac{1}{ab} = \dfrac{1}{cd}$ by substitution.

3. $\boxed{C}$ Square rooting both sides, we get $x < 5$, but we have to take into account negative values. It should be easy enough to see that $x > -5$ as well. So, $-5 < x < 5$.

4. $\boxed{C}$
$$2x(x - y)(x + y) = 2x(x^2 - y^2) = 2x^3 - 2xy^2$$

5. $\boxed{B}$ The number 5 refers to the slope of -5, which means the tank loses 5 gallons of water each hour.

6. $\boxed{D}$ Converting $3x + 4y = 6$ to slope-intercept form, we get $y = -\dfrac{3}{4}x + \dfrac{3}{2}$. The slope is $-\dfrac{3}{4}$. For the lines to be perpendicular, m must be the negative reciprocal, $\dfrac{4}{3}$.

7. $\boxed{B}$ When $x = 1$, $y = f(1) + 1 = (1 - 1)^2 + 1 = 1$. Therefore, the point $(1, 1)$ must lie on the graph of y. Only the graph in answer B crosses the point $(1, 1)$. The graph of y is just the graph of f shifted up by 1 unit.

8. $\boxed{D}$ In t hours, the car travels $65t$ miles. In doing so, the car consumes $65t$ miles $\times \dfrac{1 \text{ gallon}}{32 \text{ miles}} = \dfrac{65t}{32}$ gallons of gas.

9. $\boxed{D}$ Applying the quadratic formula to $x^2 - x - 4 = 0$,
$$x = \dfrac{1 \pm \sqrt{(-1)^2 - 4(1)(-4)}}{2(1)} = \dfrac{1 \pm \sqrt{1 + 16}}{2} = \dfrac{1 \pm \sqrt{17}}{2}$$

10. $\boxed{B}$ Multiply the first equation by y to get
$$y^9 = my$$
Now substitute this into the left side of the second equation,
$$my = \dfrac{2}{3}$$
$$y = \dfrac{2}{3m}$$

11. $\boxed{B}$ To earn \$180 more, Mitch would have to work $\dfrac{180}{15}$ more hours. Working $\dfrac{180}{15}$ more hours would mean stocking $\dfrac{180}{15}(8)$ more shelves. To summarize,

$$s = \frac{180}{15}(8)$$

This is equivalent to

$$\frac{15}{8}s = 180$$

Another solution is to start from s. If s is the additional number of shelves he must stock to earn \$180 more, then it would take him $\dfrac{s}{8}$ more hours to do so. Working that many hours would earn him $\dfrac{s}{8}(15)$ dollars, which should be equal to \$180.

$$\frac{s}{8}(15) = 180$$
$$\frac{15}{8}s = 180$$

12. $\boxed{C}$ The slope of the line is $\dfrac{16-0}{12-0} = \dfrac{4}{3}$. It goes up 4 units for every 3 units to the right. Starting from $(0,0)$ (which is on the line) and using the slope, we can easily see that $(3,4)$ will be on the line.

13. $\boxed{B}$ To get y in terms of k, we need to eliminate x. We could use either substitution or elimination here, but we'll choose elimination. Multiply the second equation by 3 and subtract to get

$$ky - 3(4y) = 8 - 3(-1)$$
$$ky - 12y = 8 + 3$$
$$y(k - 12) = 11$$
$$y = \frac{11}{k - 12}$$

14. $\boxed{A}$ Apply the identity $\cos y = \sin\left(\dfrac{\pi}{2} - y\right)$ to the equation.

$$\sin x = \cos y$$
$$\sin x = \sin\left(\frac{\pi}{2} - y\right)$$
$$x = \frac{\pi}{2} - y$$

15. $\boxed{D}$ If there are a ounces of Arabica beans in the blend, then there must be $\dfrac{a}{2}$ ounces of Robusta beans. The corresponding amounts of caffeine are then $40a$ milligrams and $60 \cdot \dfrac{a}{2} = 30a$ milligrams, respectively. Since the total amount of caffeine in a large cup must be less than 280 milligrams,

$$40a + 30a < 280$$
$$70a < 280$$
$$a < 4$$

And since there must be more than zero beans in a cup of coffee (otherwise it wouldn't be coffee), $0 < a < 4$.

16. $\boxed{19}$ First, distribute the b. Then expand.

$$b(2a+3)(2+5a) = (2ab + 3b)(2+5a) = 4ab + 10a^2b + 6b + 15ab = 19ab + 10a^2b + 6b$$

The coefficient of the ab term is 19.

17. $\boxed{100}$ Expand.

$$x^2 + 3x - 3x - 9 = 91$$
$$x^2 = 100$$

18. $\boxed{40}$ $\triangle ABE$ and $\triangle ACD$ are congruent since $AB = AC$, $AD = AE$, and the triangles both share $\angle A$. You may remember this as side-angle-side congruency from your geometry class. Even if you don't, it's not a big deal on the SAT because these congruencies are generally easy to see intuitively. Now because the triangles are congruent, $\angle E$ is also 35°. Looking at $\triangle ABE$, we can then calculate the measure of $\angle ABE$ to be $180 - 70 - 35 = 75°$. Finally, $\angle DBF = 180 - 75 = 105°$ and $\angle BFD = 180 - 35 - 105 = 40°$.

19. $\boxed{7}$ First, plug in $(-1, 4)$ to get $4 = a(-1)^3 + b$. Next, plug in $(1, 10)$ to get $10 = a(1)^3 + b$. We now have two equations and two unknowns:

$$4 = -a + b$$
$$10 = a + b$$

Add the two equations together to get $14 = 2b$. Finally, $b = 7$.

20. $\boxed{10}$ In the first equation, we can multiply both sides by $y + 2$ to get $x = 2(y + 2)$. Substituting this into the second equation,

$$3(y - 5) - 2(y + 2) = -16$$
$$3y - 15 - 2y - 4 = -16$$
$$y - 19 = -16$$
$$y = 3$$

Finally, $x = 2(3 + 2) = 10$.

Section 4

1. $\boxed{C}$ Move m to the right-hand side and multiply both sides by $\frac{3}{2}$. Note the parentheses.

$$\frac{2}{3}t + m = 40$$

$$\frac{2}{3}t = 40 - m$$

$$t = \frac{3}{2}(40 - m)$$

2. $\boxed{B}$ $a(3 - a) + 2(a + 5) = 3a - a^2 + 2a + 10 = -a^2 + 5a + 10$

3. $\boxed{C}$ There are 3 sophomores for every 8 juniors and 7 seniors for every 5 juniors. Therefore, there must be $\frac{3}{8} \times 120 = 45$ sophomores and $\frac{7}{5} \times 120 = 168$ seniors at the school. The seniors outnumber the sophomores by $168 - 45 = 123$.

4. $\boxed{B}$ The diameter, which always goes through the center, is always the longest segment in a circle. $\overline{AD}$ is the only answer choice that's a diameter.

5. $\boxed{B}$ If we let x be the number of nails required by the second desk, then the first desk required $x - 62$ nails. Since a total of 258 nails were used,

$$x + (x - 62) = 258$$
$$2x - 62 = 258$$
$$2x = 320$$
$$x = 160$$

Therefore, the first desk required $160 - 62 = 98$ nails.

6. $\boxed{A}$ Since Jones starts at the bottom of the mountain and ends up at the bottom, the correct graph must start at the x-axis and return to the x-axis. Only graphs (A) and (B) do that. Since Jones comes down at twice the speed, the later portion of the graph should be steeper than the initial portion. Graph (B) does not reflect that, but graph (A) does.

7. $\boxed{D}$ Choice (D) is the only one that's true. There are 11 players with more than 5 years of training (to the right of 5 on the x-axis). There are 9 players with less than 5 years of training (to the left of 5 on the x-axis).

8. $\boxed{D}$ The total amount she spends is $3(14) + 10x = 42 + 10x$. Now,

$$100 \leq 42 + 10x \leq 150$$

We could split these inequalities up and handle them separately, but we'll just do it all at once by subtracting each part by 42 and dividing by 10.

$$100 \leq 42 + 10x \leq 150$$

$$58 \leq 10x \leq 108$$

$$5.8 \leq x \leq 10.8$$

Of the answer choices, 12 is the only one that falls outside this range.

9. $\boxed{C}$ Anytime we're asked for a minimum or a maximum, think of the vertex or vertex form. To get vertex form, we need to complete the square. Divide the middle term by 2 to get 5 and square that result to get 25. Put the 5 inside the parentheses with x and subtract the 25 at the end.

$$y = (x+5)^2 + 16 - 25$$

$$y = (x+5)^2 - 9$$

10. $\boxed{A}$ The line of best fit has a negative slope, which means that as x increases, y tends to decrease. In the context of this problem, as the average number of advertisements per issue increases, the number of subscribers tends to decrease.

11. $\boxed{D}$ Be wary when using the line of best fit to make predictions based on values outside the gathered data set. Oftentimes, you will get predictions that don't reflect reality. The point $(55, -1)$, which has a negative y-value, is just one example. Obviously, you cannot have a negative number of subscribers. Answers A, B, and C give statements that we cannot be certain about. There might be a magazine out there with 100 advertisements per issue and a million subscribers, but we don't know. Therefore, D is the correct answer.

12. $\boxed{A}$ Because the line passes through the origin and its slope is $\dfrac{1}{2}$, any point on the line will have an x-coordinate that is twice its y-coordinate. Since $(t, t+5)$ lies on the line,

$$t = 2(t+5)$$
$$t = 2t + 10$$
$$-t = 10$$
$$t = -10$$

13. $\boxed{C}$ From the graph, $f(3) = 2$. Where else does the graph have a y-value of 2? When $x = -1$. Therefore, $c = -1$.

14. $\boxed{B}$ Over 8 seconds, the kinetic energy of the object rose by a total of $1,700 \times 8 = 13,600$ joules. That's equivalent to $13,600 \text{ joules} \times \dfrac{1,000 \text{ calories}}{4,187 \text{ joules}} \approx 3,250$ calories.

15. $\boxed{C}$ Put the scores for each class in order. History class: $79, 82, 87, 91, 93$. Chemistry class: $82, 82, 85, 95,$ 98. The median is the middle number and the range is the difference between the highest and the lowest. Thus, $m_1 = 87$ and $m_2 = 85$, and $r_1 = 93 - 79 = 14$ and $r_2 = 98 - 82 = 16$. Comparing the respective values, $m_1 > m_2$ and $r_1 < r_2$.

16. $\boxed{C}$ Because $\triangle ABC$ is isosceles, the remaining $160°$ is split between the two remaining angles: $\angle ABC = \angle ACB = 80°$. Now $\angle ACD = 180 - 80 = 100°$ and because $\triangle ACD$ is isosceles, the remaining $80°$ is split so that $\angle ACD = \angle ADC = 40°$. Finally, $\angle ADE = 180 - 40 = 140°$ and because $\triangle ADE$ is isosceles, the remaining $40°$ is split so that $\angle DAE = \angle E = 20°$. Therefore, $x = 20$.

17. $\boxed{D}$ Let the number of wallets be w and the number of keychains be k. With the information given, we can set up the following system of equations:

$$12w + 8k = 160$$
$$w + k = 18$$

The second equation gives $w = 18 - k$. Substituting this into the first equation, we get

$$12(18 - k) + 8k = 160$$
$$216 - 12k + 8k = 160$$
$$216 - 4k = 160$$
$$-4k = -56$$
$$k = 14$$

18. $\boxed{C}$ The volume of the glass rectangular prism is $10 \times 15 \times 20 = 3,000$ cubic inches. The sculptor removes 880 cubic inches to form the cylinder, so the volume of the cylinder must be $3,000 - 880 = 2,120$ cubic inches. Since the volume of a right circular cylinder is $\pi r^2 h$, we can set up the following equation and solve for the radius.

$$\pi r^2 h = 2,120$$
$$\pi r^2 (8) = 2,120$$
$$\pi r^2 = 265$$
$$r = \sqrt{\frac{265}{\pi}} \approx 9.2$$

19. $\boxed{A}$ Using our rules for exponents, we can turn the equation into

$$y^{b - \frac{1}{2}} = y^{-2}$$

Equating the exponents,

$$b - \frac{1}{2} = -2$$
$$b = -2 + \frac{1}{2} = -\frac{3}{2}$$

20. $\boxed{D}$ Triangles ABE and DCE are similar. Therefore, the ratio of their respective sides is $4 : 6$, or $2 : 3$. If we let $BE = 2x$, then $EC = 3x$.

$$2x + 3x = 15$$
$$5x = 15$$
$$x = 3$$

Therefore, $EC = 3(3) = 9$.

21. $\boxed{A}$ Each day, Tom's collection grows by $7 - 2 = 5$ cards. Because this is a constant increase, the relationship is linear growth.

22. $\boxed{D}$ $\dfrac{\text{Work in Boston}}{\text{Total surveyed}} = \dfrac{110}{250} = \dfrac{11}{25}$

23. $\boxed{C}$ Let's start with Boston. The probability that an office worker in Boston brings lunch to work is $\dfrac{44}{110} = \dfrac{2}{5} = 0.4$. The probability that an office worker in Chicago brings lunch to work is $\dfrac{35}{140} = \dfrac{1}{4} = 0.25$. Therefore, it is $\dfrac{0.4}{0.25} = 1.6$ times more likely for an office worker in Boston to bring lunch to work than for an office worker in Chicago to bring lunch to work.

24. $\boxed{D}$ For the first 30 minutes, she's charged $0.25, leaving $1.35 - \$0.25 = \$1.10$ to account for. Every additional 5 minutes costs $0.10 so

$$\$1.10 \times \dfrac{5 \text{ minutes}}{\$0.10} = 55 \text{ minutes}$$

$1.10 is the cost for an additional 55 minutes, making the total number of minutes $30 + 55 = 85$.

25. $\boxed{B}$ The standard form of a circle with center (h, k) and radius r is $(x - h)^2 + (y - k)^2 = r^2$.

26. $\boxed{B}$ The results are flawed because the gym wanted to evaluate the class's appeal to all its members and yet only those interested attended the class. The opinions of these interested attendees are likely not representative of all the gym's members. Maybe they were already interested in the topic of the class or they happened to have free time in their schedules to attend. For the results to be unbiased, the class attendees need to be randomly selected members of the gym.

27. $\boxed{B}$ The 1.6 refers to the slope, which means each additional gram of potassium hydroxide Jane wishes to produce from the reaction requires an additional 1.6 milliliters of water.

28. $\boxed{B}$ Because this question is asking for the change in "x" per change in "y" (the reverse of slope), we need to rearrange the equation to get a in terms of w:

$$w = 1.6a + 10$$

$$w = \dfrac{8}{5}a + 10$$

$$5w = 8a + 50$$

$$5w - 50 = 8a$$

$$a = \dfrac{5}{8}w - \dfrac{50}{8}$$

What we care about is the slope, which is $\dfrac{5}{8}$, or 0.625. This is the additional amount of potassium hydroxide that would be produced if one more milliliter of water were used in the reaction.

29. $\boxed{B}$ Multiply both sides by 2 and then square both sides.

$$\frac{\sqrt{2x^2 - 14}}{2} = 3$$
$$\sqrt{2x^2 - 14} = 6$$
$$2x^2 - 14 = 36$$
$$2x^2 = 50$$
$$x^2 = 25$$
$$x = 5$$

30. $\boxed{D}$ Let the length of the rectangle be l and the width be w. Let's say that Tammy picks two "lengths" and one "width". Gladys picks two "widths" and one "length."

$$\begin{cases} 2l + w = 140 \\ l + 2w = 100 \end{cases}$$

Adding these two equations together,

$$3l + 3w = 240$$

Dividing both sides by 3,

$$l + w = 80$$

Keeping in mind that the perimeter of a rectangle is $2l + 2w$, we multiply both sides by 2.

$$2l + 2w = 160$$

31. $\boxed{35}$ The missing angle in the triangle on the right is $180 - 40 - 40 = 100°$. Because vertical angles are equal, the angle on the left is also $100°$. Therefore, $x = 180 - 45 - 100 = 35$.

32. $\boxed{770}$

$$42,000 \text{ email} \times \frac{11 \text{ lost}}{600 \text{ emails}} = 770 \text{ lost}$$

33. $\boxed{2009}$ The lines intersect in the year 2009, which means the number of applications was the same in both countries during that year.

34. $\boxed{39}$

$$f(n) = 3$$
$$\frac{\sqrt{n - 3}}{2} = 3$$
$$\sqrt{n - 3} = 6$$
$$n - 3 = 36$$
$$n = 39$$

194

35. $\boxed{27}$

$$-4k + 12 \geq -24$$
$$-4k \geq -36$$
$$k \leq 9$$

The maximum value of k is 9, so the maximum value of $3k$ is 27.

36. $\boxed{13}$

$$
\begin{array}{r}
3x \quad + \quad 4 \\
x - 1 \overline{\smash{\big)}\ 3x^2 \quad + \quad x \quad + \quad 2} \\
\underline{3x^2 \quad - \quad 3x} \\
4x \quad + \quad 2 \\
\underline{4x \quad - \quad 4} \\
6
\end{array}
$$

This result can be expressed as $3x + 4 + \dfrac{6}{x - 1}$. Therefore, $a = 3, b = 4, c = 6$, and $a + b + c = 13$.

37. $\boxed{1.8}$ If x represents the number of burritos sold during lunch, then let d represent the number of burritos sold during dinner.

$$x = 1.25d$$

Solving for d,

$$d = \frac{x}{1.25} = 0.8x$$

Therefore, the total number of burritos sold on a typical day is $x + d = x + 0.8x = 1.8x$.

38. $\boxed{450}$

$$\text{Lunch} = (1.25)(\text{Dinner})$$
$$\text{Lunch} = (1.25)(360) = 450$$

Practice Test 4 Answers

Question categories correspond to chapters in *The College Panda's SAT Math: The Advanced Guide and Workbook*. To estimate your score, visit *thecollegepanda.com/sat-score-calculator*

Section 3

1. $\boxed{D}$ More Equation Solving Strategies

2. $\boxed{D}$ Constructing Models

3. $\boxed{B}$ Interpreting Linear Models

4. $\boxed{C}$ Functions

5. $\boxed{D}$ Systems of Equations

6. $\boxed{D}$ Expressions

7. $\boxed{B}$ Lines

8. $\boxed{C}$ Circles

9. $\boxed{B}$ Exponents & Radicals

10. $\boxed{D}$ Triangles

11. $\boxed{A}$ Trigonometry

12. $\boxed{B}$ Lines

13. $\boxed{C}$ Complex Numbers

14. $\boxed{B}$ Inequalities

15. $\boxed{B}$ Quadratics

16. $\boxed{\frac{1}{5}}$ Manipulating & Solving Equations

17. $\boxed{140}$ Angles

18. $\boxed{60}$ Expressions

19. $\boxed{\frac{1}{2}}$ More Equation Solving Strategies

20. $\boxed{\frac{3}{5}}$ Manipulating & Solving Equations

Section 4

1. $\boxed{C}$ Percent

2. $\boxed{B}$ Reading Data

3. $\boxed{D}$ Exponential vs. Linear Growth

4. $\boxed{C}$ Percent

5. $\boxed{C}$ Manipulating & Solving Equations

6. $\boxed{A}$ Interpreting Linear Models

7. $\boxed{B}$ Inequalities

8. $\boxed{B}$ Probability

9. $\boxed{A}$ Manipulating & Solving Equations

10. $\boxed{C}$ Expressions

11. $\boxed{B}$ Inequalities

12. $\boxed{C}$ Statistics II

13. $\boxed{A}$ Statistics II

14. $\boxed{A}$ Interpreting Linear Models

15. $\boxed{C}$ Manipulating & Solving Equations

16. $\boxed{A}$ Rates

17. $\boxed{D}$ Functions

18. $\boxed{D}$ Triangles

19. $\boxed{C}$ Word Problems

20. $\boxed{B}$ Lines

21. $\boxed{C}$ Functions

22. $\boxed{D}$ Statistics I

23. $\boxed{B}$ Volume

24. $\boxed{B}$ Statistics II

25. $\boxed{B}$ Statistics II

26. $\boxed{D}$ Ratio & Proportion

27. $\boxed{D}$ Trigonometry

28. $\boxed{C}$ Lines

29. $\boxed{C}$ Percent

30. $\boxed{C}$ Systems of Equations

31. $\boxed{2}$ Circles

32. $\boxed{3}$ Manipulating & Solving Equations

33. $\boxed{5}$ Quadratics

34. $\boxed{12}$ Systems of Equations

35. $\boxed{1}$ Functions

36. $\boxed{17.5}$ Minimum & Maximum Word Problems

37. $\boxed{47}$ Percent / Reading Data

38. $\boxed{7200}$ Word Problems / Reading Data

Practice Test 4 Answer Explanations

Section 3

1. $\boxed{D}$ Both sides of the equation are the same (the terms are just in a different order), so the equation must be true for any value of x.

2. $\boxed{D}$ Ellie has collected $\dfrac{m}{2}$ coins, which is 5 more than Robert. So Robert must have collected $\dfrac{m}{2} - 5$ coins.

3. $\boxed{B}$ The slope of the equation is 10, which means a student's score increases by 10 for each additional hour of study.

4. $\boxed{C}$ From the graph, the x-intercepts of g are $-2, 0$, and 2. The correct $g(x)$ should output a value of zero when those numbers are plugged in. The only answer choice that does that is (C).

5. $\boxed{D}$ Multiply the first equation by 2 and subtract to get $-9x = -36$, $x = 4$. Plugging this value back into the first equation,

$$-2(4) - y = -9$$
$$-8 - y = -9$$
$$y = 1$$

6. $\boxed{D}$ Since $(x - y)^2 = x^2 - 2xy + y^2$,

$$(\sqrt{a} - 2\sqrt{b})^2 = (\sqrt{a})^2 - 2(\sqrt{a})(2\sqrt{b}) + (2\sqrt{b})^2 = a - 4\sqrt{ab} + 4b$$

7. $\boxed{B}$ Only graphs (B), (D), and (E) have negative slopes. A line with a slope of $-\dfrac{1}{2}$ will not be very steep, 1 unit down for every 2 units to the right. Graph (B) is the one that shows this correctly.

8. $\boxed{C}$ **Solution 1:** Since the x-coordinate is 0, we can use the equation to solve for the y-coordinate.

$$(0 + 6)^2 + (y - 4)^2 = 100$$
$$36 + (y - 4)^2 = 100$$
$$(y - 4)^2 = 64$$
$$y - 4 = \pm 8$$
$$y = 4 \pm 8 = -4 \text{ or } 12$$

Therefore, $(0, 12)$ and $(0, -4)$ are the two y-intercepts, and $c = -4$.

Solution 2: The center of the circle is at $(-6, 4)$. The y-intercepts must be evenly spaced from the center in the vertical direction. In other words, the difference between 12 and 4 must be the same difference between 4 and c. Since 12 is 8 away from 4 in the positive direction, c must be 8 away from 4 in the negative direction: $c = 4 - 8 = -4$.

9. $\boxed{B}$

$$k^2 x^{2a} = x^{2a+2}$$
$$k^2 x^{2a} = x^{2a} \cdot x^2$$

Divide both sides by x^{2a},

$$k^2 = x^2$$

Since k and x are both positive, $k = x$. Therefore, $x - k = 0$.

10. $\boxed{D}$ The short side of the rectangle is the hypotenuse of a 45–45–90 triangle with legs of length 2. Therefore, the short side has a length of $2\sqrt{2}$ (you could've also used the pythagorean theorem to calculate this length). Similarly, the long side of the rectangle is the hypotenuse of a 45–45–90 triangle with legs of length 5. So the long side has a length of $5\sqrt{2}$. The area of the rectangle is then base times height: $5\sqrt{2} \times 2\sqrt{2} = 10 \times 2 = 20$.

11. $\boxed{A}$ Using the 30–60–90 triangle relationship to find the values,

$$\sin 30° - \cos 60° = \frac{1}{2} - \frac{1}{2} = 0$$

12. $\boxed{B}$ Using the given point, we plug in $x = 2b$ and $y = -9$ into the equation:

$$y = 2x - b$$
$$-9 = 2(2b) - b$$
$$-9 = 3b$$
$$-3 = b$$

13. $\boxed{C}$

$$\frac{(2i + 1)}{(3i - 2)} \cdot \frac{(3i + 2)}{(3i + 2)} = \frac{6i^2 + 4i + 3i + 2}{9i^2 + 6i - 6i - 4} = \frac{6i^2 + 7i + 2}{9i^2 - 4} = \frac{-6 + 7i + 2}{-9 - 4} = \frac{-4 + 7i}{-13} = \frac{4}{13} - \frac{7}{13}i$$

Therefore, $b = -\dfrac{7}{13}$.

14. $\boxed{B}$ Isolate x in the first equation: $x < 11 - 2y$. As y gets bigger and bigger, x gets smaller and smaller. Therefore, the upper bound of x occurs when $y = 3$, the lower bound of y.

$$x < 11 - 2(3) \implies x < 5$$

An alternate solution is to test out different values of x and solve for y until you find the answer choice that works.

15. $\boxed{B}$ Substituting the first equation into the second,

$$4y = (1 - 2y)^2 + 3$$
$$4y = 1 - 4y + 4y^2 + 3$$
$$0 = 4y^2 - 8y + 4$$
$$0 = y^2 - 2y + 1$$

From here, it's pretty easy to finish solving for y, but for learning purposes, we'll use the discriminant to determine the number of solutions.

$$b^2 - 4ac = (-2)^2 - 4(1)(1) = 4 - 4 = 0$$

Because the discriminant is 0, there is only one value of y that satisfies the equation above, and therefore only one solution to the system of equations.

16. $\boxed{\dfrac{1}{5}}$

17. $\boxed{140}$ Because vertical angles are equal, the missing angle between $y°$ and $40°$ must have the same measure as angle z. Because the angles form a straight line,

$$y + z + 40 = 180$$
$$y + z = 140$$

18. $\boxed{60}$ Here's the easiest way: $c^2 - d^2 = (c + d)(c - d) = (-5)(-12) = 60$. The much more difficult way is to solve the system of equations to find the individual values of c and d.

19. $\boxed{\dfrac{1}{2}}$ Multiply both sides by $6x$.

$$\frac{3}{2x}(6x) - \frac{2}{3x}(6x) = \frac{5}{3}(6x)$$
$$3(3) - 2(2) = 10x$$
$$5 = 10x$$
$$\frac{1}{2} = x$$

20. $\boxed{\dfrac{3}{5}}$ Factor out a 5 from the left hand side.

$$7(2.5x - 1.5) = 12(0.5x - 0.3)$$
$$35(0.5x - 0.3) = 12(0.5x - 0.3)$$
$$23(0.5x - 0.3) = 0$$

From this equation, we can see that $0.5x - 0.3 = 0$. We can multiply both sides by 10 to get $5x - 3 = 0$ and $x = \dfrac{3}{5}$.

Section 4

1. $\boxed{C}$ When the tank is $100 - 70 = 30\%$ full, it contains 12 gallons. Let x be the number of gallons a full tank holds.

$$\frac{3}{10}x = 12$$
$$x = 40$$

2. $\boxed{B}$ From the graph, we can estimate the increase to be 130 million $-$ 76 million $= 54$ million. It's clear that B is closest as long as we make reasonable estimations.

3. $\boxed{D}$ Scatterplot D shows exponential growth.

4. $\boxed{C}$ $\frac{5}{24} \approx 0.208 = 20.8\%$.

5. $\boxed{C}$

$$10xy - 3y + 6 = 41 + 2y$$
$$10xy - 3y = 35 + 2y$$
$$10xy - 5y = 35$$
$$2xy - y = 7$$

6. $\boxed{A}$ John's initial consultation fee must be a non-zero y-intercept, where the number of hours worked is 0. From the graph, the only non-zero y-intercept is 100. The other line must represent Will's wages.

7. $\boxed{B}$ John's wages are less than Will's after the intersection point of the two lines, $h = 4$. Therefore, it is less expensive to hire John when the work is more than 4 hours, $h > 4$.

8. $\boxed{B}$ The total number of students in the group is $27 + 30 + 51 + 42 = 150$. The number of students who chose to have a cold sandwich is $30 + 42 = 72$. Therefore, the percentage is $\frac{72}{150} = 0.48 = 48\%$.

9. $\boxed{A}$ Cross multiply.

$$4(2a + 3b) = 3(a - b)$$
$$8a + 12b = 3a - 3b$$
$$5a = -15b$$
$$\frac{a}{b} = -3$$

10. $\boxed{C}$ Combining like terms, $2x^3y^2 - 3x^3y^2 = -x^3y^2$ and $-3x^2y^3 + 2x^2y^3 = -x^2y^3$, giving us $-x^3y^2 - x^2y^3$.

11. $\boxed{B}$ Test each answer choice. Only answer B satisfies both inequalities:

$$4(-3) < -1 - 5 \quad \Rightarrow \quad -12 < -6$$
$$-1 < 2 - (-4) \quad \Rightarrow \quad -1 < 6$$

12. $\boxed{C}$ Because the committee surveyed only <u>computer science</u> teachers, the survey results may not accurately reflect the opinions of all teachers in the school district. For example, computer science teachers probably use more technology in their classrooms than other teachers do. Answer D is wrong because we cannot say for certain that exactly 90 percent of all computer science teachers in the school district are in favor of adopting electronic whiteboards. When inferring from a sample, we can only say that the percentage is approximately 90.

13. $\boxed{A}$ Drawing a line of best fit, we can establish a linear model from the grid points.

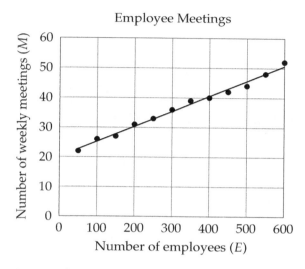

The line of best fit passes through $(200, 30)$ and $(400, 40)$. These are examples of points you would estimate from your line.

$$\text{Slope} = \frac{40 - 30}{400 - 200} = \frac{10}{200} = 0.05$$

So the line has an equation in the form of

$$M = 0.05E + b$$

Using the point $(200, 30)$, we can solve for b to get

$$M = 0.05E + 20$$

Another way to solve this problem is to test the two points with each of the answer choices. Only answer (A) gives accurate results.

14. $\boxed{A}$ The slope tells us the change in cost that results from a change of one unit sold. And because it's a positive slope, the total cost falls as the quantity of units sold falls. So, $14 \times 5 = 70$ is the decrease in total cost.

15. $\boxed{C}$

$$20Q = 14Q + 114$$
$$6Q = 114$$
$$Q = 19$$

16. $\boxed{A}$ Jane would receive $2.75 \times 500 = 1,375$ dollars in rent for one month. For one year, she would receive $1,375 \times 12 = 16,500$ dollars.

17. $\boxed{D}$ Draw a line at $y = 2$.

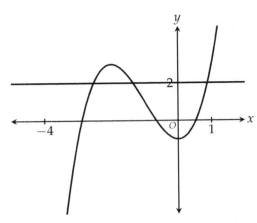

The two graphs intersect at 3 different points, which means there are 3 different values of x for which $f(x) = 2$.

18. $\boxed{D}$ $\angle A$ and $\angle C$ must add up to $180 - 110 = 70°$. Because $AB = BC$, $\angle A = \angle C$, which means they're each $70 \div 2 = 35°$. $y = 180 - 35 = 145°$.

19. $\boxed{C}$ Let the length be x. The width is then $x + 35$.

$$2x + 2(x + 35) = 110$$
$$4x + 70 = 110$$
$$4x = 40$$
$$x = 10$$

The length is 10 and the width is $10 + 35 = 45$. Finally, the area is $10 \times 45 = 450$.

20. $\boxed{B}$ Adjusting the equation, we get

$$y = -2x$$

which is a line with a slope of -2 that passes through the origin. If you graph it, it will run through quadrants II and IV.

21. $\boxed{C}$ Plug 4 into each of the answer choices to see which one doesn't give -2. Answer (C) gives 2 instead of -2.

22. $\boxed{D}$ The standard deviation says nothing about how the mean or the median of one data set compares with the mean or the median of another. The only thing it measures is how spread out, or variable, a data set is. A higher standard deviation implies that the data is more variable.

23. $\boxed{B}$ Finding the radius from the circumference,

$$2\pi r = 5\pi$$
$$r = 2.5$$

The volume of the cylinder is then $\pi r^2 h = \pi (2.5)^2 (4) = 25\pi$

24. $\boxed{B}$ Looking at the scatterplot, there are 4 points that are more than 5 units away vertically from the line of best fit. From left to right, they are the 2nd point, 3rd point, 5th point, and 6th point.

25. $\boxed{B}$ Agency A spends $5,000 \times 22.5 = 112,500$ minutes processing all its requests. Agency B spends $6,500 \times 30 = 195,000$ minutes. Agency C spends $7,000 \times 17.5 = 122,500$ minutes. Agency D spends $9,000 \times 20 = 180,000$ minutes. Of these 4 agencies, Agency B spends the most time processing all its requests.

26. $\boxed{D}$ Alfred's favorite drink is $\dfrac{2}{7}$ lime and $\dfrac{5}{7}$ raspberry soda, which means the bottle Jenny has currently contains $\dfrac{2}{7}(21) = 6$ ounces of lime and $\dfrac{5}{7}(21) = 15$ ounces of raspberry soda. Given that the ratio of lime juice to raspberry soda in Jenny's favorite drink is 1:4, and there are 6 ounces of lime juice currently in the bottle, there would need to be a total of $6 \times 4 = 24$ ounces of raspberry soda in the bottle for Jenny's ratio to be met. Therefore, Jenny must add $24 - 15 = 9$ ounces of raspberry soda.

27. $\boxed{D}$ The triangle is isosceles. Draw a line down the middle to split the base in half.

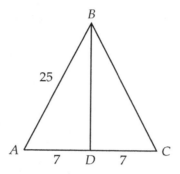

Using the pythagorean theorem to find BD,

$$AD^2 + BD^2 = AB^2$$
$$7^2 + BD^2 = 25^2$$
$$BD^2 = 576$$
$$BD = \sqrt{576} = 24$$

Finally, $\sin A = \dfrac{24}{25} = 0.96$

28. $\boxed{C}$ The rate of decrease (slope) is $\dfrac{84,200 - 93,600}{360 - 320} = \dfrac{-9,400}{40} = -235$ per dollar. Since the quantity demanded is 93,600 when the price is \$320, we can use the point-slope form of a line to determine the equation:

$$y - y_1 = m(x - x_1)$$
$$y - 93,600 = -235(x - 320)$$
$$y = 93,600 - 235(x - 320)$$
$$Q(p) = 93,600 - 235(p - 320)$$

29. $\boxed{C}$ The account will earn 3 percent for the first 5 years and then 7 percent for the remaining $t - 5$ years. In the first five years, the total amount accumulated will be $1,000(1.03)^5$. Taking that result and treating it as the initial value for the remaining years, we get $1,000(1.03)^5(1.07)^{t-5}$.

30. $\boxed{C}$ We want a 100 gallons at the end, so $a + b = 100$. One hundred gallons of a solution that is 55% acid contains 55 gallons of acid. Therefore, the acid from solution A and the acid from solution B must total 55: $0.6a + 0.4b = 55$.

31. $\boxed{2}$ The circumference of the track is $2\pi(25) \approx 157$ meters.

$$157 \text{ meters} \times \frac{1 \text{ minute}}{75 \text{ meters}} \approx 2 \text{ minutes}$$

32. $\boxed{3}$ Setting up an equation to solve for x, we get

$$2x + (x - 4) = x + 10$$
$$3x - 4 = x + 10$$
$$2x = 14$$
$$x = 7$$

The length of $\overline{BC}$ is then $x - 4 = 7 - 4 = 3$.

33. $\boxed{5}$ We have two cases: either $a = 3$ or $a = 8$. If $a = 3$, then for 8 to also be a solution,

$$8 - a - b = 0$$
$$8 - 3 - b = 0$$
$$5 - b = 0$$
$$b = 5$$

Since this meets the condition that $b > 0$, $b = 5$. What if we let $a = 8$? Then for 3 to also be a solution,

$$3 - a - b = 0$$
$$3 - 8 - b = 0$$
$$-5 - b = 0$$
$$b = -5$$

In this case, b is not greater than zero, confirming that $b = 5$ is indeed correct.

34. $\boxed{12}$ For the lines to be the same, their equations must be equivalent. For the equations to be equivalent, the second equation has to be 4 times the first, as we can see below.

$$2y - 3x = 5$$
$$8y - ax = 20$$

Therefore, $a = 3 \times 4 = 12$.

35. $\boxed{1}$

$$f(m+1) = 5$$
$$(m+1)^2 - (m+1) + 3 = 5$$
$$m^2 + 2m + 1 - m - 1 + 3 = 5$$
$$m^2 + m - 2 = 0$$
$$(m+2)(m-1) = 0$$
$$m = -2, 1$$

Since $m > 0$, $m = 1$.

36. $\boxed{17.5}$ Because the width of each parking space must be between 17 and 20 feet, the maximum number of parking spaces is $630 \div 17 \approx 37.05 \to 37$ (we have to round down), and the minimum number of parking spaces is $630 \div 20 = 31.5 \to 32$ (we have to round up). Since the number of parking spaces must be a multiple of 6, the number of parking spaces has to be 36. The width of each parking space is then $630 \div 36 = 17.5$ feet.

37. $\boxed{47}$ Let x be the total number of students at the university. From the graph, $0.40x$ students were living on campus and $(1 - 0.40)x = 0.60x$ students were not living on campus in 2013. Since 80% of the students living on campus purchased meal plans, $(0.80)(0.40x) = 0.32x$ represents the number of students living on campus who purchased meal plans. Since 25% of the students not living on campus purchased meal plans, $(0.25)(0.60x) = 0.15x$ represents the number of students not living on campus who purchased a meal plan. Adding up our two expressions, we get $0.32x + 0.15x = 0.47x$, which equates to 47% of all the students at the university.

38. $\boxed{7200}$ In 2015, there were 18,000 students and 35% of the students lived on campus. In 2016, there were $18,000 + x$ students and 25% of the students lived on campus. Since the number of students living on campus each year was the same, we can set up the following equation:

$$0.35(18,000) = 0.25(18,000 + x)$$
$$6,300 = 4,500 + 0.25x$$
$$1,800 = 0.25x$$
$$x = 7,200$$

Practice Test 5 Answers

Question categories correspond to chapters in *The College Panda's SAT Math: The Advanced Guide and Workbook*. To estimate your score, visit *thecollegepanda.com/sat-score-calculator*

Section 3

1. $\boxed{C}$ Expressions
2. $\boxed{D}$ Constructing Models
3. $\boxed{C}$ Exponents & Radicals
4. $\boxed{B}$ Interpreting Linear Models
5. $\boxed{A}$ Lines
6. $\boxed{A}$ Systems of Equations
7. $\boxed{B}$ Manipulating & Solving Equations
8. $\boxed{C}$ Functions
9. $\boxed{B}$ Expressions
10. $\boxed{A}$ Systems of Equations
11. $\boxed{C}$ Inequalities
12. $\boxed{A}$ Triangles
13. $\boxed{D}$ Complex Numbers
14. $\boxed{B}$ Quadratics
15. $\boxed{B}$ Synthetic Division
16. $\boxed{30}$ Rates
17. $\boxed{4}$ Functions
18. $\boxed{45}$ Manipulating & Solving Equations
19. $\boxed{25}$ Quadratics
20. $\boxed{7 \text{ or } 8}$ More Equation Solving Strategies

Section 4

1. $\boxed{D}$ Rates
2. $\boxed{B}$ Percent
3. $\boxed{D}$ Manipulating & Solving Equations
4. $\boxed{D}$ Constructing Models
5. $\boxed{B}$ Functions
6. $\boxed{C}$ Reading Data
7. $\boxed{D}$ Reading Data
8. $\boxed{A}$ Lines
9. $\boxed{D}$ Inequalities
10. $\boxed{B}$ Statistics I
11. $\boxed{A}$ Percent
12. $\boxed{C}$ Probability
13. $\boxed{C}$ Probability
14. $\boxed{D}$ Rates
15. $\boxed{C}$ Circles
16. $\boxed{B}$ Functions
17. $\boxed{A}$ Expressions
18. $\boxed{A}$ Exponential vs. Linear Growth
19. $\boxed{D}$ Statistics II
20. $\boxed{A}$ Statistics II
21. $\boxed{C}$ Quadratics
22. $\boxed{D}$ More Equation Solving Strategies
23. $\boxed{B}$ Percent

24. $\boxed{B}$ Circles
25. $\boxed{B}$ Volume
26. $\boxed{B}$ Lines
27. $\boxed{B}$ Reading Data
28. $\boxed{C}$ Rates
29. $\boxed{A}$ Trigonometry
30. $\boxed{B}$ Inequalities
31. $\boxed{385}$ Percent / Statistics II
32. $\boxed{20}$ Angles
33. $\boxed{1}$ Manipulating & Solving Equations
34. $\boxed{20}$ Systems of Equations
35. $\boxed{30}$ Percent / Statistics I
36. $\boxed{30}$ Triangles
37. $\boxed{3000}$ Manipulating & Solving Equations
38. $\boxed{4}$ Manipulating & Solving Equations

Practice Test 5 Answer Explanations

Section 3

1. $\boxed{C}$ $\dfrac{x}{y} \div \dfrac{y}{z} = \dfrac{x}{y} \times \dfrac{z}{y} = \dfrac{xz}{y^2}$

2. $\boxed{D}$ Each month, Alex spends a total of $15 + 3x$ on movie rentals. So in one year, he'll spend $12(15 + 3x)$.

3. $\boxed{C}$

$$\frac{x^{a^2} \cdot x^{b^2}}{x^{2ab}} = x^{25}$$

$$x^{a^2 - 2ab + b^2} = x^{25}$$

$$a^2 - 2ab + b^2 = 25$$

$$(a - b)^2 = 25$$

$$a - b = \pm 5$$

And 5 is the only one in the answer choices.

4. $\boxed{B}$ The slope of 25 means that each hour brings 25 more visitors to the store. So two hours would bring $25 \times 2 = 50$ more visitors to the store.

5. $\boxed{A}$ There are two cases: the line has a positive slope but a negative y-intercept, OR the line has a negative slope but a positive y-intercept. Try drawing both cases. In either case, the line never touches the negative side of the x-axis. Therefore, $(-1, 0)$ is the answer.

6. $\boxed{A}$ Multiplying the first equation by 3, we can see that the coefficients of x and y match up but the constants on the right side do not. Therefore, there is no solution.

7. $\boxed{B}$

$$\frac{2x}{x^3 n} = 1$$

$$\frac{2}{x^2 n} = 1$$

$$\frac{2}{x^2} = n$$

8. $\boxed{C}$ In answer (C), $(x - 1)^2$ is always greater than or equal to zero. Adding the 1 to it ensures the result is always positive. Therefore, $f(x) = (x - 1)^2 + 1$ does not cross the x-axis. It's easy to see that the other answer choices have values of x that make $f(x) = 0$, which means they cross the x-axis.

9. $\boxed{B}$

$$\left(\frac{1}{xy}\right)(2x + 2y) = \left(\frac{1}{xy}\right)(2x) + \left(\frac{1}{xy}\right)(2y) = \frac{2}{y} + \frac{2}{x}$$

10. $\boxed{A}$ To get rid of the fractions, multiply the first equation by 6 and the second equation by 5. The result is

$$2x + y = 30$$
$$3x + y = -20$$

Subtract the equations to get $-x = 50$, $x = -50$. We can plug this result back into the first equation to get

$$2(-50) + y = 30$$
$$-100 + y = 30$$
$$y = 130$$

11. $\boxed{C}$ The cost of the television ads will be $800x$ and the cost of the radio ads will be $300y$. Since the budget is \$12,000, $800x + 300y \leq 12,000$. Since the number of radio ads should be no more than 24, $y \leq 24$. Finally, the total number of ads must be at least 3 times the number of television ads: $x + y \geq 3x$.

12. $\boxed{A}$ This is a question involving similar triangles. $\triangle ABC$ and $\triangle DAC$ are similar since $\angle ABC = \angle CAD$ and the triangles both share $\angle C$. Since those angles are equal, $\angle BAC$ and $\angle ADC$ must also be equal. The takeaway here is that $\triangle ABC$ is just a bigger version of $\triangle DAC$.

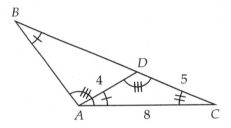

If you're having a hard time figuring out the corresponding sides, let the angles guide you. In $\triangle ABC$, $\overline{AB}$ is opposite the angle marked with two "dashes," and $\overline{BC}$ is opposite the angle marked with three "dashes." In $\triangle CAD$, $\overline{AD}$ is opposite the angle marked with two "dashes," and $\overline{AC}$ is opposite the angle marked with three "dashes." Therefore, AB corresponds with AD, and BC corresponds with AC, giving

$$\frac{AB}{BC} = \frac{AD}{AC} = \frac{4}{8} = \frac{1}{2}.$$

13. $\boxed{D}$

$$\frac{4i}{(i-1)} \cdot \frac{(i+1)}{(i+1)} = \frac{4i^2 + 4i}{i^2 + i - i - 1^2} = \frac{-4 + 4i}{-2} = 2 - 2i$$

14. $\boxed{B}$ If a parabola is defined by $y = a(x - b)^2 + c$, then (b, c) is the vertex and the sign of a determines whether the graph opens upward or downward. From the graph, the parabola opens downward so a is negative. Because the vertex is in the second quadrant, b is negative and c is positive. Now we shift our attention to the parabola represented by $y = c(x + a)(x + b)$. Since c is positive, this parabola opens upward. Since a and b are both negative, this parabola has two positive x-intercepts. To see this more concretely, just make up some numbers. Let $a = -2, b = -3$, and $c = 2$. Then the equation becomes $y = 2(x - 2)(x - 3)$, which represents a parabola that opens upward and has x-intercepts at 2 and 3.

15. $\boxed{B}$ x, which can be written as $x - 0$, is a factor of $p(x)$ only if $p(0) = 0$ (the remainder theorem). Setting up an equation,

$$(3(0)^2 - 5)(0 + k) - 20 = 0$$
$$(-5)(k) - 20 = 0$$
$$-5k = 20$$
$$k = -4$$

16. $\boxed{30}$ Matt needs $100 - 40 = 60$ more rare cards to meet his goal. If each pack contains 2 rare cards, he needs to buy $60 \div 2 = 30$ more packs.

17. $\boxed{4}$

$$\frac{2x - 5}{6} = \frac{1}{2}$$
$$2x - 5 = 3$$
$$2x = 8$$
$$x = 4$$

18. $\boxed{45}$

$$\frac{3c}{d} = 4$$
$$3c = 4d$$
$$d = \frac{3c}{4}$$

Now make the substitution:

$$\frac{60d}{c} = \frac{60 \cdot \dfrac{3c}{4}}{c} = \frac{45c}{c} = 45$$

19. $\boxed{25}$ If a parabola is tangent to the x-axis, its equation only has one solution when set to 0.

$$x^2 - 10x + k = 0$$

The discriminant, $b^2 - 4ac$, must equal 0 for the equation above to have one solution.

$$(-10)^2 - 4(1)(k) = 0$$
$$100 - 4k = 0$$
$$k = 25$$

20. $\boxed{7 \text{ or } 8}$ Multiply both sides by $(x+3)(x-2)$.

$$22(x-2) - 6(x+3) = (x+3)(x-2)$$
$$22x - 44 - 6x - 18 = x^2 + x - 6$$
$$16x - 62 = x^2 + x - 6$$
$$0 = x^2 - 15x + 56$$
$$0 = (x-7)(x-8)$$

The two possible solutions are 7 and 8.

Section 4

1. $\boxed{D}$ $6,650 \div 400 \approx 16.63$ pesos.

2. $\boxed{B}$ Harry consumed $x - y$ ounces. To get the percentage of the bottle he drank, we divide by the original amount in the bottle, x, and multiply by 100: $\dfrac{100(x-y)}{x}$

3. $\boxed{D}$

$$\frac{x-10}{5} = 12$$
$$x - 10 = 60$$
$$x = 70$$

4. $\boxed{D}$ Over t years, the car loses $2300t$ dollars in value. Since its initial value is \$65,000, $V = 65,000 - 2,300t$.

5. $\boxed{B}$ What values of x make $f(x) = 0$? We have $3, 1$, and -2. That's three times.

6. $\boxed{C}$ The greatest change occurs between 2011 and 2012.

$$1.1 \text{ million} - 0.9 \text{ million} = 0.2 \text{ million} = \$200,000$$

7. $\boxed{D}$ The value of Painting A was \$800,000 in 2009 and \$1,100,000 in 2014.

$$\text{Average Rate of Change} = \frac{1,100,000 - 800,000}{2014 - 2009} = \frac{300,000}{5} = \$60,000 \text{ per year}$$

8. $\boxed{A}$ Line l goes 3 units up for every 4 units to the right, which means it has a slope of $\dfrac{3}{4}$. Line m is perpendicular so its slope must be the negative reciprocal of line l's. The negative reciprocal of $\dfrac{3}{4}$ is $-\dfrac{4}{3}$.

9. $\boxed{D}$ Setting up the inequality,

$$1,500 + 12x > 2,800$$
$$12x > 1,300$$
$$x > 108.333$$

Since dress shirts are sold as whole units, $x \geq 109$.

10. $\boxed{B}$ The mean and the median get closer together when outliers, the data points furthest away from all the others, are removed. The outlier here is Town B.

11. $\boxed{A}$ An increase of 35 percent means the resulting price is $1.35p$. A discount of 35 percent then brings the price to $(0.65)(1.35p)$, which is the same as answer A.

12. $\boxed{C}$ $\dfrac{\text{Without fertilizer and weighs less than 6 oz}}{\text{Total number of harvested potatoes}} = \dfrac{187}{720} \approx 0.26$

13. $\boxed{C}$ $\dfrac{\text{With fertilizer and} \geq 6 \text{ oz}}{\text{With fertilizer}} - \dfrac{\text{Without fertilizer and} \geq 6 \text{ oz}}{\text{Without fertilizer}} = \dfrac{236}{236 + 159} - \dfrac{138}{138 + 187} \approx 0.173$

14. $\boxed{D}$ In 1 hour, the plant can process $90 \times 60 = 5400$ tons of coal. Now that we are comparing hours to hours, the rest is simple:

$$5400 \text{ tons} \times \frac{3 \text{ trucks}}{135 \text{ tons}} = 120 \text{ trucks}$$

15. $\boxed{C}$

$$2\pi r = 20\pi$$
$$r = 10$$

The standard form of a circle with center (h, k) and radius r is $(x - h)^2 + (y - k)^2 = r^2$. So the equation of the circle is $(x - 2)^2 + (y + 3)^2 = 100$.

16. $\boxed{B}$

$$f(b) = 29$$
$$b^3 + 2 = 29$$
$$b^3 = 27$$
$$b = \sqrt[3]{27}$$
$$b = 3$$

$$g(b) = 2b = 2(3) = 6$$

17. $\boxed{A}$ Combine like terms. $-4x^2y + 2xy^2 + (3x^2y^2 - 5x^2y^2) = -4x^2y + 2xy^2 - 2x^2y^2$

18. $\boxed{A}$ With linear growth, the population in the third year would be $600 + 400 = 1,000$. With exponential growth, the population triples each year, making the total 1,800 in the third year. The difference is $1,800 - 1,000 = 800$ turtles.

19. $\boxed{D}$ At a speed of 90 miles per hour, the line of best fit gives a fine of 100 dollars.

20. $\boxed{A}$ The slope is rise over run. Because the line of best fit has a positive slope, it's the increase in the fine for each additional mile per hour over the speed limit.

21. $\boxed{C}$ From the graph, we can see that the x-intercepts are -6 and 3, which means that two factors of the quadratic are $(x + 6)$ and $(x - 3)$. Answer (C) is the only one with both of these factors.

22. $\boxed{D}$ First, simplify the equation by distributing the $\frac{1}{10}$ on the left hand side and combining like terms on the right hand side.

$$\frac{1}{10}(11x - 5) = 3x - 1.9x - 5$$
$$1.1x - 0.5 = 1.1x - 5$$

As you can see, the left hand side will never equal the right hand side. They're inconsistent. Therefore, there are no solutions. Note that if we subtracted $1.1x$ from each side, we would get $-0.5 = -5$, which is never true and confirms that there are no solutions.

23. $\boxed{B}$ Let x be the amount of the initial deposit.

$$x(1.05)^8 = 4,000$$
$$x = \frac{4,000}{(1.05)^8}$$

24. $\boxed{B}$ Because $\triangle ACB$ is isosceles (radii are equal), $\angle CBA = 50°$ and $\angle ACB = 180 - 50 - 50 = 80°$.

$$\text{Area of sector} = \frac{80}{360} \times 54\pi = 12\pi$$

25. $\boxed{B}$

$$\text{Volume of ring} = \text{Area of base} \times \text{Height}$$
$$V = (\text{Area of square} - \text{Area of circle}) \times \text{Height}$$
$$V = (2.5^2 - \pi(1)^2) \times 0.5 \approx 1.55 \text{ cm}^3$$

26. $\boxed{B}$ Line l is perpendicular to $y = -3x + c$, which means its slope must be $\frac{1}{3}$. Since line l also passes through $(0, 0)$, its y-intercept is 0 and its equation must be $y = \frac{1}{3}x$. Finally, we plug in $(k, k - 4)$, which is also on line l.

$$y = \frac{1}{3}x$$
$$k - 4 = \frac{1}{3}k$$
$$\frac{2}{3}k = 4$$
$$2k = 12$$
$$k = 6$$

27. $\boxed{B}$ Driving along a circular road around the post office means that Pat's distance from the post office should stay the same during that time. That happens only during the portion from 1 hour to 3 hours.

28. **C** Note that the 48 minutes John and Nick already worked is irrelevant because they both worked for that same amount of time. What matters is the difference in how fast they finish the remaining records. John can enter 120 remaining records in $120 \div 40 = 3$ hours $= 180$ minutes. Nick can enter 120 remaining records in $120 \div 50 = 2.4$ hours $= 144$ minutes. The difference in their job completion times will be $180 - 144 = 36$ minutes.

29. **A** Here's the identity you need to use: the cosine of an angle is equal to the sine of the complementary angle and vice versa. In other words, $\cos x = \sin(90 - x)$.

Because $ABCD$ is a parallelogram, opposite angles $\angle A$ and $\angle C$ are congruent, which means $\cos \angle C = \cos \angle A$. Since $\angle A$ and $\angle ABE$ are complementary angles (they sum to 90°), $\cos \angle A = \sin \angle ABE$. Therefore, $\cos \angle C = \cos \angle A = \sin \angle ABE = n$.

30. **B** From the given inequality, $x < n$. Subtracting both sides by n gives $x - n < 0$. Multiplying both sides by -1 gives $n - x > 0$ (note the sign change). Therefore, I is not true.

From the given inequality, $3n - 8 < n$, which gives $2n - 8 < 0$, $2n < 8$, $n < 4$. Therefore, II is true.

We can disprove III by making up some numbers. Let $n = 1$. Then $-5 < x < 1$ and $4n - 8 = -4$. But if we let $x = 0$, then $2x$ is also 0, which is greater than the -4 we got from $4n - 8$. Because we found one case where $2x \not< 4n - 8$, III is not always true.

31. **385** If 30% DO include fries, then $100 - 30 = 70\%$ do not include fries.

$$70\% \text{ of } 550 = (0.70)(550) = 385$$

32. **20**

$$x = \frac{2}{5}(x + 30)$$
$$5x = 2(x + 30)$$
$$5x = 2x + 60$$
$$3x = 60$$
$$x = 20$$

33. **1**

$$\frac{4}{5} - 3\left(\frac{1}{2} + x\right) = \frac{3}{10} - 4x$$
$$\frac{4}{5} - \frac{3}{2} - 3x = \frac{3}{10} - 4x$$
$$x = \frac{3}{10} - \frac{4}{5} + \frac{3}{2} = \frac{3}{10} - \frac{8}{10} + \frac{15}{10} = \frac{10}{10} = 1$$

34. $\boxed{20}$ Substitute the second equation into the first. Then multiply both sides by 2 to get rid of the fraction.

$$2x = \frac{1}{2}x^2 - 3x$$

$$4x = x^2 - 6x$$

$$0 = x^2 - 10x$$

$$0 = x(x - 10)$$

Therefore, $x = 0$ or $x = 10$. When $x = 10$, $y = 2(10) = 20$, which means $b = 20$.

35. $\boxed{30}$ The fact that this question deals with percents is a hint that making up a number may be useful. We don't know the number of students in the class so let's say there are 100, in which case 20 students answered all the questions, leaving 80 students. Of the 80, 40 answered two-fifths of the questions (20 questions) and the remaining 40 answered three-fifths (30 questions).

$$\text{average} = \frac{\text{total number of questions answered}}{\text{number of students}} = \frac{20 \times 50 + 40 \times 20 + 40 \times 30}{100} = \frac{3000}{100} = 30$$

36. $\boxed{30}$ Outer triangle BAC is a multiple of the 3–4–5 right triangle: 9–12–15. You could have used the pythagorean theorem to find the sides if you didn't notice this. In any case, AC is 12. Inner triangle BDE is similar to outer triangle BAC. Using this similarity to find the length of DE,

$$\frac{DE}{BD} = \frac{AC}{BA}$$

$$\frac{DE}{6} = \frac{12}{6+3}$$

Cross multiplying,

$$9DE = 72$$

$$DE = 8$$

The area of the trapezoid is the area of the outer triangle minus the area of the inner triangle:

$$\frac{1}{2}(12)(9) - \frac{1}{2}(8)(6) = 54 - 24 = 30$$

37. $\boxed{3000}$ $S = 2,400 + (0.12)(5,000) = 3,000$

38. $\boxed{4}$

$$4,500 = 2,400 + 0.05x$$
$$2,100 = 0.05x$$
$$42,000 = x$$

So the salesperson brought in $42,000 in sales. Now we can set up a second equation to determine the necessary years of experience.

$$9,960 = 2,400 + c(42,000)$$
$$7,560 = 42,000c$$
$$0.18 = c$$

which means he would have needed a total of 5 years of experience. That's $5 - 1 = 4$ more years than he currently has.

Practice Test 6 Answers

Question categories correspond to chapters in *The College Panda's SAT Math: The Advanced Guide and Workbook*. To estimate your score, visit *thecollegepanda.com/sat-score-calculator*

Section 3

1. [C] Manipulating & Solving Equations
2. [A] Constructing Models
3. [B] Ratio & Proportion
4. [C] Triangles
5. [B] Constructing Models
6. [C] Functions
7. [C] Interpreting Linear Models
8. [B] Exponents & Radicals
9. [D] Manipulating & Solving Equations
10. [C] Constructing Models
11. [B] Systems of Equations
12. [A] Trigonometry
13. [C] Expressions
14. [A] Inequalities
15. [A] More Equation Solving Strategies
16. [24] Rates
17. [1 or 2] Exponents & Radicals
18. [9] Expressions
19. [5] Systems of Equations
20. [14] Word Problems

Section 4

1. [B] Exponential vs. Linear Growth
2. [D] Rates
3. [B] Percent
4. [A] Probability
5. [C] Expressions
6. [B] Statistics I
7. [A] Rates
8. [C] Reading Data
9. [A] Circles
10. [C] Inequalities
11. [D] Word Problems
12. [C] Reading Data
13. [B] Interpreting Linear Models
14. [B] Constructing Models
15. [D] Exponential vs. Linear Growth
16. [B] Manipulating & Solving Equations
17. [D] Systems of Equations
18. [A] Volume
19. [B] Statistics II
20. [D] Lines
21. [C] Lines
22. [D] Percent
23. [D] Functions

24. [B] Statistics I
25. [B] Statistics II
26. [C] Statistics II / Quadratics
27. [B] Functions
28. [B] Rates
29. [C] Word Problems
30. [A] Quadratics
31. [72] Angles
32. [55] Percent
33. [29] Functions
34. [$\frac{1}{2}$] Manipulating & Solving Equations
35. [16] Triangles
36. [6] Systems of Equations
37. [5] Inequalities
38. [20] Trigonometry

Practice Test 6 Answer Explanations

Section 3

1. $\boxed{C}$

$$12y^2 = \frac{12}{49}$$

$$y^2 = \frac{1}{49}$$

$$y = \frac{1}{7}$$

2. $\boxed{A}$ $\dfrac{36a}{12} + \dfrac{24w}{6} = 3a + 4w$

3. $\boxed{B}$ For answer choice (B), $\dfrac{m}{n} = \dfrac{\frac{2}{8}}{3} = 2 \times \dfrac{3}{8} = \dfrac{6}{8} = \dfrac{3}{4}$

4. $\boxed{C}$ The two right triangles are similar. The sides of the triangle on the right are one-fourth the length of those of the triangle on the left. Therefore, $a = \dfrac{1}{4}b$, which gives $b = 4a$.

5. $\boxed{B}$ Jacob reads at a rate of $23 \div 50 = 0.46$ pages per minute. Therefore, he reads $0.46t$ pages in t minutes. The number of remaining pages is the total number of pages minus what he has read: $740 - 0.46t$

6. $\boxed{C}$ $f(x^2 + 4)$ means "replace x with $x^2 + 4$." So, $f(x^2 + 4) = \sqrt{x^2 + 4} + 1$. There is no simplification that can be done.

7. $\boxed{C}$ The number 3 refers to the slope, which means each additional form a doctor has to fill out reduces the average time the doctor spends with each patient by 3 minutes.

8. $\boxed{B}$ $\sqrt[4]{h^{8b}k^3} = (h^{8b}k^3)^{\frac{1}{4}} = h^{\frac{8b}{4}}k^{\frac{3}{4}} = h^{2b}k^{\frac{3}{4}}$

9. $\boxed{D}$

$$\frac{2a + 2b}{3c + 3d} = 1$$

Multiply both sides by 3 and then divide both sides by 2:

$$\frac{a + b}{c + d} = \frac{3}{2}$$

Now multiply both sides by 3 and divide both sides by 4 to get the desired fraction:

$$\frac{3a + 3b}{4c + 4d} = \frac{3}{2} \cdot \frac{3}{4} = \frac{9}{8}$$

10. $\boxed{C}$ Pre-tax, the total price of the tacos is $5x$. The price of each burger is $2x$, so 7 burgers cost $14x$. The total pre-tax price is then $5x + 14x = 19x$. After tax, the total bill is $1.05(19x)$.

11. $\boxed{B}$ Multiply the first equation by 2 and subtract to get $9y = 36$, $y = 4$. Substituting this into the first equation,

$$5x + 4 = 9$$
$$5x = 5$$
$$x = 1$$

12. $\boxed{A}$ Draw a line from point A to the x-axis to form a right triangle. We're given the hypotenuse and n happens to be the length of the opposite side to angle θ. What trig function relates the opposite side to the hypotenuse? Sine!

$$\sin \theta = \frac{n}{5}$$
$$5 \sin \theta = n$$

13. $\boxed{C}$ The common denominator is $(x + 2)(x - 1)$.

$$\frac{x + 1}{x + 2} - \frac{x - 2}{x - 1} = \frac{(x + 1)(x - 1) - (x - 2)(x + 2)}{(x + 2)(x - 1)}$$
$$= \frac{(x^2 - 1) - (x^2 - 4)}{(x + 2)(x - 1)}$$
$$= \frac{3}{(x + 2)(x - 1)}$$

14. $\boxed{A}$ The 20 jars of jelly have a total minimum weight of $20(0.8) = 16$ pounds and a total maximum weight of $20(2) = 40$ pounds. And since, in terms of w, the jars of jelly weigh a total of $w - 12$ pounds (subtract out the weight of the crate),

$$16 \leq w - 12 \leq 40$$

That's it. Here's another path to the solution: the entire shipment, including the crate, has a minimum weight of $16 + 12$ pounds and a maximum weight of $40 + 12$ pounds:

$$16 + 12 \leq w \leq 40 + 12$$

Subtracting 12 from each part of the inequality, we get the same answer as before:

$$16 \leq w - 12 \leq 40$$

15. $\boxed{A}$ **Solution 1:** Factor the right-hand side (how to factor is outside the scope of this book).

$$(mx + c)(nx + 3) = (3x - 1)(4x + 3)$$

By comparing the coefficients on both sides, we can see that $m = 3$ and $n = 4$. Finally, $m + n = 7$.

Solution 2: Expand the left hand side to compare coefficients.

$$mnx^2 + cnx + 3mx + 3c = 12x^2 + 5x - 3$$
$$mnx^2 + (cn + 3m)x + 3c = 12x^2 + 5x - 3$$

So, $3c = -3$ and $cn + 3m = 5$ and $mn = 12$. So, $c = -1$ and we're left with the following two equations:

$$\begin{cases} 3m - n = 5 \\ mn = 12 \end{cases}$$

You could solve these by substituting the first equation into the second, but with a little mental trial and error, it's easy to guess that $m = 3, n = 4$. Therefore, $m + n = 7$.

16. $\boxed{24}$ The computer will have a total of $2 + 4 = 6$ memory cards, which will contribute a total $6 \times 4 = 24$ gigabytes of memory.

17. $\boxed{1 \text{ or } 2}$ Since $c^{-3d} = \dfrac{1}{c^{3d}} = \dfrac{1}{64}$,

$$c^{3d} = 64$$

Using intuition or guess-and-check, both $4^3 = 64$ and $2^6 = 64$. In the first case, $c = 4$ and $3d = 3$, which gives $d = 1$. In the second case, $c = 2$ and $3d = 6$, which gives $d = 2$.

18. $\boxed{9}$

$$(75x^2 - 20) - 10(6 + 7x^2) = 75x^2 - 20 - 60 - 70x^2 = 5x^2 - 80 = 5(x^2 - 16) = 5(x + 4)(x - 4)$$

Therefore, $a + b = 5 + 4 = 9$.

19. $\boxed{5}$ For the system to have infinitely many solutions, the equations must be the same. We divide the first equation by 4 to get the 36 to match the 9 in the second equation. Doing this gives $c = \dfrac{5}{4}$ and $d = 16 \div 4 = 4$. Finally, $cd = \dfrac{5}{4} \times 4 = 5$

20. $\boxed{14}$ The tank currently contains $0.20(7)$ liters of acid. If we let x be the number of liters of 35% acid solution that should be added, then the tank will contain an additional $0.35x$ liters of acid.

$$\frac{0.20(7) + 0.35x}{7 + x} = 0.30$$
$$1.4 + 0.35x = 0.30(7 + x)$$
$$1.4 + 0.35x = 2.1 + 0.30x$$
$$0.05x = 0.7$$
$$x = 14$$

Section 4

1. $\boxed{B}$ Scatterplot B is more spread apart and doesn't form a straight line as closely as the other answer choices do.

2. $\boxed{D}$ $2 \text{ gallons} \times \dfrac{128 \text{ fluid ounces}}{1 \text{ gallon}} \times 0.75 = 192 \text{ fluid ounces}$

3. $\boxed{B}$ $\dfrac{447 - 292}{292} \approx 0.53 = 53\%$

4. $\boxed{A}$

$$\frac{\text{Received 2 shots and contracted the flu}}{\text{All students}} = \frac{6}{108} = \frac{1}{18}$$

5. $\boxed{C}$ Expand and combine like terms.

$$6xy + 3xyz + 3yz - 3xy - 5xyz + 2yz = 3xy - 2xyz + 5yz$$

6. $\boxed{B}$

$$\frac{(20 \times 1) + (21 \times 3) + (22 \times 4) + (24 \times 1) + (25 \times 1)}{1 + 3 + 4 + 1 + 1} = \frac{220}{10} = 22$$

7. $\boxed{A}$ $\dfrac{120 \text{ feet}}{1 \text{ minute}} \times \dfrac{1 \text{ lap}}{160 \text{ feet}} \times \dfrac{60 \text{ minutes}}{1 \text{ hour}} = \dfrac{45 \text{ laps}}{1 \text{ hour}}$

8. $\boxed{C}$ From the graph, the density of Liquid X at 9 degrees Celsius is 60 kg/L. Ten liters of Liquid X has a mass of

$$10 \text{ L} \times \frac{60 \text{ kg}}{L} = 600 \text{ kg}$$

This is closest to the 500 in answer choice (C).

9. $\boxed{A}$ Converting radians to degrees,

$$\frac{\pi}{10} \text{ radians} \times \frac{180°}{\pi \text{ radians}} = 18°$$

Because segment $\overline{AB}$ is tangent to the circle, $\angle OAB = 90°$. The central angle AOB is then $180 - 18 - 90 = 72°$, which is $\dfrac{72°}{360°} = \dfrac{1}{5}$ of $360°$. This means that the sector is $\dfrac{1}{5}$ of the circle. Since the area of the sector is π, the area of the entire circle must be 5π.

10. $\boxed{C}$ The estimated maximum heart rate for a 30-year-old is $220 - 30 = 190$. Fifty percent of that is 95 and eighty percent of that is 152. Therefore, $95 \le h \le 152$.

11. $\boxed{D}$ Let the number of pages of the smaller book be x. The larger book then has $x + 50$ pages.

$$x + (x + 50) = 400$$
$$2x + 50 = 400$$
$$2x = 350$$
$$x = 175$$

The longer book has $175 + 50 = 225$ pages.

12. $\boxed{C}$ Since 2011 is 6 years after 2005, we look at the values at $t = 6$. From the graph, Brazil consumed 50 tons of lithium and 90 tons of nickel, giving a combined total of $50 + 90 = 140$ tons.

13. $\boxed{B}$ Since a is the slope, the change in "y" (nickel consumption) over the change in "x" (years), a must represent the change in nickel consumption per year. In other words, it's the predicted annual increase in nickel consumption.

14. $\boxed{B}$ When $t = 0$, the annual difference d is $30 - 20 = 10$. When $t = 1$, the annual difference d is about $40 - 25 = 15$. Therefore, if d is modeled by the equation of a line, its slope should be $15 - 10 = 5$ and its y-intercept should be 10: $d = 5t + 10$.

15. $\boxed{D}$ The number of ants doubles every 4 months—a case of exponential growth. The standard equation for exponential growth is $y = ab^{\frac{t}{k}}$, where a is the initial population and k is the time required for the population to increase by one factor of b. Note that t and k must have the same units (e.g. months). In the context of this problem, $a = 3000$, $b = 2$, and $k = 4$. Therefore, $A(t) = 3,000 \cdot 2^{\frac{t}{4}}$.

An alternative solution is to test the answer choices by plugging in enough values from the table to narrow them down to one. For example, testing answer (D), we plug in $t = 8$ to get $3,000 \cdot 2^{8/4} = 3,000 \cdot 2^2 = 12,000$, which lines up with the number listed in the table. In fact, answer (D) is the only one that gives the correct result for all the values of t in the table.

16. $\boxed{B}$ Divide both sides by 3,

$$(a + b) = \frac{2}{9}$$

Then

$$\frac{a + b}{2} = \frac{\frac{2}{9}}{2} = \frac{1}{9}$$

17. $\boxed{D}$ Getting the first equation into $y = mx + b$ form,

$$y = -\frac{3}{2}x + \frac{5}{2}$$

Doing the same for the second equation,

$$y = \frac{3}{2}x + \frac{5}{2}$$

The slopes are not the same nor is one the negative reciprocal of the other. Therefore, the two lines intersect but are not perpendicular.

18. $\boxed{A}$ At a depth of half the cone's height, the radius is 3 (similar triangles).

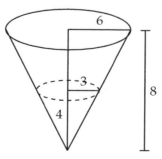

The volume of the water (the smaller cone) is $V = \frac{1}{3}\pi r^2 h = \frac{1}{3}\pi(3)^2(4) = 12\pi$.

19. $\boxed{B}$ I does not have to be true. Just because 40 employees walk to work does not mean that the remaining 160 drive a car to work. Maybe they commute by bus. II does not have to be true either. Doubling the sample size from 200 to 400 does not mean that you'll get exactly double the number of employees who walk to work (from 40 to 80). It's likely you'll get a number near 80 instead. III must be true since 160 out of the 200 surveyed do not walk to work.

20. $\boxed{D}$ Continuing the line, you should see that the slope is -2 and the y-intercept is 4.

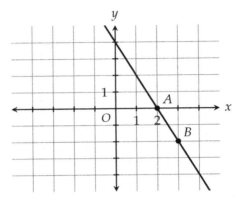

21. $\boxed{C}$ A slope of 6 means up 6 units for every 1 unit to the right, or down 6 units for every 1 unit to the left. Starting from point A, the point $(3,6)$ is 6 units up and 1 unit to the right. Therefore, $(3,6)$ is on line l.

22. $\boxed{D}$

$$\text{this year} = (0.70)(\text{last year})$$
$$270{,}000 = (0.70)(\text{last year})$$
$$386{,}000 \approx \text{last year}$$

23. $\boxed{D}$ The graph of g is 2 units up from where f is.

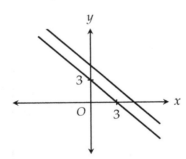

It's easy to see that both the x and y intercepts are increased by 2. Therefore, the x-intercept is 5.

24. $\boxed{B}$ The distribution of jean sizes for Store A is more clustered around a single number (29) than the distribution for Store B, which is spread out equally over all sizes. Therefore, the standard deviation for Store B is larger.

25. $\boxed{B}$ At a value of 20 along the x-axis, the best fit curve gives a value of 15 along the y-axis.

26. $\boxed{C}$ In this case, the vertex is the lowest point on the best fit curve. Furthermore, none of the data points fall below the vertex. Therefore, the vertex can be interpreted as the number of applications for a job that requires the least amount of time to fill. Note that the answer is not (B). From the point $(10, 15)$ on the best fit curve, the minimal number of applications required to fill a job within 15 days is 10, and this point is clearly not the vertex.

27. $\boxed{B}$ To compress $g(x)$ horizontally by a factor of 2, substitute $2x$ for x:

$$g(2x)$$

To shift $g(x)$ to the right by 1 unit, substitute $x - 1$ for x:

$$f(x) = g(2(x - 1)) = g(2x - 2)$$

28. $\boxed{B}$ On the original test, it would take Aaron $42 \div 3.5 = 12$ minutes to finish the 42 medium questions. After these medium questions are replaced with 42 hard questions, it will take him $42 \div 2.4 = 17.5$ minutes instead. That's a difference of $17.5 - 12 = 5.5$ minutes for those 42 questions. Note that we don't care about the 28 easy questions or the original 30 hard questions because they didn't change. Aaron would take the same amount of time on those questions regardless. Therefore, Aaron will take 5.5 more minutes to finish the test.

29. $\boxed{C}$ Let the number of students be s.

$$\frac{s}{10} + \frac{s}{15} + \frac{s}{30} = k$$
$$3s + 2s + s = 30k$$
$$6s = 30k$$
$$s = 5k$$

30. $\boxed{A}$ The x-intercepts of the parabola are $\frac{1}{2}$ and $\frac{11}{2}$. The x-coordinate of the vertex is the average of these two values.

$$\left(\frac{1}{2} + \frac{11}{2}\right) \div 2 = 6 \div 2 = 3$$

At $x = 3$, $y = (2(3) - 1)(2(3) - 11) = (5)(-5) = -25$. Therefore, the vertex is at $(3, -25)$.

31. $\boxed{72}$ Because MN is a line,

$$5a = 180$$
$$a = 36$$

Now, $b = 2a = 2(36) = 72$.

32. $\boxed{55}$ Calculators that require AAA batteries: $550(0.10) = 55$. Alarm clocks that require AAA batteries: $440(0.25) = 110$. Difference: $110 - 55 = 55$.

33. $\boxed{29}$ If $2f(b) = 28$, then $f(b) = 14$. Solving for b,

$$f(b) = 3b - 1$$
$$14 = 3b - 1$$
$$15 = 3b$$
$$5 = b$$

Finally, $f(2b) = f(10) = 3(10) - 1 = 29$.

34. $\boxed{\dfrac{1}{2}}$ Multiply both sides by x.

$$10x + 6 = 22x$$
$$6 = 12x$$
$$\frac{1}{2} = x$$

35. $\boxed{16}$ From the 6–8–10 triangle and the $30°$–$60°$–$90°$ triangle relationship, $BD = 16$.

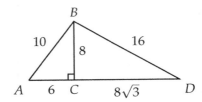

36. $\boxed{6}$ To get the intersection points, solve the system consisting of the two equations.

$$y = x^2 - 7x + 9$$
$$y = 9 - x$$

Substituting the second equation into the first, we get

$$9 - x = x^2 - 7x + 9$$
$$0 = x^2 - 6x$$
$$0 = x(x - 6)$$

Therefore, the x-coordinates of the intersection points are 0 and 6, which means $m = 6$.

37. $\boxed{5}$ Split the inequality up into two parts. In the first part,

$$9 \leq -5x - 6$$
$$15 \leq -5x$$
$$-3 \geq x$$

In the second part,

$$-5x - 6 \leq 34$$
$$-5x \leq 40$$
$$x \geq -8$$

Putting the two results together, $-8 \leq x \leq -3$. The greatest possible value of x is -3 and the least possible value of x is -8.

$$a - b = -3 - (-8) = 5$$

38. $\boxed{20}$ Since $\sin D = \dfrac{4}{5}$, $CE{:}DE$ = 4:5 (opposite over hypotenuse), and because we're dealing with a right triangle, $DC{:}CE{:}DE$ = 3:4:5 by the pythagorean theorem (it works even when we're dealing with ratios). Hopefully you have the 3–4–5 triangle memorized. Now $\overline{AB}$ and $\overline{CD}$ are parallel, so $\angle BAE \cong \angle CDE$. Vertical angles $\angle AEB$ and $\angle CED$ are also congruent. Therefore, triangles $\triangle ABE$ and $\triangle DCE$ are similar, and the ratio of the corresponding sides of $\triangle ABE$ must also be 3:4:5. Since AB corresponds with DC, BE corresponds with CE, and AE corresponds with DE, $AB{:}BE{:}AE$ = 3:4:5. Finally, $AB = 12$, so AE must be $(12 \div 3) \times 5 = 20$.

Practice Test 7 Answers

Question categories correspond to chapters in *The College Panda's SAT Math: The Advanced Guide and Workbook*. To estimate your score, visit *thecollegepanda.com/sat-score-calculator*

Section 3

1. C Exponents & Radicals
2. D Constructing Models
3. C Expressions
4. B Interpreting Linear Models
5. C Expressions
6. D Lines
7. A Expressions
8. A Percent
9. B Manipulating & Solving Equations
10. C Interpreting Linear Models
11. B Lines
12. C Trigonometry
13. D Inequalities
14. C Quadratics
15. C Circles / Manipulating & Solving Equations
16. 800 Rates
17. 4 Systems of Equations
18. $\frac{1}{3}$ Triangles
19. $5 \text{ or } 13$ Functions
20. 2 Synthetic Division

Section 4

1. A Statistics I
2. C Rates
3. C Reading Data
4. D Statistics II
5. C Expressions
6. B Reading Data
7. A Reading Data / Percent
8. C Functions
9. A Circles
10. D Exponential vs. Linear Growth
11. D Quadratics
12. D Statistics II
13. C Percent
14. B Rates
15. C Functions
16. B Systems of Equations
17. B Lines
18. D Statistics II
19. A Manipulating & Solving Equations
20. C Ratio & Proportion
21. C Statistics I
22. B Functions
23. B Manipulating & Solving Equations
24. A Probability
25. B Absolute Value
26. B Systems of Equations
27. B Word Problems
28. D Inequalities
29. B Inequalities
30. D Triangles
31. $\frac{5}{4}$ Manipulating & Solving Equations
32. 4 Reading Data
33. 8.75 Interpreting Linear Models
34. 11 Rates
35. 50 Angles
36. 7 Functions
37. 5 Statistics II
38. 3 Statistics II

Practice Test 7 Answer Explanations

Section 3

1. $\boxed{C}$

$$\sqrt[3]{x^2} \cdot \sqrt{x^3} = x^{\frac{2}{3}} \cdot x^{\frac{3}{2}} = x^{\frac{2}{3}+\frac{3}{2}} = x^{\frac{13}{6}}$$

2. $\boxed{D}$ After m months, he loses mx pounds. His total weight is then $230 - mx$.

3. $\boxed{C}$

$$ab = (b+c) \cdot b = b^2 + bc$$

4. $\boxed{B}$ The slope of the line is 25, which means the monthly insurance premium increases by 25 for each car accident.

5. $\boxed{C}$ Split the fraction up into two parts.

$$\frac{3x-2}{12x^2} = \frac{3x}{12x^2} - \frac{2}{12x^2} = \frac{1}{4x} - \frac{1}{6x^2}$$

6. $\boxed{D}$ A line that is perpendicular to the y-axis is a horizontal one. Since it passes through $(3,4)$, the horizontal line must be $y = 4$.

7. $\boxed{A}$ The given expression is in the pattern of $(a+b)(a-b) = a^2 - b^2$, where $a = m+n$ and $b = 1$. Therefore, the expression is equivalent to $(m+n)^2 - 1^2$, which is equal to $m^2 + 2mn + n^2 - 1$.

8. $\boxed{A}$ Jonas bought the jacket for $0.8x$. Together, the two jackets cost $x + 0.8x = 1.8x$. After the 10 percent tax, the final price is $1.1(1.8x)$. Remember from the percent chapter that we multiply by 1.1 for a 10 percent increase.

9. $\boxed{B}$

$$p = at^3 - bt + c$$

$$p - at^3 - c = -bt$$

$$\frac{at^3 + c - p}{t} = b$$

10. $\boxed{C}$ The number 16,000 is the y-intercept of the equation, Jake's total monthly revenue when he has no franchise locations. The 16,000 must be the monthly revenue generated by Jake's own restaurant.

11. $\boxed{B}$ Since the function is linear, $f(x)$ must go up (or down) by the same amount for each unit change in x. From $x = 5$ to $x = 6$, $f(x)$ increases by 4. Therefore, m must be $-10 + 4 = -6$ and n must be $2 + 4 = 6$, which means $m + n = -6 + 6 = 0$.

12. $\boxed{C}$

$$c \sin \theta = c \times \frac{a}{c} = a$$

13. $\boxed{D}$ The students as a whole receive $3s$ textbooks and the teachers as a whole receive $2t$ textbooks. Since the school has no more than 800 textbooks, $3s + 2t \leq 800$. Now, there is at least one teacher for every 15 students, which means $t \geq \dfrac{s}{15}$. Notice that when $s = 15$, $t \geq 1$ and when $s = 30$, $t \geq 2$, as required. Multiplying both sides of this inequality by 15, we get $s \leq 15t$.

14. $\boxed{C}$ Using the quadratic formula,

$$x = \frac{-3b \pm \sqrt{(3b)^2 - 4(1)(2b^2)}}{2(1)} = \frac{-3b \pm \sqrt{9b^2 - 8b^2}}{2} = \frac{-3b \pm b}{2}$$

So,

$$x = \frac{-3b - b}{2} = -2b \text{ or } x = \frac{-3b + b}{2} = -b$$

We also could've factored to get directly to the answer.

$$x^2 + 3bx + 2b^2 = (x + 2b)(x + b)$$

15. $\boxed{C}$ The perimeter of a semicircle is half the circumference of a circle and two radii: $\pi r + 2r$

$$P = \pi r + 2r$$
$$P = r(\pi + 2)$$
$$\frac{P}{\pi + 2} = r$$

16. $\boxed{800}$ Four printers of the same type can print $50 \times 4 = 200$ pages in 3 minutes.

$$12 \cancel{\text{ minutes}} \times \frac{200 \text{ pages}}{3 \cancel{\text{ minutes}}} = 800 \text{ pages}$$

17. $\boxed{4}$ Multiply the second equation by 2 and add to get $-y = -3$, which means $y = 3$. Plugging this value into the second equation,

$$-x + 3 = -1$$
$$-x = -4$$
$$x = 4$$

18. $\boxed{\dfrac{1}{3}}$ Because the angles of a triangle add up to $180°$, which is equivalent to π radians, the measure of the third angle must be $\pi - \dfrac{\pi}{6} - \dfrac{\pi}{2} = \dfrac{6}{6}\pi - \dfrac{1}{6}\pi - \dfrac{3}{6}\pi = \dfrac{2}{6}\pi = \dfrac{1}{3}\pi$. Therefore, $k = \dfrac{1}{3}$.

19. $\boxed{5 \text{ or } 13}$

$$f(a-2) = 25$$
$$((a-2)-7)^2 + 9 = 25$$
$$(a-9)^2 = 16$$
$$a-9 = \pm 4$$
$$a = 9 \pm 4 = 5 \text{ or } 13$$

20. $\boxed{2}$ If $x+1$ is a factor of $p(x)$, then the remainder is 0 when $p(x)$ is divided by $x+1$. Using the remainder theorem,

$$p(-1) = 0$$
$$4(-1)^3 - k(-1) + k = 0$$
$$-4 + 2k = 0$$
$$2k = 4$$
$$k = 2$$

Section 4

1. $\boxed{A}$

$$\frac{\text{Total} - \text{Sat} - \text{Sun}}{5} = \frac{27,615 - 6,230 - 5,695}{5} = 3,138$$

2. $\boxed{C}$

$$3 \text{ miles} \times \frac{5280 \text{ feet}}{1 \text{ mile}} \times \frac{61 \text{ cm}}{2 \text{ feet}} = 483,120 \text{ cm}$$

3. $\boxed{C}$ The peak of the graph occurs at around age 25.

4. $\boxed{D}$ If 37.5% think that new computers are a higher priority, then $100 - 37.5 = 62.5\%$ think new textbooks are a higher priority.

$$62.5\% \text{ of } 2,200 = (0.625)(2,200) = 1,375$$

5. $\boxed{C}$ Since $(a+b)^2 = a^2 + 2ab + b^2$ and $(a-b)^2 = a^2 - 2ab + b^2$,

$$(1.4x + 2.5)^2 = (1.4x)^2 + 2(1.4x)(2.5) + (2.5)^2 = 1.96x^2 + 7x + 6.25$$
$$(1.4x - 2.5)^2 = (1.4x)^2 - 2(1.4x)(2.5) + (2.5)^2 = 1.96x^2 - 7x + 6.25$$

Therefore, $(1.4x + 2.5)^2 - (1.4x - 2.5)^2 = (1.96x^2 + 7x + 6.25) - (1.96x^2 - 7x + 6.25) = 14x$.

6. $\boxed{B}$ Bates: $\frac{40}{60} = \frac{2}{3}$. Bentley: $\frac{60}{80} = \frac{3}{4}$. Collins: $\frac{50}{75} = \frac{2}{3}$. Only Bates and Collins.

7. $\boxed{A}$ In 2012, the total budget was $35 + 60 + 80 + 75 = 250$. In 2013, the total budget was $50 + 40 + 60 + 50 = 200$. The percent decrease is

$$\frac{200 - 250}{250} \times 100 = -20\%$$

8. $\boxed{C}$ You have to do a little guessing and checking. There are two outputs for $f(x)$: $x + 2$ and $x - 2$. Let's try to get the output to be 1. For the output to be 1, x must equal -1 if we're looking at $x + 2$. However, this can't be possible because $x + 2$ is the output only if $x \geq 0$. In the second case, $x = 3$ if we're looking at $x - 2$. However, this also can't be possible because $x - 2$ is the output only if $x < 0$. Therefore, 1 can never be the output of $f(x)$. All the other answer choices are possible to obtain using valid values of x.

9. $\boxed{A}$ The center of the circle is at $(0,3)$. Its radius is $\sqrt{25} = 5$. Therefore, the circle intersects the y-axis at $(0, 3 + 5) = (0, 8)$ and $(0, 3 - 5) = (0, -2)$.

10. $\boxed{D}$ The value of the house is always 0.75 of what it was the previous year. Because this rate is less than 1, it is exponential decay.

11. $\boxed{D}$ There are two ways to do this question. We could expand everything out and complete the square, but the faster way is find the x-coordinate of the vertex by averaging the x-intercepts, -4 and 6, to get 1. The only answer choice that contains 1 as a constant is answer (D). It's also the only answer choice in vertex form.

12. $\boxed{D}$ The customers who chose the sandwich themselves are probably not representative of all the customers of the restaurant. People who regularly buys salads, for example, would likely be excluded from the results.

13. $\boxed{C}$ The total balance in the account after 3 years is $1000(1.04)^3$. Subtracting the initial deposit of \$1,000 from the total balance gives us the total interest earned: $1000(1.04)^3 - 1000 \approx \$125$.

14. $\boxed{B}$ At the official exchange rate, James would receive

$$800 \text{ U.S. dollars} \times \frac{1 \text{ euro}}{1.40 \text{ U.S. dollars}} \approx 571.54 \text{ euros}$$

At the airport rate, he would receive

$$800 \text{ U.S. dollars} \times \frac{1 \text{ euro}}{1.55 \text{ U.S. dollars}} \approx 516.13 \text{ euros}$$

That's a difference of $571.54 - 516.13 \approx 55$ euros.

15. $\boxed{C}$

$$f(k) = g(k)$$
$$k^2 - 3k = 2k + 14$$
$$k^2 - 5k - 14 = 0$$
$$(k - 7)(k + 2) = 0$$
$$k = 7, -2$$

There are two values of k for which $f(k) = g(k)$, which means f and g intersect two times.

16. $\boxed{B}$ Let d be the cost of a doll and c be the cost of a toy car. Based on the information, we can form the following two equations:

$$2d + 3c = 88$$
$$3d + 2c = 62$$

Add the two equations to get $5d + 5c = 150$. Divide both sides by 5 to get $d + c = 30$.

17. $\boxed{B}$ The slope between the first and second points must be the same as the slope between the second and third points.

$$\frac{7-3}{-2-0} = \frac{k-7}{5-(-2)}$$

$$-2 = \frac{k-7}{7}$$

$$-14 = k-7$$

$$-7 = k$$

18. $\boxed{D}$ Answer D is the most reasonable. Since the <u>mean</u> salary for the sample was \$100,000 with a \$10,000 margin of error, it's likely that the <u>mean</u> salary for all Chicago engineers is \$100,000, give or take \$10,000. Answers A, B, and C are wrong because the given data only allow us to draw conclusions about the mean salary, not the actual salaries of Chicago engineers. For instance, it's possible for the mean to be \$100,000 without any engineer actually having a \$100,000 salary (e.g. half the engineers have \$50,000 salaries while the other half have \$150,000 salaries). That's why answer A is wrong. Answer B is wrong for pretty much the same reason. A mean salary between \$90,000 and \$110,000 does not require that all Chicago engineers have a salary in that range. Finally, answer C is wrong because the mean doesn't tell us anything about how likely any given engineer is above or below it. It's possible that all Chicago engineers have salaries below \$100,000 except a few who make millions of dollars and skew the mean upwards.

19. $\boxed{A}$

$$T = \frac{2m_1 m_2}{m_1 + m_2} g$$

$$T(m_1 + m_2) = 2m_1 m_2 g$$

$$\frac{T(m_1 + m_2)}{2m_1 m_2} = g$$

20. $\boxed{C}$ The tension would be doubled.

$$T_{old} = \frac{2m_1 m_2}{m_1 + m_2} g$$

$$T_{new} = \frac{2(2m_1)(2m_2)}{2m_1 + 2m_2} g = \frac{4(2m_1 m_2)}{2(m_1 + m_2)} g = 2T_{old}$$

21. $\boxed{C}$ For these types of questions, we must calculate the lower limit and the upper limit of the average.

$$\text{Lower Limit} = \frac{(30 \times 2) + (60 \times 4) + (90 \times 3) + (120 \times 1) + (150 \times 5)}{15} = 96$$

$$\text{Upper Limit} = \frac{(60 \times 2) + (90 \times 4) + (120 \times 3) + (150 \times 1) + (180 \times 5)}{15} = 126$$

The only answer choice between these two limits is 123.

22. $\boxed{B}$

$$f(5) = f(2+3) = f(2) - 3 = 10 - 3 = 7$$

23. $\boxed{B}$ Expand.

$$(x^2 + 2xy + y^2) - (x^2 - 2xy + y^2) = 60$$
$$4xy = 60$$
$$xy = 15$$

$x + y$ is 8 when $x = 3$ and $y = 5$.

24. $\boxed{A}$ For marketing, the proportion is $\dfrac{6+7}{24} \approx 0.54$. For engineering, the proportion is $\dfrac{4+4}{25} = 0.32$. For accounting, the proportion is $\dfrac{1+15}{37} \approx 0.43$. For human resources, the proportion is $\dfrac{2+5}{14} \approx 0.50$. The department with the highest proportion is marketing.

25. $\boxed{B}$ Here's the rule: the distance between two points on a number line is equal to the absolute value of their difference. The difference between a and -5 is $a - (-5) = a + 5$. Therefore, $|a + 5| = 8$. Done another way, a must be 8 units from -5 so the two possible values are $-5 - 8 = -13$ and $-5 + 8 = 3$. When we plug in those values for a in each of the answer choices, only answer B checks out for both.

26. $\boxed{B}$ We can factor the first equation into $(x + y)(x - y) = 48$. Since the second equation tells us that $x + y = 12$, we can use this in the first equation: $12(x - y) = 48$, $x - y = 4$. We now have the following two equations:

$$x + y = 12$$
$$x - y = 4$$

Subtracting the two equations to eliminate x, we get $2y = 8$, $y = 4$. From here, $x = 8$ and $xy = 32$.

27. $\boxed{B}$ If we let x be the number of ounces a medium glass holds, then each large glass holds $x + 3$ ounces. Since both pitchers contained an equal amount of water, we can set up the following equation:

$$8x = 6(x + 3)$$
$$8x = 6x + 18$$
$$2x = 18$$
$$x = 9$$

Therefore, each pitcher contained $8x = 8(9) = 72$ ounces of water originally.

28. $\boxed{D}$ The minimum value of T is $60(1) + 80(6) = 540$ minutes, which is $540 \div 60 = 9$ hours. The maximum value of T is $60(5) + 80(12) = 1,260$ minutes, which is $1,260 \div 60 = 21$ hours. Therefore, $9 \le T \le 21$.

29. $\boxed{B}$ If the processing times are cut in half, then for the 60 orders, $0.5 \le t \le 2.5$, and for the 80 orders, $3 \le t \le 6$. Therefore, the processing time of an order cannot be between 2.5 minutes and 3 minutes. The only answer choice in this interval is (B). By the way, the processing time also can't be under 0.5 minutes or above 6 minutes, but none of the answer choices are outside these bounds.

30. $\boxed{D}$ $\triangle ABC$ is a 3–4–5 triangle.

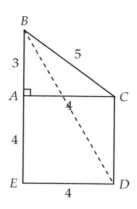

Using the pythagorean theorem to find BD,

$$BE^2 + ED^2 = BD^2$$
$$7^2 + 4^2 = BD^2$$
$$65 = BD^2$$
$$\sqrt{65} = BD$$

31. $\boxed{\dfrac{5}{4}}$ Substitute the first equation into the second:

$$\left(\frac{2}{3b}\right)x = \frac{5}{6b}$$
$$\frac{2}{3}x = \frac{5}{6}$$
$$x = \frac{5}{6} \cdot \frac{3}{2} = \frac{5}{4}$$

32. $\boxed{4}$ From the graph, 279 kelvin is equivalent to 6 degrees Celsius. This is $6 - 2 = 4$ degrees greater than what the student calculated.

33. $\boxed{8.75}$ The slope of the equation is $\dfrac{7}{4}$, or 1.75, which means the length of a garden snake increases by 1.75 inches each month. So over 5 months, the length increases by $5 \times 1.75 = 8.75$.

34. $\boxed{11}$ Alice bought $\dfrac{108}{12} = 9$ chairs. Since the store gives away a free chair for every four chairs purchased, she received an extra 2 chairs for a total of 11 chairs.

35. $\boxed{50}$

$$5x + 4x = 180$$
$$9x = 180$$
$$x = 20$$

So, the measure of $\angle A$ is $2x = 2(20) = 40$. Using $\triangle ABC$,

$$y = 180 - 40 - 90 = 50$$

36. $\boxed{7}$ The maximum value (highest y-value) is 4. The minimum value (lowest y-value) is -3. The difference is $4 - (-3) = 7$.

37. $\boxed{5}$ To understand what this question is asking for, let's analyze each data point one by one.

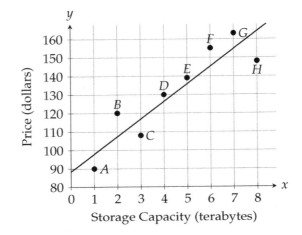

For Brandon to consider a hard drive device, there must be no other device in the scatterplot that has both greater storage capacity and lower price. So will Brandon consider device A? Yes, because while all the other devices have greater storage capacities, none of them have a lower price. How about device B? No, because device C has greater storage capacity and a lower price. And will device C be considered? Yes, because none of the devices with greater storage capacities (D through H) have a lower price. The same logic applies for devices D and E. They will be considered. Device F won't be considered because device H has greater storage capacity and a lower price. The same goes for device G. Finally, device H will be considered. In summary, Brandon will choose from devices A, C, D, E, and H—a total of 5 devices.

38. $\boxed{3}$ Draw a horizontal line at the price of 120 dollars. Notice that this splits the scatterplot into two intervals. In the first interval, the horizontal line is above the line of best fit. In the second interval, the horizontal line is below the line of best fit. Since the price of the device is more than that predicted by the line of best fit, the device must have a storage capacity in the first interval (to the left of the intersection point between the horizontal line and the line of best fit). The greatest storage capacity over this interval is 3 terabytes (it must be a whole number).

Practice Test 8 Answers

Question categories correspond to chapters in *The College Panda's SAT Math: The Advanced Guide and Workbook*. To estimate your score, visit *thecollegepanda.com/sat-score-calculator*

Section 3

1. $\boxed{D}$ Manipulating & Solving Equations
2. $\boxed{A}$ Exponents & Radicals
3. $\boxed{C}$ Lines
4. $\boxed{D}$ Interpreting Linear Models
5. $\boxed{B}$ Absolute Value
6. $\boxed{B}$ Expressions
7. $\boxed{B}$ Functions
8. $\boxed{B}$ Constructing Models
9. $\boxed{C}$ Word Problems
10. $\boxed{C}$ Manipulating & Solving Equations
11. $\boxed{B}$ Functions
12. $\boxed{C}$ Inequalities
13. $\boxed{D}$ Manipulating & Solving Equations
14. $\boxed{A}$ Quadratics
15. $\boxed{C}$ Synthetic Division
16. $\boxed{19}$ Rates
17. $\boxed{8}$ Systems of Equations
18. $\boxed{1.2}$ Expressions
19. $\boxed{80}$ Circles
20. $\boxed{\dfrac{2}{5}}$ Word Problems

Section 4

1. $\boxed{B}$ Expressions
2. $\boxed{D}$ Manipulating & Solving Equations
3. $\boxed{C}$ Interpreting Linear Models
4. $\boxed{B}$ Statistics II
5. $\boxed{D}$ Percent
6. $\boxed{A}$ Rates
7. $\boxed{D}$ Reading Data
8. $\boxed{C}$ Reading Data
9. $\boxed{B}$ Percent
10. $\boxed{D}$ Probability
11. $\boxed{C}$ Ratio & Proportion
12. $\boxed{B}$ Inequalities
13. $\boxed{D}$ Probability
14. $\boxed{B}$ Constructing Models
15. $\boxed{C}$ Constructing Models
16. $\boxed{A}$ Rates
17. $\boxed{D}$ Systems of Equations
18. $\boxed{B}$ Triangles
19. $\boxed{A}$ Statistics I
20. $\boxed{A}$ Quadratics
21. $\boxed{D}$ Statistics II
22. $\boxed{C}$ Statistics II
23. $\boxed{C}$ Exponential vs. Linear Growth
24. $\boxed{C}$ Inequalities
25. $\boxed{A}$ Functions
26. $\boxed{B}$ Circles
27. $\boxed{C}$ Systems of Equations
28. $\boxed{B}$ Statistics II
29. $\boxed{C}$ Manipulating & Solving Equations
30. $\boxed{B}$ Inequalities
31. $\boxed{48}$ Rates
32. $\boxed{144}$ Angles
33. $\boxed{20}$ Trigonometry
34. $\boxed{1.2}$ Systems of Equations
35. $\boxed{3}$ Functions
36. $\boxed{36}$ Word Problems
37. $\boxed{25.6}$ Manipulating & Solving Equations
38. $\boxed{5}$ Manipulating & Solving Equations

Practice Test 8 Answer Explanations

Section 3

1. $\boxed{D}$

$$9x^2 = 40$$
$$x^2 = \frac{40}{9}$$
$$x = \sqrt{\frac{40}{9}}$$

2. $\boxed{A}$

$$\sqrt[3]{b^{\frac{1}{2}}} = \left(b^{\frac{1}{2}}\right)^{\frac{1}{3}} = b^{\frac{1}{6}}$$

3. $\boxed{C}$ If line k has a negative slope, any line perpendicular to it will have a positive slope.

4. $\boxed{D}$ The number 500 is the y-intercept of the equation, the number of shirts left in inventory on days when no coupons are given out.

5. $\boxed{B}$ Test each of the answer choices, making sure to include the negative possibilities. For example, the answer is not (A) because when $x = 1$ or -1, $|x + 3|$ is not less than 2. However, $|x + 3|$ is less than 2 when $x = -4$.

6. $\boxed{B}$ $(a + b)^2 - (a - b)^2 = (a^2 + 2ab + b^2) - (a^2 - 2ab + b^2) = 4ab$

7. $\boxed{B}$ The best way to do this question is to plug $x + 1$ into each of the answer choices and see which one gives $3x + 2$. Looking at answer (B), for example, $f(x + 1) = 3(x + 1) - 1 = 3x + 3 - 1 = 3x + 2$.

8. $\boxed{B}$ Each pen costs $\dfrac{4}{x}$ dollars and each notebook costs $\dfrac{6}{y}$ dollars. So 9 pens and 7 notebooks will cost $9\left(\dfrac{4}{x}\right) + 7\left(\dfrac{6}{y}\right)$ dollars.

9. $\boxed{C}$

$$0.30 + 0.02a = 5$$
$$0.02a = 5 - 0.30$$
$$a = \frac{5 - 0.30}{0.02}$$

10. $\boxed{C}$ Square both sides.

$$m^2 = \frac{1}{n}$$
$$nm^2 = 1$$
$$n = \frac{1}{m^2}$$

11. $\boxed{B}$ Since $f(800) = 320$,

$$320 = \frac{3}{8}\left(\frac{1}{2}(800) + 4k\right) + 50$$

$$320 = \frac{3}{8}(400 + 4k) + 50$$

$$320 = 150 + \frac{3}{2}k + 50$$

$$120 = \frac{3}{2}k$$

$$80 = k$$

12. $\boxed{C}$ The 12 chapters will take up a minimum of $(12)(9) = 108$ pages and a maximum of $(12)(15) = 180$ pages. Since the introduction is 10 pages, the total number of pages x will be greater than or equal to $108 + 10$ and less than or equal to $180 + 10$. In other words, $x \geq 108 + 10$ and $x \leq 180 + 10$, which is equivalent to saying $108 \leq x - 10 \leq 180$. Another way to think about it is that the 12 chapters will take up $x - 10$ pages. Since the 12 chapters will take up between 108 and 180 pages, $108 \leq x - 10 \leq 180$.

13. $\boxed{D}$ Square both sides.

$$(\sqrt{4 + \sqrt{x}})^2 = (1 + \sqrt{3})^2$$

$$4 + \sqrt{x} = 1^2 + 2\sqrt{3} + (\sqrt{3})^2$$

$$4 + \sqrt{x} = 4 + 2\sqrt{3}$$

$$\sqrt{x} = 2\sqrt{3}$$

$$\sqrt{x} = \sqrt{12}$$

$$x = 12$$

14. $\boxed{A}$ Substituting the first equation into the second,

$$3x - 1 = (x + 1)^2$$

$$3x - 1 = x^2 + 2x + 1$$

$$0 = x^2 - x + 2$$

The number of solutions to the equation above is equal to the number of solutions to the original system of equations. For example, if there is only one value of x that satisfies the equation above, there will be only one solution to the system. Using the discriminant,

$$b^2 - 4ac = (-1)^2 - 4(1)(2) = 1 - 8 = -7$$

Because the discriminant is negative, there are no solutions to the equation above, and therefore no solutions to the system of equations.

15. $\boxed{C}$

$$
\begin{array}{r}
x \quad - \quad 2 \\
2x-1 \overline{\big)\ 2x^2 \quad - \quad 5x \phantom{{}+2}} \\
2x^2 \quad - \quad x \phantom{{}+2} \\
\hline
- \quad 4x \phantom{{}+2} \\
- \quad 4x \quad + \quad 2 \\
\hline
-2
\end{array}
$$

This result can be expressed as $x - 2 - \dfrac{2}{2x-1}$.

16. $\boxed{19}$ Maria took $11 - 7 = 4$ days to read $196 - 120 = 76$ pages. Therefore, $k = 76 \div 4 = 19$ pages.

17. $\boxed{8}$ Multiply both sides of the second equation by 4 and subtract to get $-35y = 35$, $y = -1$. Using this result in the second equation,

$$
\begin{aligned}
-x + 5(-1) &= -13 \\
-x - 5 &= -13 \\
-x &= -8 \\
x &= 8
\end{aligned}
$$

18. $\boxed{1.2}$

$$
\frac{3x+7}{5} - \frac{1-2x}{5} = \frac{3x+7-1+2x}{5} = \frac{5x+6}{5} = \frac{5x}{5} + \frac{6}{5} = x + 1.2
$$

This expression comes out to be 1.2 more than x.

19. $\boxed{80}$ There are 9 arcs in the figure. Since $\angle AOC$ intercepts 2 of them, its measure is two-ninths of a circle: $\dfrac{2}{9} \times 360° = 80°$. Since $\angle EOH$ intercepts 3 of the arcs, its measure is three-ninths, or one-third, of a circle: $\dfrac{1}{3} \times 360° = 120°$. Now since $\triangle AOC$ is isosceles ($\overline{OA}$ and $\overline{OC}$ are radii), the measures of $\angle OCA$ and $\angle CAO$ are equal. Therefore, $y = \dfrac{180 - 80}{2} = 50°$. And since $\triangle EOH$ is also isosceles, the measures of $\angle OEH$ and $\angle OHE$ are equal, giving $x = \dfrac{180 - 120}{2} = 30°$. Finally, $x + y = 30 + 50 = 80$.

20. $\boxed{\dfrac{2}{5}}$ Let the average population of the islands be x. Then the population of the mainland is $6x$ and the total population of the islands is $9x$.

$$
\frac{\text{Mainland population}}{\text{Total population of the country}} = \frac{6x}{6x + 9x} = \frac{6}{15} = \frac{2}{5}
$$

Section 4

1. $\boxed{B}$ Distribute and combine like terms: $(-2a^2 + 5) - (3 - 8a^2) = -2a^2 + 5 - 3 + 8a^2 = 6a^2 + 2$

2. $\boxed{D}$ The ball will stop once it reaches the top of its upward motion, at which point the velocity v will equal 0.

$$0 = 550 - 9.8t$$
$$-550 = -9.8t$$
$$56.1 \approx t$$

3. $\boxed{C}$ Since dividing y, the total number of glass bottles, by x, the total number of hours, gives 90, 90 must be the number of glass bottles that can be sorted in one hour. Another way to think about it is to rearrange the equation to $y = 90x$, where 90 is the slope (rate of change).

4. $\boxed{B}$ Every year, the seal population hovers around 350, so it's reasonable to approximate the seal population in 2005 to also be around 350.

5. $\boxed{D}$ In Portuguese, vowels make up $\dfrac{14}{37} \approx 0.38 = 38\%$ of the alphabet.

6. $\boxed{A}$

$$25 \text{ miles} \times \frac{2.5 \text{ hours}}{10 \text{ miles}} = 6.25 \text{ hours} = 6 \text{ hours and } 15 \text{ minutes}$$

7. $\boxed{D}$ From 1950 to 1960, the number of patient visits increased from 200 to 400 million. This is a percent increase of $\dfrac{400 - 200}{200} = 100\%$, not 50%.

8. $\boxed{C}$ In 1990, there were 700 million patient visits and 5,000 hospitals. $\dfrac{700,000,000}{5,000} = 140,000$ patient visits per hospital.

9. $\boxed{B}$ $\dfrac{12 - 16}{16} = -\dfrac{4}{16} \approx -0.25 = 25\%$ decrease

10. $\boxed{D}$

$$\frac{\text{Lamb over rice orders during dinner}}{\text{Lamb over rice orders}} = \frac{108}{144} = \frac{3}{4}$$

11. $\boxed{C}$ **Solution 1:** The ratio of the length to the width is 3:2, which can be expressed as 6:4. Since the ratio of the width to the height is 4:9, the ratio of the length to the height is 6:9, which reduces to 2:3. The above steps can be visualized as follows:

length   width   height
$\boxed{6}$:   4   : $\boxed{9}$
2   :   3

The height is then $80 \times \dfrac{3}{2} = 120$.

Solution 2: Since the ratio of the length to the width is 3:2, the width is $80 \times \dfrac{2}{3} = \dfrac{160}{3}$. Since the ratio of the width to the height is 4:9, the height is $\dfrac{160}{3} \times \dfrac{9}{4} = 40 \times 3 = 120$.

12. $\boxed{B}$ Over the 2-week period, Amy works a total of $2x$ hours at \$60 per hour and earns a minimum of \$3,600.

$$60(2x) \geq 3,600$$
$$120x \geq 3,600$$
$$x \geq 30$$

13. $\boxed{D}$ The station was correct when it forecasted rain and it actually rained and when it forecasted no rain and it didn't rain, a total of $75 + 220 = 295$ times out of 365.

$$\frac{295}{365} = \frac{59}{73}$$

14. $\boxed{B}$ After the first 50 square feet, $k + 75 - 50 = k + 25$ square feet remain.

$$120(50) + 200(k + 25) = 6,000 + 200k + 5,000 = 200k + 11,000$$

15. $\boxed{C}$ The line should have a slope of 120 for the first 50 square feet and then a steeper slope of 200 thereafter. Graph (C) is the only one that shows a segment with a positive slope followed by another with an even more positive (steeper) slope.

16. $\boxed{A}$ $200,000 \text{ cubic feet} \times \dfrac{1 \text{ cubic meter}}{35 \text{ cubic feet}} \times \dfrac{12.5 \text{ grams of lead}}{800 \text{ cubic meters}} \approx 89 \text{ grams of lead}$

17. $\boxed{D}$ The solution to the system of equations will be the intersection point. Multiply both sides of the second equation by 3 to get rid of the fraction. Then flip the equation so that we get the x's on the left side and the y's on the right side:

$$5x = 273 - 6y$$
$$4x = 3y$$

Now multiply both sides of the second equation by 2 ($8x = 6y$) and add both equations to get $13x = 273$, which gives $x = 21$. Finally, $y = \dfrac{4}{3}x = \dfrac{4}{3}(21) = 28$.

18. $\boxed{B}$ Draw the height to B.

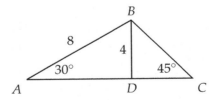

$\triangle ABD$ is 30–60–90, which means $BD = \dfrac{1}{2}AB = \dfrac{1}{2}(8) = 4$. Because $\triangle BDC$ is 45–45–90, $BC = 4\sqrt{2}$.

19. $\boxed{A}$ The range does not change because the minimum and the maximum stay the same. Before the 18 is added, the median is represented by the 8th student (18) and the mean is 17. After the 18 is added, the median is represented by the average of the 8th and 9th students (still 18). However, the mean must change because we've added a number (18) that's different from the original mean (17).

20. $\boxed{A}$ The minimum must occur at the midpoint of the two x-intercepts. The midpoint of -4 and 4 is 0. Plugging this into the equation, we get $y = -k$.

21. $\boxed{D}$ When $x = 0$, the line of best fit gives a y-value of 47. Therefore, the y-intercept is 47. Since the line of best fit crosses the points $(2, 50)$ and $(5, 55)$, we can approximate its slope to be $\dfrac{55 - 50}{5 - 2} = \dfrac{5}{3}$. The equation of the line of best fit is then $y = \dfrac{5}{3}x + 47$. Note that this is an approximation and you could've used other points to find the slope.

22. $\boxed{C}$ The y-intercept of a line refers to the value of y when x is 0. In this problem, $x = 0$ means that the year is 1997, and y represents the percentage of adults with retirement savings. Since the line of best fit gives predicted values and not actual values, its y-intercept can be interpreted as the predicted percentage of adults with retirement savings in 1997.

23. $\boxed{C}$ Keep track of the greeting cards being sent at each stage in the scenario given by choice C: 3, 9, 27, ... Because it triples each time, the scenario is one of exponential growth.

24. $\boxed{C}$ The number of medium refrigerators that can be delivered is $4a + 3b$, so $4a + 3b \geq 20$ (there may be extra capacity). The number of large refrigerators that can be delivered is $5a + 2b$, so $5a + 2b \geq 30$.

25. $\boxed{A}$ Plugging in $(a, 7)$,

$$7 = a^2 + 3$$
$$4 = a^2$$
$$a = \pm 2$$

Plugging in $(b, 12)$,

$$12 = b^2 + 3$$
$$9 = b^2$$
$$b = \pm 3$$

The minimum value of $a + b$ occurs when $a = -2$ and $b = -3$. Therefore, $a + b = -5$.

26. $\boxed{B}$ Complete the square for the terms with x:

$$(x - 2)^2 - 4 + y^2 + 6y = 12$$

Now complete the square for the terms with y:

$$(x - 2)^2 - 4 + (y + 3)^2 - 9 = 12$$
$$(x - 2)^2 + (y + 3)^2 = 25$$

The radius is $\sqrt{25} = 5$. The circumference is $2\pi(5) = 10\pi$.

27. $\boxed{C}$ Since the intersection point $(3, 4)$ lies on both lines, we can plug it into the equations of both lines to get the following system:

$$4 = 3a + b$$
$$4 = 2b(3) + a$$

Subtracting the second equation from the first,

$$0 = 2a - 5b$$
$$-2a = -5b$$
$$\frac{a}{b} = \frac{-5}{-2} = \frac{5}{2}$$

28. $\boxed{B}$ A mean recovery time of 3.5 days and a margin of error of 1.25 days for the sample suggest that the true mean recovery time is between 2.25 and 4.75 days (3.5 ± 1.25). The other answers are too absolute to be correct. The sample mean only allows us to estimate the true mean. It doesn't say anything about the actual recovery times for all patients (for example, it's possible the actual times are all very far from the mean). It also doesn't imply that the true mean recovery time for all patients is exactly 3.5 days. After all, there is a margin of error of 1.25 days.

29. $\boxed{C}$ For $(mx - 10)^2 = 0$, $mx - 10$ must equal 0. The equation $mx - 10 = 0$ has integer solutions when $m = 1, 2, 5,$ and 10. That's four different values.

30. $\boxed{B}$ Split the inequality up into two parts. In the first part,

$$-1 \leq x + y$$
$$-1 - x \leq y$$

In the second part,

$$x + y \leq 1$$
$$y \leq -x + 1$$

So, $y \geq -x - 1$ and $y \leq -x + 1$, which means the solution set (shaded region) must be in between those two lines. The graph in answer (B) correctly shows this.

31. $\boxed{48}$ The bus's morning route is $40 \times 3 = 120$ miles. To travel this distance in 2.5 hours, its average speed must be $120 \div 2.5 = 48$ miles per hour.

32. $\boxed{144}$ The angles in a pentagon sum to $180(5 - 2) = 540$. In a regular pentagon, each angle is then $540 \div 5 = 108$. Line l splits the pentagon into a top part and a bottom part. The bottom part is a quadrilateral whose angles sum to 360. Therefore,

$$a + b = 360 - 108 - 108 = 144$$

33. $\boxed{20}$ Given the trig identity $\sin x° = \cos(90 - x)°$, $\sin 24° = \cos 66°$. Setting up an equation,

$$\cos 66° = \cos(3k + 6)°$$
$$66 = 3k + 6$$
$$60 = 3k$$
$$k = 20$$

34. ☐1.2 For this system to have no solution, the coefficients of x and y should be able to match, but not the constants. Comparing the coefficients of the y's, we see that we should multiply the first equation by 4 ($2.8 \div 0.7 = 4$) to make the coefficients match. The equations then look like this:

$$1.2x - 2.8y = 4$$
$$kx - 2.8x = 3$$

It's now easy to see that the constants are different and that $k = 1.2$.

35. ☐3 $g(f(a)) = g(a^2 + 2) = 4(a^2 + 2) - 3 = 4a^2 + 8 - 3 = 4a^2 + 5$. Now,

$$4a^2 + 5 = 41$$
$$4a^2 = 36$$
$$a^2 = 9$$
$$a = \pm 3$$

Since $a > 0$, $a = 3$.

36. ☐36 Let the side of the square be x. Setting the areas of the square and the rectangle equal to each other,

$$x^2 = (2x - 8)(x + 3)$$
$$x^2 = 2x^2 + 6x - 8x - 24$$
$$0 = x^2 - 2x - 24$$
$$0 = (x - 6)(x + 4)$$
$$x = 6, -4$$

Since it doesn't make sense for the side of a square to be a negative number, it must be 6. The area of the square is then $6^2 = 36$.

37. ☐25.6 First, we need to solve for k.

$$10 = \frac{1}{2}k(0.05)^2$$
$$20 = (0.05)^2 k$$
$$8000 = k$$

Now, $P = \frac{1}{2}(8000)(0.08)^2 = 25.6$ joules

38. ☐5 The spring currently has a potential energy of 10 joules. When this potential energy is transferred to the block as kinetic energy,

$$\frac{1}{2}mv^2 = 10$$
$$\frac{1}{2}(0.8)v^2 = 10$$
$$v^2 = 25$$
$$v = 5$$

Practice Test 9 Answers

Question categories correspond to chapters in *The College Panda's SAT Math: The Advanced Guide and Workbook*. To estimate your score, visit *thecollegepanda.com/sat-score-calculator*

Section 3

1. $\boxed{A}$ Manipulating & Solving Equations
2. $\boxed{D}$ Expressions
3. $\boxed{C}$ Interpreting Linear Models
4. $\boxed{D}$ Exponents & Radicals
5. $\boxed{B}$ Constructing Models
6. $\boxed{C}$ Functions
7. $\boxed{B}$ Manipulating & Solving Equations
8. $\boxed{D}$ Inequalities
9. $\boxed{B}$ Triangles
10. $\boxed{B}$ Circles
11. $\boxed{A}$ Trigonometry
12. $\boxed{B}$ Functions
13. $\boxed{A}$ Word Problems
14. $\boxed{C}$ Expressions
15. $\boxed{A}$ Systems of Equations
16. $\boxed{\frac{1}{3}}$ Manipulating & Solving Equations
17. $\boxed{5}$ Lines
18. $\boxed{1 \text{ or } 6}$ Systems of Equations
19. $\boxed{22}$ Quadratics
20. $\boxed{10}$ Synthetic Division

Section 4

1. $\boxed{B}$ Rates
2. $\boxed{B}$ Percent
3. $\boxed{C}$ Minimum & Maximum Word Problems
4. $\boxed{B}$ Reading Data
5. $\boxed{C}$ Manipulating & Solving Equations
6. $\boxed{D}$ Constructing Models
7. $\boxed{D}$ Statistics II
8. $\boxed{B}$ Percent
9. $\boxed{D}$ Word Problems
10. $\boxed{C}$ Lines / Triangles
11. $\boxed{C}$ Functions
12. $\boxed{B}$ Functions
13. $\boxed{C}$ Rates
14. $\boxed{C}$ Reading Data
15. $\boxed{D}$ Probability
16. $\boxed{A}$ Statistics I
17. $\boxed{D}$ Inequalities
18. $\boxed{C}$ Systems of Equations
19. $\boxed{A}$ Statistics I
20. $\boxed{A}$ Interpreting Linear Models
21. $\boxed{B}$ Statistics II
22. $\boxed{C}$ Functions
23. $\boxed{A}$ Triangles
24. $\boxed{B}$ Triangles
25. $\boxed{B}$ Inequalities
26. $\boxed{D}$ Statistics II
27. $\boxed{B}$ Constructing Models
28. $\boxed{B}$ Manipulating & Solving Equations
29. $\boxed{A}$ Functions
30. $\boxed{B}$ Quadratics
31. $\boxed{25}$ Rates
32. $\boxed{15}$ Circles
33. $\boxed{7}$ Expressions
34. $\boxed{11}$ Systems of Equations
35. $\boxed{16}$ Statistics I
36. $\boxed{9}$ Word Problems
37. $\boxed{.9}$ Percent
38. $\boxed{27.1}$ Percent

Practice Test 9 Answer Explanations

Section 3

1. $\boxed{A}$ If $4b = 7$, then multiply both sides by 3 to get $12b = 21$. Then, $12b - 3 = 21 - 3 = 18$.

2. $\boxed{D}$

$$\frac{2a^2b - 3ab^2 + ab}{ab} = \frac{2a^2b}{ab} - \frac{3ab^2}{ab} + \frac{ab}{ab} = 2a - 3b + 1$$

3. $\boxed{C}$ The number 16.8 refers to the slope of the equation, which means John increased his average number of points per game by 16.8 each year.

4. $\boxed{D}$ Raise both sides to the -3 power.

$$(c^{-\frac{1}{3}})^{-3} = x^{-3}$$
$$c = \frac{1}{x^3}$$

5. $\boxed{B}$ $\dfrac{3.50}{1,000}g + 12 = 0.0035g + 12$

6. $\boxed{C}$ The graph is below the x-axis when $-2 < x < 0$ and $3 < x \le 4$.

7. $\boxed{B}$

$$8a^2 = 3(a^2 + b)$$
$$8a^2 = 3a^2 + 3b$$
$$5a^2 = 3b$$
$$\frac{a^2}{b} = \frac{3}{5}$$

8. $\boxed{D}$ Altogether, the sandwich platters served up to $9x$ people and the seafood platters served up to $6y$ people. Since there was more than enough food for all 300 attendees, $9x + 6y > 300$. And because the total number of platters was less than 40, $x + y < 40$.

9. $\boxed{B}$ Triangle BCP is similar to triangle ADP. Since the side lengths of $\triangle ADP$ are twice those of $\triangle BCP$, the length of $\overline{AD}$ is $8 \times 2 = 16$. Since $AB = 8 \div 2 = 4$ and $CD = 12 \div 2 = 6$, the perimeter of $ABCD$ is $AB + BC + CD + AD = 4 + 8 + 6 + 16 = 34$.

10. $\boxed{B}$ The standard form of a circle is $(x - h)^2 + (y - k)^2 = r^2$, where (h, k) is the center and r is the radius. Since the radius of the circle is 5, the equation of the circle should look like $(x - h)^2 + (y - k)^2 = 25$. This eliminates answer A. Of the remaining answers, only B is satisfied when you plug in $(2, 2)$: $(2 + 2)^2 + (2 - 5)^2 = 16 + 9 = 25$.

11. $\boxed{A}$ From the coordinates, $BC = 4 - (-3) = 7$ and $AC = 7 - (-5) = 12$.

$$\tan A = \frac{BC}{AC} = \frac{7}{12}$$

12. $\boxed{B}$ Answers A and B have x-intercepts at -1 and 2. Answers C and D have x-intercepts at -1, 0, and 2. Because the given graph only has x-intercepts at -1 and 2, the answer must be either A or B. When $x = 0$, the given graph gives a positive y-value. Plugging $x = 0$ into answers A and B, we see that only B gives a positive y-value. Therefore, the answer must be B.

13. $\boxed{A}$ If Bob can paint a house in 4 days, then he paints $\frac{1}{4}$ of a house in one day. If Carl can paint a house in 6 days, then he paints $\frac{1}{6}$ of a house in one day. Working together, they would paint $\frac{1}{4} + \frac{1}{6}$ of a house in one day. If d is the number of days they would need to finish painting one house, then

$$\left(\frac{1}{4} + \frac{1}{6}\right) d = 1$$

14. $\boxed{C}$ Factor out a $\frac{1}{4}$ from each term like so:

$$\frac{1}{4}x^2 + 3x + 9 = \frac{1}{4}(x^2 + 12x + 36) = \frac{1}{4}(x+6)(x+6) = \frac{1}{4}(x+6)^2$$

Therefore, $a = 6$.

15. $\boxed{A}$ Divide the first equation by 2 to get $-x + 3y = 5$. Divide the second equation by 3 to get $-x + 3y = 6$. The coefficients of x and y match but the constants on the right side do not. Therefore, there is no solution.

16. $\boxed{\dfrac{1}{3}}$

$$5 - \frac{6}{k} = -13$$
$$-\frac{6}{k} = -18$$
$$6 = 18k$$
$$\frac{1}{3} = k$$

17. $\boxed{5}$ The slope of the first line is $\dfrac{2-0}{1-0} = 2$. The slope of the second line is $\dfrac{2-0}{1-k}$. Since the two lines are perpendicular, the slope of the second line must be $-\dfrac{1}{2}$. Setting up an equation,

$$\frac{2}{1-k} = -\frac{1}{2}$$

Cross multiplying,

$$4 = -(1-k)$$
$$4 = -1 + k$$
$$5 = k$$

18. $\boxed{1 \text{ or } 6}$ We can factor the first equation to get $(x+y)^2 = 25$. Taking the square root of both sides, $x + y = \pm 5$. If $x + y = 5$, then we add this equation to the second equation to get $2x = 12$, $x = 6$. If $x + y = -5$, then we add this equation to the second equation to get $2x = 2$, $x = 1$.

19. $\boxed{22}$ The x-coordinate of the vertex is the average of the two x-intercepts, $(3 + 15) \div 2 = 9$. Since the line passes through the vertex, the y-coordinate can be found by using the equation of the line, $y = 3(9) - 5 = 22$.

20. $\boxed{10}$ From the remainder theorem, if $3x - 2$ is a factor of a polynomial, then $\frac{2}{3}$ must be a root of the polynomial. This means that when $x = \frac{2}{3}$, the value of the polynomial is 0. Hence,

$$9\left(\frac{2}{3}\right)^3 - k\left(\frac{2}{3}\right) + 4 = 0$$

$$9\left(\frac{8}{27}\right) - \frac{2}{3}k + 4 = 0$$

$$\frac{8}{3} - \frac{2}{3}k + \frac{12}{3} = 0$$

$$\frac{20}{3} = \frac{2}{3}k$$

$$20 = 2k$$

$$k = 10$$

Section 4

1. $\boxed{B}$ $30 \text{ minutes} \times \dfrac{4 \text{ feet}}{1 \text{ minute}} \times \dfrac{12 \text{ inches}}{1 \text{ foot}} = 1,440 \text{ inches}$

2. $\boxed{B}$ $\dfrac{94 - 84}{84} = \dfrac{10}{84} \approx .119 = 11.9\%$

3. $\boxed{C}$ If he edits at the slowest pace, he'll finish $15 \times 7 = 105$ essays. If he edits at the fastest pace, he'll finish $18 \times 7 = 126$ essays. The only answer between 105 and 126 is 112.

4. $\boxed{B}$ The line representing Minnesota has two data points that are higher than the respective ones for Missouri.

5. $\boxed{C}$ When the ball reaches the bottom of the ramp, the distance d it has traveled is equal to the length of the ramp. Solving for d,

$$6 = \sqrt{\frac{3d}{4}}$$

$$36 = \frac{3d}{4}$$

$$144 = 3d$$

$$d = 48$$

6. $\boxed{D}$ As the ball rolls down the ramp, it travels faster and faster, which means its height drops faster and faster. Therefore, a graph of the height should get steeper and steeper in the negative direction over time. Only the graph in answer D meets this description.

7. $\boxed{D}$ Using proportions, the number of subscribers for whom football is the favorite sport to watch is

$$\frac{150}{400} \times 2,000,000 = 750,000$$

The other answers do not conform to the proportions set by the survey.

8. $\boxed{B}$ The expected number of balls he hits is $(0.25)n$. Using that result, the expected number of home runs he hits is $(0.05)(0.25)n$. Answer B is the equivalent.

9. $\boxed{D}$ Let x be the number of weeks that pass.

$$650 - 16x = 100 + 6x$$
$$-22x = -550$$
$$x = 25$$

10. $\boxed{C}$ The y-intercept of the line is 8. By setting $y = 0$ and solving for x, we find that the x-intercept of the line is -6. Using the pythagorean theorem,

$$AO^2 + BO^2 = AB^2$$
$$6^2 + 8^2 = AB^2$$
$$100 = AB^2$$
$$10 = AB$$

11. $\boxed{C}$ Based on the pattern, when $x = 5$, $y = \dfrac{(4)(6)}{10} = 2.4$

12. $\boxed{B}$ The numerator is the product of the numbers on either side of x and the denominator is 2 times the value of x. Therefore, $y = \dfrac{(x-1)(x+1)}{2x}$.

13. $\boxed{C}$ 30 pounds $\times \dfrac{2 \text{ cups}}{\frac{2}{3} \text{ pounds}} \times \dfrac{1 \text{ bottle}}{5 \text{ cups}} = 18$ bottles

14. $\boxed{C}$

$$A: \quad \frac{2,000}{600} \approx 3.33$$

$$B: \quad \frac{5,000}{800} = 6.25$$

$$C: \quad \frac{7,000}{1,000} = 7$$

$$D: \quad \frac{9,000}{1,300} \approx 6.92$$

Flight C is the one with the greatest ratio.

15. $\boxed{D}$ $\dfrac{2+3+6}{20} = \dfrac{11}{20} = 0.55$

16. $\boxed{A}$ $\dfrac{1(4)+2(5)+3(2)+4(3)+5(6)}{20} = \dfrac{62}{20} = 3.1$

17. $\boxed{D}$ We could solve like so,

$$\frac{4}{2x-7} > 3$$
$$4 > 3(2x-7)$$
$$4 > 6x - 21$$
$$25 > 6x$$
$$4\frac{1}{6} > x$$

But this seems to suggest that all of the answer choices could be possible values of x! Did we do something wrong? When variables are in the denominator, weird things can happen, especially in inequalities. Beware of these situations. Looking back at the answer choices, we can simply plug them in to see that answers (A), (B), and (C) give us negative values that do not satisfy the inequality. Answer (D) is the only one that works.

18. $\boxed{C}$ Let the price of a puppy be p and the price of a kitten be k. We can then make two equations:

$$\begin{cases} 3p + 2k = 240 \\ p + 5k = 210 \end{cases}$$

From the second equation, we can get $p = 210 - 5k$. Substituting this into the first equation,

$$3(210 - 5k) + 2k = 240$$
$$630 - 15k + 2k = 240$$
$$-13k = -390$$
$$k = 30$$

The price of a kitten is \$30. Then $p = 210 - 5(30) = 60$. The price of a puppy is \$60.

19. $\boxed{A}$ Notice that the dots have the same distribution except for one dot at the far right for Factory A and one dot at the far left for Factory B. That means Factory A must have a higher mean than Factory B.

20. $\boxed{A}$ Because this question is asking for the change in "x" for each change in "y" (the reverse of slope), we need to rearrange the equation to get a in terms of w.

$$w = \frac{5}{7}(2a + 1)$$

$$7w = 5(2a + 1)$$
$$7w = 10a + 5$$
$$10a = 7w - 5$$
$$a = \frac{7}{10}w - \frac{5}{10}$$

The slope here is 0.7, which means each additional inch in wingspan takes 0.7 years.

21. $\boxed{B}$ Drawing a line of best fit, we can establish a linear model from the grid points.

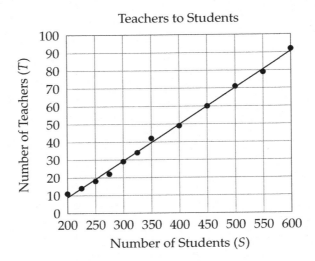

The line of best fit passes through $(400, 50)$ and $(500, 70)$. These are examples of points you would estimate from your line.

$$\text{Slope} = \frac{70 - 50}{500 - 400} = \frac{20}{100} = 0.2$$

So the line has an equation in the form of

$$T = 0.2S + b$$

Using the point $(400, 50)$, we can solve for b to get

$$T = 0.2S - 30$$

Another way to solve this problem is to test the two points with each of the answer choices. Only answer (B) gives accurate results.

22. $\boxed{C}$ A horizontal line at $y = -3$ intersects f at 2 points (2 solutions). A horizontal line at $y = 0$ intersects f at 3 points (3 solutions). A horizontal line at $y = 2.5$ intersects f at 2 points (2 solutions). I and III only.

23. $\boxed{A}$ To convert from degrees to radians, multiply by $\frac{\pi}{180}$.

$$\frac{180(n - 2)}{n} \times \frac{\pi}{180} = \frac{\pi(n - 2)}{n}$$

24. $\boxed{B}$ $\triangle ABC$ is a 45–45–90 triangle so $BC = 5$. Using the pythagorean theorem to find CD,

$$BC^2 + CD^2 = BD^2$$

$$5^2 + CD^2 = 10^2$$

$$CD^2 = 75$$

$$CD = \sqrt{75}$$

$$CD = 5\sqrt{3}$$

Note that $\triangle BCD$ is a 30–60–90 triangle.

25. $\boxed{B}$ If x tickets are for reserved seats, then $1,200 - x$ tickets are for general admission seats. Ticket sales are $40x$ for the reserved seats and $15(1,200 - x)$ for the general admission seats. Setting up the inequality,

$$40x + 15(1,200 - x) \geq 30,000$$
$$40x + 18,000 - 15x \geq 30,000$$
$$25x \geq 12,000$$
$$x \geq 480$$

26. $\boxed{D}$ No conclusion about cause and effect can be made about the reduction in mosquito bites for Anne and her family (or anyone else for that matter). There are numerous problems with this experiment. First, Anne and her family are not a random sample of people and not enough of a sample size. Second, individual members weren't randomly assigned to use the new repellent or the old repellent. This opens the experiment up to other factors such as the temperature during Week 2 or whether they wore different clothes during Week 2. The purpose of random sampling and random assignment is to "average out," or "cancel out," all these factors.

27. $\boxed{B}$ When $n = 2$, 4 pins are needed. When $n = 3$, 8 pins are needed. When $n = 4$, 12 pins are needed. See the pattern? The number of pins needed goes up by 4 each time. Now we could use the values we already have to filter through the answer choices, or we could come up with the expression ourselves. Let's start with the former. If we plug $n = 2$ into each of the answer choices, only B and D evaluate to 4. Now if we plug $n = 3$ into B and D, only B evaluates to 8. Therefore, the answer is B. To come up with the expression ourselves, let y be the number of pins needed. Using point-slope form with 4 as the slope and $(2, 4)$ as the point,

$$y - y_1 = m(n - n_1)$$
$$y - 4 = 4(n - 2)$$
$$y = 4n - 8 + 4$$
$$y = 4n - 4$$

28. $\boxed{B}$ The fact that all the answer choices deal with y is a hint that we should isolate y. To do so, we multiply both sides by y and group all the y terms on the right-hand side so that we can factor it out.

$$\frac{x - y}{y} = x$$
$$x - y = xy$$
$$x = xy + y$$
$$x = y(x + 1)$$
$$\frac{x}{x + 1} = y$$

Since x is positive, y must be a positive fraction less than 1 (the denominator is always larger than the numerator).

29. $\boxed{A}$ Plugging in $(a, 3)$,

$$f(a) = \frac{1}{2}a + a$$
$$3 = \frac{3}{2}a$$
$$6 = 3a$$
$$a = 2$$

So, $f(x) = \frac{1}{2}x + 2$, and $f(8) = \frac{1}{2}(8) + 2 = 6$.

30. $\boxed{B}$ One of the x-intercepts is -2. Because the x-coordinate of the vertex is the midpoint of the two x-intercepts, the other x-intercept is 8. So the equation of the parabola is of the form

$$y = a(x + 2)(x - 8)$$

where a is a constant. We can plug in the vertex $(3, 25)$ to find a.

$$25 = a(3 + 2)(3 - 8)$$
$$25 = -25a$$
$$a = -1$$

The final equation is $y = -(x + 2)(x - 8)$.

31. $\boxed{25}$ Let t be the number of seconds it takes to slow down to the residential speed limit. Then,

$$80 - 2t = 30$$
$$-2t = -50$$
$$t = 25$$

32. $\boxed{15}$ Each wedge is $\frac{20}{360} = \frac{1}{18}$ of the disk. Therefore, each wedge weighs $\frac{1}{18} \times 270 = 15$ grams.

33. $\boxed{7}$ Distribute and combine like terms.

$$\frac{1}{2}(x - 2) + 6\left(\frac{1}{4}x + 1\right) = \frac{1}{2}x - 1 + \frac{3}{2}x + 6 = 2x + 5$$

Therefore, $p = 2$, $q = 5$, and $p + q = 7$.

34. $\boxed{11}$ Substituting the second equation into the first,

$$\frac{1}{2}(-4y)^2 - 3y^2 = 55$$
$$\frac{1}{2}(16y^2) - 3y^2 = 55$$
$$8y^2 - 3y^2 = 55$$
$$5y^2 = 55$$
$$y^2 = 11$$

35. $\boxed{16}$ The logic behind this question can be a bit tricky to follow so if you get confused, just keep reading this explanation the whole way through before coming back to process the steps you didn't understand initially. First, choose one of the printers with an input capacity of 400 to be the median printer. To maximize x while maintaining a median of 400, we need to put as many printers as possible to the "right" of the median printer:

$$3 + x \text{ printers} \qquad \text{median printer} \qquad 19 \text{ printers}$$
$$400$$

This means all the printers with input capacities 400 or greater should be considered as "above" the median. As shown above, there are $10 + 5 + 5 - 1 = 19$ of these printers (we exclude the printer designated as the median). By maximizing the right side, we also maximize the left side, since by definition, there must be an equal number of printers on either side of the median. Therefore, $3 + x = 19$ and the maximum value of x is $19 - 3 = 16$.

36. $\boxed{9}$ Let x be the number of students in the initial group. They each had $\dfrac{900}{x}$ square feet of space. After the 3 students joined, each student then had $\dfrac{900}{x+3}$ square feet of space. Since the before-and-after difference was 25 square feet, we can set up the following equation:

$$\frac{900}{x} - 25 = \frac{900}{x+3}$$

To solve the equation, first multiply everything by $x(x+3)$ to get rid of the fractions.

$$900(x+3) - 25x(x+3) = 900x$$
$$900x + 2700 - 25x^2 - 75x = 900x$$
$$-25x^2 - 75x + 2700 = 0$$
$$x^2 + 3x - 108 = 0$$
$$(x+12)(x-9) = 0$$

Since x must be positive, $x = 9$.

37. $\boxed{.9}$ Every time the price is reduced by 10 percent, 90 percent remains.

38. $\boxed{27.1}$ After 3 months, $P = a(0.9)^3 = 0.729a$. This translates to a percent decrease of $1 - 0.729 = 0.271 = 27.1\%$. Note that the percent decrease is the same after any 3 month period, not just after the first 3 months. It doesn't matter what the starting value of P is.

Practice Test 10 Answers

Question categories correspond to chapters in *The College Panda's SAT Math: The Advanced Guide and Workbook*. To estimate your score, visit *thecollegepanda.com/sat-score-calculator*

Section 3

1. B Manipulating & Solving Equations
2. C Rates
3. C Lines
4. A Exponents & Radicals
5. C Manipulating & Solving Equations
6. B Functions
7. D Interpreting Linear Models
8. B Lines
9. D Inequalities
10. B Manipulating & Solving Equations
11. B Systems of Equations
12. A Expressions
13. A Lines
14. A Quadratics
15. C Triangles
16. 8 Manipulating & Solving Equations
17. 8 More Equation Solving Strategies
18. $\frac{2}{3}$ Circles
19. 10 Word Problems
20. $3 \text{ or } 4$ Systems of Equations

Section 4

1. D Reading Data
2. B Rates
3. A Percent
4. B Expressions
5. B Exponential vs. Linear Growth
6. B Reading Data
7. D Constructing Models
8. C Statistics II
9. B Inequalities
10. C Reading Data
11. A Functions
12. C Probability
13. A Statistics II
14. B Inequalities
15. C Interpreting Linear Models
16. D Reading Data
17. B Quadratics
18. D Statistics I
19. C Statistics I
20. D Inequalities
21. C Percent
22. B Minimum & Maximum Word Problems
23. D Systems of Equations
24. D Rates

25. A Rates
26. B Functions
27. B Circles
28. B Synthetic Division
29. D Volume / Ratio & Proportion
30. C Lines / Systems of Equations
31. 120 Percent / Word Problems
32. 71 Functions
33. 160 Angles
34. 12 Minimum & Maximum Word Problems
35. 21 Systems of Equations / Word Problems
36. $.6$ Trigonometry
37. 2.4 Manipulating & Solving Equations
38. $\frac{2}{3}$ Manipulating & Solving Equations

Practice Test 10 Answer Explanations

Section 3

1. $\boxed{B}$ $y = \dfrac{27}{35} - \dfrac{3}{5} = \dfrac{27}{35} - \dfrac{21}{35} = \dfrac{6}{35}$

2. $\boxed{C}$

$$15 \ \cancel{\text{dollars}} \times \frac{8 \text{ magazines}}{d \ \cancel{\text{dollars}}} = \frac{120}{d} \text{ magazines}$$

3. $\boxed{C}$ When $x = 0, y = \dfrac{5}{6}$. Therefore, the y-intercept is $\dfrac{5}{6}$. When $y = 0, x = \dfrac{5}{2}$. Therefore, the x-intercept is $\dfrac{5}{2}$. Note that the slope is $-\dfrac{1}{3}$.

4. $\boxed{A}$ We could square both sides, but I'll move the 3 back inside the square root to show you the result is the same:

$$3\sqrt{x^3} = \sqrt{72}$$
$$\sqrt{9x^3} = \sqrt{72}$$
$$9x^3 = 72$$
$$x^3 = 8$$
$$x = 2$$

5. $\boxed{C}$ The best way to do this question is to try out the answer choices and see if they work. Only 1 and 6 work.

6. $\boxed{B}$ The graph has a y-value of -2 when x is between -1 and 0. Answer (B) is the only choice between -1 and 0.

7. $\boxed{D}$ The number 120 refers to the y-intercept of the equation, when no checks have been written. Therefore, 120 is the initial number of checks in Anna's checkbook.

8. $\boxed{B}$ Since the relationship is linear, the tax rate increases at a constant rate: $\dfrac{0.023 - 0.014}{2003 - 1995} = \dfrac{0.009}{8} = \dfrac{0.009}{8} \times \dfrac{1,000}{1,000} = \dfrac{9}{8,000}$ per year. When $t = 0$, the tax rate was 0.014. Therefore, the y-intercept is 0.014 and the slope is $\dfrac{9}{8,000}$. The equation is then $R = \dfrac{9}{8,000}t + 0.014$.

9. $\boxed{D}$ The total price of John's order will be np. To qualify for free shipping,

$$np \geq 75$$
$$n \geq \frac{75}{p}$$

10. $\boxed{B}$ Expand and cross multiply.

$$\frac{3(-h+3)+2}{4} = \frac{5-(1-2h)}{10}$$

$$\frac{-3h+11}{4} = \frac{4+2h}{10}$$

$$10(-3h+11) = 4(4+2h)$$

$$-30h+110 = 16+8h$$

$$-38h = -94$$

$$h = \frac{47}{19}$$

11. $\boxed{B}$ Multiply the second equation by 3 and add the equations to get $8y = 16$, $y = 2$. Plug this result back into the second equation (the original one) to get $x = 0$.

12. $\boxed{A}$ First, combine the fractions on the right. yz is the common denominator.

$$\frac{1}{y} - \frac{1}{z} = \frac{z-y}{yz}$$

Now,

$$\left(\frac{1}{z-y}\right)\left(\frac{z-y}{yz}\right) = \frac{1}{yz}$$

13. $\boxed{A}$ The length of the base is 4. Since the area of the rectangle is 20, the height must be 5. From A to B, the line segment goes 4 units to the right and 5 units up, which means the slope is $\frac{5}{4}$.

14. $\boxed{A}$ Since the x-intercepts are at -3 and 5, the equation must have factors $(x+3)$ and $(x-5)$. This eliminates C and D. The x-coordinate of the vertex of a parabola is always the midpoint of the x-intercepts. In this case, the midpoint of -3 and 5 is $\frac{-3+5}{2} = 1$. When $x = 1$, the equation in answer A gives $y = -\frac{1}{2}(1+3)(1-5) = 8$. Therefore, the answer is A.

15. $\boxed{C}$ $\triangle BDE$ is similar to $\triangle BAC$. The ratio of their sides is $1 : 2$. Therefore, the ratio of their areas is $1^2 : 2^2 = 1 : 4$. If we let the area of $\triangle BDE$ be x, then the area of $\triangle BAC$ would be $4x$. The area of the trapezoid would then be $4x - x = 3x$. Therefore, the area of trapezoid $ADEC$ is 3 times the area of triangle DBE.

16. $\boxed{8}$ Multiply both sides by x to get $3 = 12x$ and $x = \frac{1}{4}$. Then, $\frac{2}{x} = \frac{2}{\frac{1}{4}} = 8$.

17. $\boxed{8}$ For the equation to have infinitely many solutions, the equation must be true no matter what the value of x is. For that to be the case, both sides of the equation must be the same. First, let's get rid of the fraction by multiplying both sides by 2.

$$10x + 24 = 10x + 3c$$

Now it's easy to see that for both sides to be the same, $3c = 24$, $c = 8$.

18. $\boxed{\dfrac{2}{3}}$ The circumference of the circle is $2\pi r = 2\pi(6) = 12\pi$. Arc $\overset{\frown}{AB}$ is $\dfrac{4\pi}{12\pi} = \dfrac{1}{3}$ of the circumference, which means $\angle ACB$ is $\dfrac{1}{3}$ of the circle. Since a circle is $360° = 2\pi$ radians, the measure of $\angle ACB$ must be $\dfrac{1}{3} \times 2\pi = \dfrac{2}{3}\pi$ radians, which gives $k = \dfrac{2}{3}$.

19. $\boxed{10}$

$$\frac{20 - x}{50 - x} = \frac{1}{4}$$

Cross multiplying,

$$4(20 - x) = 50 - x$$
$$80 - 4x = 50 - x$$
$$-3x = -30$$
$$x = 10$$

20. $\boxed{3 \text{ or } 4}$ In the first equation, we can shift things around to get $y = x + 2$. Substituting this into the second equation,

$$y^2 - 7y + 25 = 4y - 5$$
$$y^2 - 11y + 30 = 0$$
$$(y - 6)(y - 5) = 0$$

y can be either 5 or 6. Therefore, x can be either 3 or 4.

Section 4

1. $\boxed{D}$ The points at 2003 and 2010 are at the same level along the y-axis.

2. $\boxed{B}$ If 4 out of every 15 pose a safety hazard, that means 11 out of 15 do not. $6 \times \dfrac{11}{15} = 4.4$ million dolls.

3. $\boxed{A}$ If Rachel discarded 45%, she kept $100 - 45 = 55\%$, which can be expressed as $\dfrac{55}{100}$ or $\dfrac{11}{20}$. That means she kept 11 pens out of every 20. The total number of pens she kept must be a multiple of 11. After all, the assumption is that you can't keep half a pen (or any other fraction). The only multiple of 11 in the answer choices is 22.

4. $\boxed{B}$ Because $\sqrt{x} \geq 0$, $\sqrt{x} + 1$ can never equal 0. The other answer choices are equal to 0 when $x = -1$.

5. $\boxed{B}$ The number of criminal cases decreases by 50 each year. This is linear decay (decreasing linear).

6. $\boxed{B}$ $40(30,000) - 20(40,000) = \$400,000$

7. $\boxed{D}$ As the price increases, the projected number of toys sold decreases and then stays the same. Only graph (D) exhibits this correctly.

8. $\boxed{C}$ Answer (C) is the only choice that gives a valid conclusion supported by the study. Answers (A) and (B) give reasons for the results, but these reasons are mere conjectures that are not supported at all by the study. Answer (D) is wrong because the study did not deal with the specific types of reading the students did.

9. $\boxed{B}$

$$1,100x + 150x > 180,000$$
$$1,250x > 180,000$$
$$x > 144$$

10. $\boxed{C}$ From 10 to 15 minutes, the temperature increases from $-4°$F to $1°$F, a change of 5 degrees.

11. $\boxed{A}$ From the graph, the y-value is -4 when $x = 3$.

12. $\boxed{C}$ Let x be the number of employees who commute by car. The number of employees who commute by train is then $x + 50$.

$$x + (x + 50) = 260$$
$$2x + 50 = 260$$
$$2x = 210$$
$$x = 105$$

Filling in the table,

	Car	Train	Total
Late	20	15	35
On time	85	140	225
Total	105	155	260

$$\frac{\text{On time and took the train}}{\text{On time}} = \frac{140}{225} = \frac{28}{45}$$

13. $\boxed{A}$ The most that we can conclude is that there is a negative association between water pollution levels and the number of fish for rivers in China (as one goes up, the other goes down). We CANNOT conclude that there is a cause and effect relationship between the two. We can't say that one causes the other. Nor can we generalize to all rivers.

14. $\boxed{B}$ The shaded regions cover all x values greater than 3 and all x values less than -3. The y-values are irrelevant. The only inequality that reflects this is $|x| \geq 3$.

15. $\boxed{C}$ The solution $(9, 0)$ means $s = 0$ when $a = 9$. So when 9 milliliters of sulfuric acid are used in the reaction, no sugar is left afterwards. Because the block of sugar is 27 grams (as indicated by the y-intercept), it takes 9 milliliters of sulfuric acid to react with 27 grams of sugar.

16. $\boxed{D}$ The line is at its steepest from 3:30 P.M. to 4:00 P.M., which means Amy traveled the fastest during that time. In other words, the slope, distance over time, is at its greatest (in absolute value) from 3:30 P.M. to 4:00 P.M.

17. $\boxed{B}$ This question is asking for vertex form, since the vertex is where the maximum is. To get vertex form, we need to complete the square. First, divide everything by -6 to get 1 as the coefficient of t.

$$\frac{h}{-6} = t^2 - 6t - 2$$

Then divide the middle term by 2 to get -3 and square that result to get 9. We put the -3 inside the parentheses with x and subtract the 9 at the end.

$$\frac{h}{-6} = (t-3)^2 - 2 - 9$$
$$\frac{h}{-6} = (t-3)^2 - 11$$
$$h = -6(t-3)^2 + 66$$

18. $\boxed{D}$ The mode is the number that shows up the most often. In this case, it's 30 since it shows up 5 times (the most).

19. $\boxed{C}$ It should be obvious that the mean will increase since we're removing the two lowest data points. The range will decrease because the minimum will be higher. Before the data points are removed, the median is represented by the 6th soft drink (25 grams). After the data points are removed, the median is represented by the 5th soft drink (30 grams). Therefore, only the mean and median will increase.

20. $\boxed{D}$ Total sales are $5m$ for the milk chocolate bars and $7d$ for the dark chocolate bars. So, $5m + 7d \geq 5,000$. Total costs are $2m$ for the milk chocolate bars and $5d$ for the dark chocolate bars. So, $2m + 5d \leq 2,800$.

21. $\boxed{C}$ $500(0.92)^{\frac{30}{5}} \approx 303$

22. $\boxed{B}$

$$P > 350$$
$$\frac{1500}{\sqrt{n}} > 350$$
$$1500 > 350\sqrt{n}$$
$$\frac{30}{7} > \sqrt{n}$$
$$\left(\frac{30}{7}\right)^2 > n$$
$$18.37 > n$$

Based on this result, the greatest possible number of "whole" rooms available is 18.

23. $\boxed{D}$ The constant a cannot be 3. Otherwise, the second equation's coefficients would be twice the first equation's coefficients, which would allow them to match. This results in a system with either zero or infinite solutions. Answer (D) is the only one where a is not set to 3.

24. $\boxed{D}$ $\$2.00 + 2.5 \text{ miles} \times \dfrac{\$1.00}{0.25 \text{ miles}} = \$2.00 + \$10.00 = \$12.00$

25. $\boxed{A}$ Since the base fare in City E is $\$3.00$, we let that be the total cost of a ride in City A. Converting this cost back to the distanced traveled, we get $\$3.00 \times \dfrac{0.25 \text{ miles}}{\$1.25} = 0.6$ miles.

26. $\boxed{B}$ To find the intersection point, we equate the two functions and solve for the x-coordinate.

$$f(x) = g(x)$$
$$x^2 - 2x + 1 = x^2 - 10x + 25$$
$$8x = 24$$
$$x = 3$$

At $x = 3$, the y-coordinate is $f(3) = 3^2 - 2(3) + 1 = 4$. So $h = 3$ and $k = 4$. $h + k = 3 + 4 = 7$.

27. $\boxed{B}$ The measure of $\angle AOD$ is $180 - 64 = 116°$. Since $\overline{OA}$ and $\overline{OD}$ are radii, $\triangle AOD$ is isosceles with $\angle OAD$ equal in measure to $\angle ODA$. Therefore, $\angle OAD$ measures $\dfrac{180 - 116}{2} = 32°$. Since $\overline{OB}$ is a radius drawn to a tangent line, $\angle OBC$ is $90°$. Therefore, $y = 180 - 32 - 90 = 58°$.

28. $\boxed{B}$ From the remainder theorem, $p(2) = 0$ and $p(-1) = 0$ if $x - 2$ and $x + 1$ are both factors of $p(x)$. Testing each answer choice, only choice (B) results in 0 when $x = 2$ and when $x = -1$.

29. $\boxed{D}$ Let r_a and r_b be the radii of cylinders A and B, respectively. Similarly, let h_a and h_b be the heights of cylinders A and B, respectively.

$$\text{Volume of cylinder A} = \text{Volume of cylinder B}$$
$$\pi(r_a)^2(h_a) = \pi(r_b)^2(h_b)$$
$$\pi(1.2r_b)^2(h_a) = \pi(r_b)^2(h_b)$$
$$\pi(1.2)^2(r_b)^2(h_a) = \pi(r_b)^2(h_b)$$
$$1.44h_a = h_b$$

The result above indicates that the height of cylinder B is 44% greater than the height of cylinder A.

30. $\boxed{C}$ **Solution 1:** The slope of the line is m. Given the two points, $m = \dfrac{\text{rise}}{\text{run}} = \dfrac{4d - 2d}{(c + 3) - c} = \dfrac{2d}{3}$. Therefore,

$$m = \frac{2d}{3}$$
$$3m = 2d$$
$$\frac{3}{2} = \frac{d}{m}$$

Solution 2: Plugging $(c, 2d)$ into the equation of the line gives $2d = mc + b$. Plugging $(c + 3, 4d)$ into the same equation gives $4d = m(c + 3) + b$, which simplifies to $4d = mc + 3m + b$. So now we have the following two equations:

$$4d = mc + 3m + b$$
$$2d = mc + b$$

By subtracting the second equation from the first, we're able to eliminate mc and b, and we get

$$2d = 3m$$
$$\frac{d}{m} = \frac{3}{2}$$

31. $\boxed{120}$ This problem is very tricky. The two numbers are NOT x and $1.2x$ because x being "20% less than the other number" is not the same as the other number being "20% more than x". In the first case, the 20% is based off of the other number, whereas 20% more than x is based off of x. Let's have the other number be y. The two numbers are then x and y, but $x = 0.8y$ (20% less than y).

$$y - x = 30$$
$$y - 0.8y = 30$$
$$0.2y = 30$$
$$y = 150$$

Finally, $x = 0.8(150) = 120$.

32. $\boxed{71}$ The function is undefined when the denominator is equal to zero.

$$\sqrt{x + 10} - 9 = 0$$
$$\sqrt{x + 10} = 9$$
$$x + 10 = 81$$
$$x = 71$$

33. $\boxed{160}$ From the triangle with points A and B,

$$y = 180 - 40 - 30 = 110$$

The top-most triangle with point B has angles with degree measures $40, 80$, and 60. Using the right-most triangle with point E,

$$x = 180 - 60 - 70 = 50$$

Therefore, $x + y = 110 + 50 = 160$

34. $\boxed{12}$ The 10 regular assortment packs contain $10 \times 18 = 180$ bolts and $10 \times 12 = 120$ washers. To satisfy their requirements, Sam and Ali still need at least $540 - 180 = 360$ bolts and at least $400 - 120 = 280$ washers. For the remaining bolts, $360 \div 40 = 9$ deluxe packs are needed. For the remaining washers, however, $280 \div 25 = 11.2 \Rightarrow 12$ deluxe packs are needed (round up because they can't buy a fraction of a pack). Therefore, the least number of deluxe packs they can buy is 12.

35. $\boxed{21}$ Let r be the number of red cards she drew and b be the number of black cards she drew. Based on the information, we can form the following two equations:

$$r = 7b$$
$$5r - 10b = 75$$

Plugging the first equation into the second, we get

$$5(7b) - 10b = 75$$
$$35b - 10b = 75$$
$$25b = 75$$
$$b = 3$$

Finally, $r = 7(3) = 21$.

36. $\boxed{.6}$ The two triangles are similar. Using the pythagorean theorem, $BD = 10$. Therefore,

$$\sin A = \sin \angle DBE = \frac{6}{10} = 0.6$$

37. $\boxed{2.4}$

$$\frac{1}{R} = \frac{1}{6} + \frac{1}{4}$$
$$\frac{1}{R} = \frac{2}{12} + \frac{3}{12}$$
$$\frac{1}{R} = \frac{5}{12}$$
$$5R = 12$$
$$R = 2.4$$

38. $\boxed{\dfrac{2}{3}}$ Let the resistance of the second resistor be x. Then the resistance of the first resistor is $2x$. Finding the total resistance,

$$\frac{1}{R} = \frac{1}{x} + \frac{1}{2x}$$
$$\frac{1}{R} = \frac{2}{2x} + \frac{1}{2x}$$
$$\frac{1}{R} = \frac{3}{2x}$$
$$3R = 2x$$
$$R = \frac{2}{3}x$$

The total resistance is two-thirds the resistance of the second resistor.

Questions by Category

Categories correspond to chapters in *The College Panda's SAT Math: The Advanced Guide and Workbook*. Some questions may belong in more than one category.

Exponents & Radicals

	Section 3	Section 4
Test 1	4	
Test 2	14	
Test 3	10	19
Test 4	9	
Test 5	3	
Test 6	8, 17	
Test 7	1	
Test 8	2	
Test 9	4	
Test 10	4	

Percent

	Section 3	Section 4
Test 1		3, 9, 16
Test 2		6, 11, 22, 26
Test 3		37, 38
Test 4		1, 4, 29, 37
Test 5		2, 11, 23, 31, 35
Test 6		3, 22, 32
Test 7	8	7, 13
Test 8		5, 9
Test 9		2, 8, 37, 38
Test 10		3, 21, 31

Exponential vs. Linear Growth

	Section 3	Section 4
Test 1		15, 31
Test 2		25
Test 3		21
Test 4		3
Test 5		18
Test 6		1, 15
Test 7		10
Test 8		23
Test 9		
Test 10		5

Rates

	Section 3	Section 4
Test 1	11	2, 23, 34
Test 2		1, 12
Test 3	8	14, 24, 32
Test 4		16
Test 5	16	1, 14, 28
Test 6	16	2, 7, 28
Test 7	16	2, 14, 34
Test 8	16	6, 16, 31
Test 9		1, 13, 31
Test 10	2	2, 24, 25

Ratio & Proportion

	Section 3	Section 4
Test 1		
Test 2		
Test 3		3
Test 4		26
Test 5		
Test 6	3	
Test 7		20
Test 8		11
Test 9		
Test 10		29

Expressions

	Section 3	Section 4
Test 1	2, 13	32
Test 2	1, 19	19, 30
Test 3	4, 16	2
Test 4	6, 18	10
Test 5	1, 9	17
Test 6	13, 18	5
Test 7	3, 5, 7	5
Test 8	6, 18	1
Test 9	2, 14	33
Test 10	12	4

Constructing Models

	Section 3	Section 4
Test 1		1
Test 2	2, 9	7, 13
Test 3		6
Test 4	2	
Test 5	2	4
Test 6	2, 5, 10	14
Test 7	2	
Test 8	8	14, 15
Test 9	5	6, 27
Test 10		7

Manipulating & Solving Equations

	Section 3	Section 4
Test 1	1, 3, 20	7, 14, 18, 29, 30
Test 2	3, 16,	3, 20, 24, 30, 37
Test 3	2, 17	1, 29
Test 4	16, 20	5, 9, 15, 32
Test 5	7, 18	3, 33, 37, 38
Test 6	1, 9	16, 34
Test 7	9, 15	19, 23, 31
Test 8	1, 10, 13	2, 29, 37, 38
Test 9	1, 7, 16	5, 28
Test 10	1, 5, 10, 16	37, 38

More Equation Solving Strategies

	Section 3	Section 4
Test 1	14	
Test 2	12	
Test 3		
Test 4	1, 19	
Test 5	20	22
Test 6	15	
Test 7		
Test 8		
Test 9		
Test 10	17	

Systems of Equations

	Section 3	Section 4
Test 1	15	20, 28
Test 2	8	34
Test 3	13, 20	17, 30
Test 4	5	30, 34
Test 5	6, 10	34
Test 6	11, 19	17, 36
Test 7	17	16, 26
Test 8	17	17, 27, 34
Test 9	15, 18	18, 34
Test 10	11, 20	23, 30, 35

Inequalities

	Section 3	Section 4
Test 1		10, 36
Test 2	15	18, 36
Test 3	3, 15	35
Test 4	14	7, 11
Test 5	11	9, 30
Test 6	14	10, 37
Test 7	13	28, 29
Test 8	12	12, 24, 30
Test 9	8	17, 25
Test 10	9	9, 14, 20

Word Problems

	Section 3	Section 4
Test 1	6	19, 35
Test 2	5	38
Test 3	11	5
Test 4		19, 38
Test 5		
Test 6	20	11, 29
Test 7		27
Test 8	9, 20	36
Test 9	13	9, 36
Test 10	19	31, 35

Minimum & Maximum Word Problems

	Section 3	Section 4
Test 1	18	
Test 2	17	
Test 3		8
Test 4		36
Test 5		
Test 6		
Test 7		
Test 8		
Test 9		3
Test 10		22, 34

Lines

	Section 3	Section 4
Test 1	7, 12	6
Test 2	10	16, 21
Test 3	6, 12	12
Test 4	7, 12	20, 28
Test 5	5	8, 26
Test 6		20, 21
Test 7	6, 11	17
Test 8	3	
Test 9	17	10
Test 10	3, 8, 13	30

Interpreting Linear Models

	Section 3	Section 4
Test 1	8	17
Test 2		15, 33
Test 3	5	27, 28
Test 4	3	6, 14
Test 5	4	
Test 6	7	13
Test 7	4, 10	33
Test 8	4	3
Test 9	3	20
Test 10	7	15

Functions

	Section 3	Section 4
Test 1	16, 19	25, 33
Test 2	7, 18	10, 29
Test 3	7, 19	13, 34
Test 4	4	17, 21, 35
Test 5	8, 17	5, 16
Test 6	6	23, 27, 33
Test 7	19	8, 15, 22, 36
Test 8	7, 11	25, 35
Test 9	6, 12	11, 12, 22, 29
Test 10	6	11, 26, 32

Quadratics

	Section 3	Section 4
Test 1	10	5
Test 2	6, 20	23
Test 3	9	9
Test 4	15	33
Test 5	14, 19	21
Test 6		26, 30
Test 7	14	11
Test 8	14	20
Test 9	19	30
Test 10	14	17

Synthetic Division

	Section 3	Section 4
Test 1	14	
Test 2		
Test 3		36
Test 4		
Test 5	15	
Test 6		
Test 7	20	
Test 8	15	
Test 9	20	
Test 10		28

Complex Numbers

	Section 3	Section 4
Test 1	9	
Test 2		
Test 3		
Test 4	13	
Test 5	13	
Test 6		
Test 7		
Test 8		
Test 9		
Test 10		

Absolute Value

	Section 3	Section 4
Test 1		
Test 2		
Test 3	1	
Test 4		
Test 5		
Test 6		
Test 7		25
Test 8	5	
Test 9		
Test 10		

Angles

	Section 3	Section 4
Test 1	17	
Test 2		31
Test 3		31
Test 4	17	
Test 5		32
Test 6		31
Test 7		35
Test 8		32
Test 9		
Test 10		33

Triangles

	Section 3	Section 4
Test 1	5	27
Test 2	4, 13	17
Test 3	18	16, 20
Test 4	10	18
Test 5	12	36
Test 6	4	35
Test 7	18	30
Test 8		18
Test 9	9	10, 23, 24
Test 10	15	

Circles

	Section 3	Section 4
Test 1		4, 11
Test 2	11	2
Test 3		4, 25
Test 4	8	31
Test 5		15, 24
Test 6		9
Test 7	15	9
Test 8	19	26
Test 9	10	32
Test 10	18	27

Trigonometry

	Section 3	Section 4
Test 1		21
Test 2		
Test 3	14	
Test 4	11	27
Test 5		29
Test 6	12	38
Test 7	12	
Test 8		33
Test 9	11	
Test 10		36

Reading Data

	Section 3	Section 4
Test 1		12, 13, 24
Test 2		4, 14
Test 3		7, 33
Test 4		2, 37, 38
Test 5		6, 7, 27
Test 6		8, 12
Test 7		3, 6, 7, 32
Test 8		7, 8
Test 9		4, 14
Test 10		1, 6, 10, 16

Probability

	Section 3	Section 4
Test 1		8
Test 2		35
Test 3		22, 23
Test 4		8
Test 5		12, 13
Test 6		4
Test 7		24
Test 8		10, 13
Test 9		15
Test 10		12

Statistics I

	Section 3	Section 4
Test 1		26
Test 2		27, 28
Test 3		15
Test 4		22
Test 5		10, 35
Test 6		6, 24
Test 7		1, 21
Test 8		19
Test 9		16, 19, 35
Test 10		18, 19

Statistics II

	Section 3	Section 4
Test 1		22, 37, 38
Test 2		8, 9
Test 3		10, 11, 26
Test 4		12, 13, 24, 25
Test 5		19, 20, 31
Test 6		19, 25, 26
Test 7		4, 12, 18, 37, 38
Test 8		4, 21, 22, 28
Test 9		7, 21, 26
Test 10		8, 13

Volume

	Section 3	Section 4
Test 1		
Test 2		32
Test 3		18
Test 4		23
Test 5		25
Test 6		18
Test 7		
Test 8		
Test 9		
Test 10		29

Uncategorized

	Section 3	Section 4
Test 1		
Test 2		5
Test 3		3
Test 4		
Test 5		
Test 6		
Test 7		
Test 8		
Test 9		
Test 10		